SCIENCE FICTION WRITING SERIES

Space Travel

Science Fiction **EDITED BY Ben Bova** Writing Series

Space Travel

Ben Bova with Anthony R. Lewis

WRITER'S DIGEST BOOKS
Cincinnati, Ohio

Other fine Writer's Digest Books are available from your local bookstore or direct from the publisher.

01   00   99   98   97   5   4   3   2   1

Library of Congress Cataloging-in-Publication Data

Bova, Ben
   Space travel / by Ben Bova with Anthony R. Lewis.—1st ed.
     p.   cm.—(Science fiction writing series)
   Includes bibliographical references and index.
   ISBN 0-89879-747-0 (alk. paper)
   1. Science fiction—Authorship. 2. Astronautics. I. Lewis, Anthony.
  II. Title. III. Series.
PN3377.5.S3B63   1997
808.3'8762—dc20   96-36003
                                             CIP

Edited by Ben Bova
Content edited by David Tompkins and David H. Borcherding
Production edited by Jennifer Lepore
Designed by Angela Lennert Wilcox
Cover illustration by Bob Eggleton

ABOUT THE EDITOR

Ben Bova is the author of *Mars, Moonrise,* and more than ninety other novels, nonfiction and instructional books, including *The Craft of Writing Science Fiction That Sells* for Writer's Digest Books. The former editor of *Analog Science Fiction* and *Omni* magazines, Bova is the six-time winner of science fiction's Hugo Award for Best Professional Editor. He is president emeritus of the National Space Society and a past president of Science Fiction and Fantasy Writers of America.

TABLE OF CONTENTS

Meteoroids and Meteorites • Space Stations • A Visit to Skylab • Space Suits • Who Are the Decision-Makers? • The Excitement of the Frontier

• Skyhook • Mass Drivers • Laser Propulsion • The MHD
Torch Ship • Storm Cellars • Imagination and Knowledge

INTRODUCTION

This book is intended to help the writer who wants to produce realistic science fiction stories that deal with space travel.

The major chapters will cover the fundamentals of space travel, starting with rockets and spacecraft and moving outward from Earth orbit to the vast reaches of cosmic space. Most of these chapters will be divided into two segments, one dealing with the technical facts, the other showing how those facts can be used in writing fiction. We will use examples from published science fiction stories to show how successful writers have used such materials in their stories.

Realize that we will only be offering a glimpse at the fundamentals. The mathematical details of rocket propulsion, interplanetary trajectories, planetology, astronomy, astrogation, cosmology, etc. are far beyond the scope of this book. The bibliography, however, gives you a list of books and reports that have many of these details and suggestions of where to dig even deeper.

There is also a references section, in which we cite each of the science fiction stories mentioned in the text.

No one can make a good writer out of you—except you yourself. Your success as a writer depends on your innate skills and drive. To become a writer, you must write; all the books, courses and workshops are tools. To succeed, you must sit down and write; there is no royal road, only hard work, skill and experience.

What this book can do for you, however, is give you a solid background in the many fascinating aspects of space travel and suggestions on how to use such material to help write believable, salable science fiction stories.

TERMS FOR BIG AND LITTLE

You probably know that a kilowatt is a thousand watts, and a megawatt is a million watts. Here are some of the prefixes used to denote large and small units.

Larger
kilo   = 1000 or 10^3
mega = 1,000,000 or 10^6
giga   = 1,000,000,000 or 10^9
tera   = 1,000,000,000,000 or 10^{12}

Smaller
deci   = 0.1 or 10^{-1}
centi = 0.01 or 10^{-2}
milli   = 0.001 or 10^{-3}
micro = 0.000001 or 10^{-6}
nano = 0.000000001 or 10^{-9}
pico   = 0.000000000001 or 10^{-12}

You can see that in the "powers of ten" notation, 10^6 (for example) means there are six digits after the one and 10^{-6} means there are six digits after the decimal place.

Temperature Scales

In the Fahrenheit scale, the freezing point of water is 32°F, and water's boiling point is 212°F.

In the Celsius, or centigrade, scale the freezing point of water is 0°C, and its boiling point is 100°C.

To go from Celsius to Fahrenheit, multiply the degrees Celsius by ⅑, then add 32. To go from Fahrenheit to Celsius, subtract 32 from the degrees Fahrenheit, then multiply the result by ⅝.

$$F = \tfrac{9}{5}C + 32$$
$$C = \tfrac{5}{9}(F - 32)$$

A comfortable room temperature of 70°F would then be:

$$\tfrac{5}{9}(70 - 32) = 21°C$$

The Kelvin, or *absolute*, scale places zero at the point where all molecular motion stops; nothing can get colder than that, so it is called *absolute zero*. Thus the Kelvin scale does not need minus numbers. Zero is as cold as anything can get.

The Kelvin scale uses the same-sized degrees as Celsius; on the Celsius scale, absolute zero is -273.15°C. The freezing point of water in the Kelvin scale, therefore, is 273.15°K. Comfortable room temperature is 300°K.

Absolute zero in the Fahrenheit scale is -459.67°F.

CHAPTER 1

Dreams Into Reality

The dream of interplanetary travel is as old as the dream of flight. . . .
Arthur C. Clarke

Writers work to make dreams seem real.

In the realm of science fiction, the dream of space travel is a constant and thrilling theme. Since the days of Jules Verne and H.G. Wells, travelling to the Moon and farther has provided much of the "sense of wonder" that excites science fiction readers.

In fact, one of the earliest stories that can be called science fiction involved a trip to the Moon. "The Other World" was written by none other than Cyrano de Bergerac and published posthumously in 1657. Cyrano, the hero of Edmond Rostand's nineteenth-century play, was a real person who lived in seventeenth-century France. He was a famous swordsman, poet and playwright and (unlike the character in Rostand's play) quite a womanizer.

Science Fiction Vs. Fantasy

We might say that Cyrano was the first true science fiction writer. Previous writers sent their heroes to other worlds in dreams or by using mystical unexplained powers. Cyrano not only was one of the earliest writers to use the Copernican view of the Solar System,[1] but he even hit upon the idea of using rockets to travel beyond the Earth. No one had thought of that before.

Although rockets could not propel a man to the Moon in the seventeenth century, rockets did exist. They were real, and an in-

---

TWO LAWS OF SCIENCE FICTION

1. Science fiction stories are those in which some aspect of future science or technology is so integral to the story that, if you take away the science or technology, the story collapses. Think of Mary Shelley's *Frankenstein*; without the scientific element, there is no story.

2. Science fiction writers are free to extrapolate from today's knowledge and to invent anything they can imagine— so long as no one can prove that what they have "invented" is wrong.

---

ventive writer like Cyrano could surmise that they might plausibly be used for space transportation some day.

The difference between rocket propulsion—something that really existed—and dreams or magic is the difference between science fiction and fantasy. Science fiction uses known scientific principles and technological capabilities as the underpinning of its stories. The writer is free to *extrapolate*, that is, to carry today's known facts forward into the future, and assume that there will be changes, improvements, in our knowledge.

Thus, Cyrano could write about rockets to the Moon three hundred years before the Saturn V rocket lifted Armstrong, Aldrin and Collins to the Sea of Tranquility. And science fiction writers today can write about starships plying the galaxy, even though most scientists blanch at the idea of travelling across interstellar distances.

Isaac Asimov was quite specific in his view of what science fiction must be:

> In my view, the best science fiction, the only valid science fiction and the science fiction I try to write depends on *legitimate* science *rationally* extrapolated. If something is wrong, distorted and illogical, it cannot be categorized as science fiction; any more than noise can be called music or a used paint rag a painting.

The Writer's Aim: Verne Vs. Wells

Within the field of science fiction, however, there are differences of attitude and approach. How closely should you stick to the known facts? How far can you extrapolate before you leave the realm of science fiction and begin writing fantasy? To a large extent, that depends on your intentions.

Jules Verne complained about H.G. Wells over these matters. Verne tried hard to stick to the known facts, extrapolating only slightly in his stories. In his novel *From the Earth to the Moon*, he described with almost engineering detail the phenomenon of weightlessness that astronauts feel. On the other hand, when Wells sent his characters to the Moon in *The First Men in the Moon*, he "invented" a substance called Cavorite that cancelled the effects of gravity—what we today would call an antigravity device. Antigravity devices did not exist then and still don't exist now.

Verne took umbrage. "I do not see the possibility of comparison between his work and mine," he told an interviewer in 1903. "We do not proceed in the same manner. It occurs to me that his stories do not repose on very scientific bases. . . . I make use of physics. He invents. I go to the moon in a cannonball, discharged from a cannon. Here there is no invention. He goes [to the Moon] in an airship, which he constructs of a metal which does away with the law of gravitation. *Ça c'est très joli,* but show me this metal. Let him produce it."

Verne's indignation at Wells' "invention" stems from the fact that Verne was writing an adventure story, where the thrill of going to the Moon was what the story really was all about. Wells was writing a social commentary. *How* his characters got to the Moon was not so important as what they found once they arrived there.

Incidentally, the tremendous acceleration of Verne's cannonball spacecraft would have crushed its occupants when it blasted off. Verne either did not understand this problem or decided to ignore it.

So it is with modern writers. Ray Bradbury's stories are almost totally innocent of scientific detail, yet they are among the most memorable that science fiction has produced. Hal Clement writes stories of such scientific intricacy that you almost expect to see equations and footnotes in them. Yet it is often such scientific detail itself that keeps the reader turning pages.

How much scientific detail you put into your stories depends on what effects you are trying to achieve. There can be a lot or a little. But it is important that you, the writer, understand the scientific underpinnings of your story if you want to make it self-consistent and interesting to read.

It's all right to break the rules, but you need to know what the rules are. Otherwise your stories will not be internally consistent. Worse still, they won't be published, because science fiction readers—and editors—will not tolerate stories in which the science is obviously incorrect or inconsistent.

Pioneers of Spaceflight

Space travel remained in the realm of imagination until the twentieth century, when three pioneers began to make the dreams of space flight real. Their work provided the basis not only for today's space programs, but for science fiction writers as well.

The Russian Konstantin Edvardovich Tsiolkovskii deserves the title "Father of Astronautics." Writing around the turn of the century, he outlined most of the concepts that eventually became the realities of today's space programs. In his writings, Tsiolkovskii worked out the basic ideas of rocketry, space suits, space stations, and the eventual human expansion into space. He even wrote a science fiction novel, *Outside the Earth.*

He prophesied, "The Earth is the cradle of mankind, but mankind cannot stay in the cradle forever."

Hermann Oberth was born in Transylvania but worked and studied most of his adult life in Germany. His books, *The Rocket Into Interplanetary Space* (published in 1923) and *Ways to Spaceflight* (1929), helped to interest many youngsters—including teenaged Wernher von Braun—in rocketry and astronautics. Von Braun, of course, went on to develop the V-2 ballistic missile for Germany during World War II and Saturn launching rockets for America's lunar program, Apollo.

Oberth built the first liquid-fueled rocket motor, which ran on gasoline and liquid oxygen, and helped to found the German Society for Space Travel. Perhaps his greatest impact, however, came when he served as the science advisor to motion picture director Fritz Lang for his seminal science fiction film *Woman in the Moon* in 1929. Thanks to Oberth, film audiences saw that it might be possible to build a rocket-driven spacecraft that could carry men—and at least one woman—to the Moon.

(Lang invented the "countdown" in this film for its dramatic effect. It was picked up in numerous stories and films before it was actually used in real rocket launches. However, Lang ignored

Oberth's advice about conditions on the lunar surface and allowed his actors to walk around on the Moon without space suits!)

It was the American Robert H. Goddard who turned theory into hardware. A professor of physics at Clark College (now Clark University) in Worcester, Massachusetts, Goddard built the first liquid-fueled rockets that actually flew. Although his 1926 gasoline/oxygen rocket lifted a scant forty feet above his aunt's farm near Worcester, it was the first liquid-fueled rocket to get off the ground. Before that, rockets had been powered by solid fuels more or less like gunpowder.

Goddard's rocketry experiments got too loud for his Massachusetts neighbors, and eventually he moved his work to New Mexico—and flew his rockets much higher.

Earlier, in 1919, Goddard had published a scientific paper about the possibility of using rockets to reach the Moon. He cautiously titled his paper "A Method of Reaching Extreme Altitudes." While the scientific world hardly noticed Goddard's paper, *The New York Times* in an editorial in its January 18, 1920, edition chided:

> That Professor Goddard . . . does not know the relation of action to reaction, and of the need to have something better than a vacuum against which to react—to say that would be absurd. Of course he only seems to lack the knowledge ladled out daily in highschools. . . .

The *Times* was dead wrong. Rockets do not need "something better than a vacuum" to push against. In fact, rockets are the *only* form of propulsion that have worked in the vacuum of space.

---

[1] The Copernican description of the Solar System places the Sun at the center, with the Earth and other planets going around it. The earlier Ptolemaic view pictured the Earth in the center with the Sun and everything else orbiting around our planet. As we know now, the Earth orbits the Sun, not vice versa.

CHAPTER 2

Rockets

. . . And the rockets' red glare. . . .

from "The Star-Spangled Banner," by Francis Scott Key

TECHNICAL FACTORS

The earliest rockets were metal tubes stuffed with burnable powder. When the powder was ignited, the tube leaped into the air with a roar and a cloud of smoke.

Rockets were invented sometime in the Middle Ages, apparently in China. The Chinese used rocket-propelled artillery against Genghis Khan's invading Mongols in the thirteenth century, and the Great Khan—knowing a good thing when he saw it—used rockets against his enemies later on. The Mongol emperor brought Chinese crews with him to handle this new and frightening weapon.

Rockets were adopted by European armies; the British fired Congreve rockets at Fort McHenry during the War of 1812, while Francis Scott Key anxiously watched the battle and then penned the poem that would become our national anthem.

All of these rockets used solid propellants, usually "black powder," a mixture of 75 percent saltpeter (potassium nitrate), 15 percent ground charcoal and 10 percent sulphur. It was not until Goddard's 1926 gasoline/oxygen flight that liquid propellants lifted a rocket off the ground.

Chemical Rockets

Whether liquid or solid, the rockets we are discussing here are *chemical rockets.* That is, they burn chemicals of one sort or another to produce hot gases and the hot gases, in turn, produce thrust.

Just about every form of engine we use is essentially a *heat*

NEWTON'S THREE LAWS OF MOTION

1. A body at rest will remain at rest, unless acted upon by an external force; a body in motion will continue to move at a constant speed in a straight line unless acted upon by an external force.

2. An unbalanced force applied to an object will give that object an acceleration that is directly proportional to, and in the direction of, the force applied, and inversely proportional to the mass of the object.

3. For every action there is an equal and opposite reaction.

---

engine, a device that transforms heat energy into mechanical or kinetic energy. Think about a steam engine, for example: Water is boiled, and the steam pushes a piston that is linked to one or more wheels (or whatever else the engine is designed to move).

In automobile engines, gasoline is ignited in the cylinders, and the rapidly expanding hot gases push the pistons which turn the crankshaft which turns the wheels. In piston-engined airplanes, much the same type of engine is used; the pistons turn the propeller shaft.

Action and Reaction

Jet engines are different, however. In a jet engine, the fuel is burned and the resulting hot gases are made to flow out a nozzle at the rear of the engine. The force of their flow pushes the engine—and whatever it is attached to—in the opposite direction.

Isaac Newton discovered the principle of jet propulsion as part of his three Laws of Motion (see sidebar). The first two laws need not concern us here; it is that third law we are interested in.

What the Third Law of Motion tells us is that, when a force is applied in one direction, another force is created that is equal in intensity but opposite in direction to the first force. Jet aircraft are propelled by this Third Law of Motion. So are squid, octopuses and cuttlefish, which use the jet propulsion principle to move through the sea. They squirt water through specialized muscular funnels to propel themselves backward.

Blow up a balloon and then let it loose. It zips around like an unguided missile, propelled by the escaping air. This occurs in accordance with Newton's third law.

Notice that the third law does not require "something to push against," as the *Times* editorial writer incorrectly assumed. In fact, a vehicle propelled by the third law will work more efficiently in the vacuum of space because there is no air resistance to hold it back.

Jet engines do not work in space, however; they need air to "breathe." Their fuel must be burned to produce the hot gases that are fired out the nozzle, and without oxygen or some other chemical that will support combustion the fuel will not burn. Jet engines burn their fuel with the oxygen in the air; oxygen makes up about 20 percent of our planet's atmosphere.

Fuel Plus Oxidizer Equals *Propellants*

A chemical rocket differs from a jet engine in one major way: A rocket carries not only its fuel but an *oxidizer* as well. The oxidizer is a chemical, such as oxygen, that will support combustion of the fuel. Thus, a rocket can work in space because it carries both its fuel and the stuff with which to burn it.

That is why we speak of rocket *propellants* rather than just rocket fuels. The fuel is necessary, of course. But without an oxidizer to make it burn, the fuel is useless. Fuels and oxidizers are called propellants.

The most common oxidizer used in liquid rockets is oxygen itself, but other oxidizers are possible. Fluorine, for example, is more energetic chemically than oxygen and has been used in a few "exotic" rocket systems. However, fluorine is a highly corrosive, dangerous chemical to handle. It is poisonous to breathe. Liquid oxygen is no fun to deal with, but fluorine—gaseous or liquified—is *nasty*.

Nitric acid and nitrogen peroxide have also been used as oxidizers. Nitrogen peroxide is relatively easy to handle and is a liquid at normal temperatures; therefore it can be stored in the rocket's own tankage for long periods of time. Most other oxidizers, including liquid oxygen, have to be pumped into the rocket during the countdown to the launch, either because they are too corrosive to stay in the rocket's tanks for long, or they are cryogenic (that is, they remain liquid only at extremely low temperatures) and would boil away in a short time.

Solid Vs. Liquid Rockets

Picture NASA's space shuttle, standing on its launch pad. The "stack" (as the launch crew calls it) consists of the shuttle orbiter—the winged spacecraft that carries the crew and cargo—plus the gigantic "egg" of the external tank that holds the propellants for the shuttle's main rocket engines, plus two tall solid-rocket boosters strapped on either side of the external tank.

The shuttle's three main engines, in the tail of the orbiter, are liquid rockets, powered by hydrogen and oxygen. The boosters are, of course, solid rockets.

Solid propellants are simpler than liquid. In principle, you just stuff a tube with your solid propellant, stick a nozzle at the end of the tube, and ignite the propellant. Whoosh! Off goes your rocket, into the wild blue yonder, until the propellant burns out entirely.

The first solid propellant used in rocketry actually was black gunpowder. Today's solid propellants look and feel more like rubber. Those "strap-on" solid rocket boosters used by the space shuttle, for example, are composed of 70 percent ammonium perchlorate (the oxidizer), 16 percent aluminum (fuel) and 14 percent polybutadine plastic, which binds the fuel and oxidizer together.

Aluminum, by the way, is a fairly good rocket fuel. It burns quite nicely, especially in pure oxygen. Although not as high in energy content as most liquid fuels, it is a common element on the Moon's surface and therefore might make a reasonably cheap, abundant rocket fuel for lunar explorers. Oxygen is also abundant on the Moon, so lunar settlers should be able to manufacture their own rocket propellants, instead of carrying them up from Earth. (More on this in chapter 7.)

Liquid-propelled rockets need tanks to hold their propellants, pumps to pump the liquids into the combustion chamber, plumbing to move the liquids where they are supposed to go, and an ignition system to start the propellants burning (see figure 1). Although this makes liquid-propelled rockets more complex than solids, liquid propellants can yield more energy per pound than solids.

Liquid-propelled rockets can also be throttled: By controlling the flow of propellants into the combustion chamber, you can control the amount of thrust produced. You can throttle down when you want to or throttle up. You can shut down the engine entirely and then start it up again. Solids will just continue to burn until they have used up all their propellant.

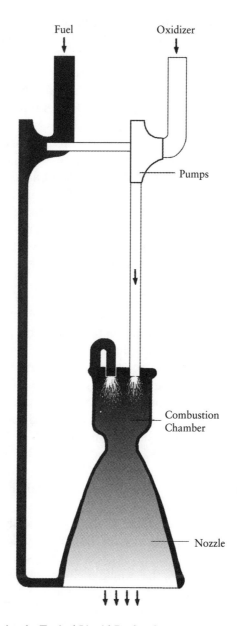

FIGURE 1 Schematic of a Typical Liquid Rocket System.
Fuel and oxidizer are pumped to combustion chamber, where they are ignited.
Their burning produces hot gas expelled through the rocket nozzle, providing
thrust. Fuel is piped through the wall of the rocket nozzle, to help cool it.

There have been times when a launch of the space shuttle had to be aborted at the very last second. On at least one occasion, the shuttle's main engines had already ignited and had to be shut down. This was possible only because those three main engines burn liquid propellants. Shut off the flow of hydrogen and oxygen, and the rocket turns off. The shuttle's solid-rocket boosters are another matter, however. Once they light off, the shuttle leaves the ground whether you like it or not! There is no way to stop them once they fire up.

Some liquid propellants, such as nitric acid and hydrazine, are "self-starters." These *hypergolic* propellants need no igniter; they burst into flame when they contact each other. The second stage of the Vanguard rocket, for example, used hypergolic propellants.

Engineers have proposed solid-rocket systems that can be throttled or even stopped and restarted, but the complications this causes wipe out the benefits of the solid rocket's simplicity.

Cryogenics[1]

The shuttle's main engines burn hydrogen and oxygen, both of which are gases at normal temperature and pressure. Rocket propellants are liquified to reduce the size of the spacecraft's tankage. When cooled to the point where they liquify, gases such as hydrogen and oxygen are reduced in volume by a factor of more than 800. This means they can be carried in much smaller tanks, which saves structural weight in spacecraft and boosters and allows the engineers to design them more compactly.

Oxygen liquifies at -297.4° Fahrenheit (-183.0° Celsius). Hydrogen must be cooled to a truly frigid temperature, -423°F (-252.8°C), which is not much above absolute zero, -459.67°F (-273.15°C), the lowest temperature possible.

In many liquid-rocket systems, the cryogenically cold propellant is piped through the walls of the rocket's nozzle, to help cool it (as shown in figure 1). Thus rockets can run safely at combustion chamber temperatures that would melt an uncooled nozzle.

Producing, storing and handling cryogenic hydrogen and oxygen causes considerable problems. One of the engineering triumphs of the space program has been the hard-gained knowledge of how to deal with cryogenic fluids.

When you see a rocket being prepared for launch, you usually see plumes of "steam" and rimes of frost on the hoses and tanks that hold the cryogenic propellants. This is a valuable point of description in a story that helps the reader to "see" the scene you are describing.

Thrust and Specific Impulse

How can you rate the performance of a rocket engine? Think about an automobile engine for a moment. An automobile engine can be rated either by the amount of power it produces—its horse-power—or its fuel efficiency, in miles per gallon. A rocket engine can also be rated by its power or its efficiency. In rocketry, power is measured in terms of *thrust*; engineers refer to a rocket's efficiency in terms of *specific impulse.*

Thrust is the pushing force that moves the space vehicle. It is usually measured in pounds. A pound of thrust will move a pound of spaceship against the gravity at Earth's surface.

Specific impulse is the measure of how long a pound of propellants will yield a pound of thrust. It is rated in seconds. Different propellant mixtures give different specific impulses. Specific impulse is also dependent on the gas pressure inside the rocket combustion chamber.

Table 1 shows the thrust and specific impulses for three liquid-propelled rocket engines and one solid: the F-1 that powered the first stage of the Saturn V moon launcher; the J-2 that powered the Saturn upper stages; the Space Shuttle Main Engine (SSME); and the Solid-Propellant Rocket Booster (SRB) that is used to help launch the space shuttle.

Notice that the thrust of a rocket engine, whether liquid or solid, has very little to do with its efficiency, or specific impulse. The thrust is mainly a matter of how large the engine is; the huge F-1 produces far more thrust than the J-2 or SSME, but those hydrogen/oxygen engines are far more efficient than either the F-1 or the SRB.

Specific impulse, the measure of rocket efficiency, is the key to future space travel. For while we can afford to use brute force, low-efficiency rockets to lift spacecraft off the surface of the Earth, when it comes to operating over the long distances between the worlds we will need much more efficient rockets. A spacecraft intended to go to Mars would not use kerosene/oxygen engines such as the F-1, for example; the amount of propellants required by such low-efficiency engines would make the mission economically impracticable, if not impossible.

Engine	Propellants	Thrust (lbs)	Specific Impulse
F-1	kerosene/oxygen	1,500,000	265 sec.
J-2	hydrogen/oxygen	208,242	426 sec.
SSME	hydrogen/oxygen	470,000	455 sec.
SRB	aluminum (fuel) ammonium perchlorate (oxidizer)	2,600,000	262 sec.

TABLE 1

It appears that even the most advanced chemical rockets will not be able to deliver specific impulses above five hundred seconds. To find more efficient interplanetary propulsion we must look beyond chemical rockets.

Nuclear Rockets

Specific impulse depends critically on the speed with which the hot gases rush out of the rocket's nozzle. In chemical rockets, the speed of the expelled gas is determined mainly by the energy of the chemical combustion—burning—and the molecular weight of the gases themselves. Gases consisting of light molecules can be accelerated, speeded up, more easily than those made of heavier molecules. You can throw a baseball harder and faster than you can throw a bowling ball, right?

Chemical combustion can heat up the rocket's fuel/oxidizer mixture only to a certain degree. To attain higher specific impulses, we need to find ways to accelerate the propellants to much higher velocities than chemical combustion can provide and/or find lighter gases to accelerate.

A nuclear-powered rocket can provide higher specific impulse than any chemical rocket because it can both heat the gases to a higher temperature than chemical combustion could, and it can use a much lighter propellant.

Nuclear reactors are excellent sources of heat; they are used on the ground to boil water and thereby provide steam for electric power plants. Smaller and more efficient nuclear reactors could be used in space to heat a propellant and provide rocket thrust (see figure 2).

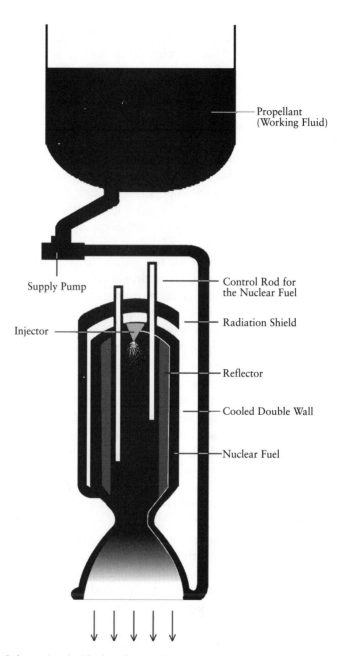

FIGURE 2 Schematic of a Nuclear Rocket System.
Propellant (also called the working fluid) is heated by the energy of nuclear fission as it is piped through the nuclear reactor. There is no combustion, as in chemical rockets.

In a chemical rocket, the energy comes from the chemical energy in the propellants. Their burning produces the thrust. In a nuclear rocket, however, the energy comes from the fissioning (splitting) of atomic nuclei inside the nuclear reactor. That produces the heat energy that powers the rocket. The only purpose of the propellant in a nuclear rocket is to provide gas to expel through the rocket nozzle. It is not necessary for the propellant to generate the system's energy, as in a chemical rocket. The nuclear reactor provides the energy, a heat exchanger imparts the energy to the propellant, and the propellant carries the energy out through the nozzle.

Thus the propellant in a nuclear rocket is often called the *working fluid*. To engineers, a fluid can be either a liquid or a gas.

The faster the molecules of the working fluid move through the nozzle, the more efficient the rocket. The lighter the molecule, the easier to accelerate it. Since hydrogen is the lightest element, a nuclear rocket could consist of a compact nuclear reactor, tanks of liquid hydrogen for the working fluid, a heat exchanger where the reactor's heat energy is transferred to the working fluid, one or more rocket nozzles, pumps and plumbing, and the shielding necessary to protect the rest of the spacecraft from the radiation produced in the nuclear reactor.

In a spacecraft that is assembled in orbit and is intended solely for space operations, never touching the Earth, it is possible to place the nuclear reactor far from the crew's modules and use a small "shadow shield" to prevent radiation from reaching the habitation area. A shadow shield can be smaller, and therefore lighter, than shielding that completely surrounds the reactor. Lightness is important when you have to lift everything from the surface of the Earth.

Nuclear rockets could provide specific impulses in the range of 1000 seconds, with thrusts comparable to those of chemical rockets.

Since their exhaust gases would be radioactive, nuclear rockets are envisioned as pure space propulsion systems, to be used only by spacecraft already in orbit. They would not be used as boosters to lift spacecraft from the ground. In the vacuum of orbital space the radioactive plume of exhaust gases would soon expand and thin to the point where its radioactivity would dwindle to a barely measurable amount.

You may, however, want to consider a story in which a powerful nuclear rocket is used to boost a spacecraft from Earth's surface. Who would want to use a "nuke" that way? Who would try to stop such a launch? Where on Earth could a relatively safe launching base be placed?

Nuclear Power for Electricity

Although no one has flown a nuclear rocket system, yet, nuclear power has been used in space to generate electricity for sensors and communications equipment aboard spacecraft. The two Viking spacecraft that landed on the surface of Mars in 1976 used *radioisotope thermal generators* in which electricity was generated from the heat caused by the natural decay of radioactive elements.[2]

Not only can nuclear power generate electricity for sensors and communications equipment; it can also be used to provide energy for electrical rockets, as we will see in a moment.

Burn, Then Coast

Chemical rockets are designed to burn their propellants as rapidly as possible, building up the spacecraft's velocity quickly. The idea is to transform all the energy of the propellants into velocity as soon as possible. Remember, the rocket engines have to lift the propellant's mass as well as the rocket's structure, equipment and payload. Get rid of the propellant fast; get the bird up to maximum velocity as quickly as you can.

Nuclear rockets would probably use the same approach, consuming all their working fluid as quickly as possible to build up the desired speed and then coasting through the vacuum of space the rest of the way.

The major restraint on this approach is the amount of acceleration the equipment (or crew, in manned craft) can survive. The human body can withstand nine times the normal force of gravity, 9g, for a few seconds at a time. For periods longer than a few minutes, anything more than normal Earth gravity, 1g, can eventually cause physical problems. Most rocket boosters, including the space shuttle, subject their crews to about 3g for a few minutes.

Putting a spacecraft into orbit, therefore, is rather like throwing a ball. All the energy is expended at the very beginning and the ball coasts the rest of the way. For a rocket booster, all the energy is expended during the few minutes between ignition and burnout, when all the propellants are used up.

Multistage rockets work the same way, except that as soon as one stage's engines burn out, the next stage lights up and the exhausted stage is dropped away.

Chemical rockets, designed to deliver all their energy in a quick burst, are the only way we have (at present) to boost payloads off Earth's surface. As we have seen, nuclear rockets will be restricted to use in space and are not being considered as boosters to launch spacecraft from Earth.

Once the spacecraft is in orbit, however, different possibilities open up.

Electrical Rockets

Electrical energy can heat a propellant. Or a working fluid that conducts electricity can be accelerated to very high velocity directly by electrical energy. This can produce rocket systems that are extremely efficient, with specific impulses in the range of 1000 to 10,000 seconds or even better.

Unfortunately, most (but not all) electrical rocket systems produce very low thrusts. Yet because they are much more efficient than chemical rockets, electrical rockets can "burn" for days or weeks or even months, chugging along like the patient tortoise. Although their thrust is low, by constantly accelerating over long periods of time, even their low thrusts can build up great velocities.

For relatively short space missions, such as a flight from the Earth to the Moon, chemical rockets give much shorter trip times than the tortoiselike electrical rockets. But electrical rockets can actually yield shorter trip times for very long interplanetary missions than the jackrabbit chemical or nuclear rockets, which burn up their propellants quickly and then coast the rest of the way.

Types of Electrical Rockets

There are several types of electrical rockets. The *resistojet* simply heats its working fluid (usually hydrogen) by electrical resistance, using a heating coil much like an electric stove or hot plate. Specific impulse is limited to about one thousand seconds, largely because it is difficult to create higher temperatures without damaging the metal heating elements. Small resistojets have been used as attitude-control thrusters on satellites, where they provide little puffs of thrust to keep the satellite pointing in the proper direction as it orbits around the Earth.

The *ion thruster* has been flown in NASA's Space Electric Rocket Test (SERT) program. A working fluid that conducts electricity, such as mercury or ionized argon gas, is accelerated directly by electrical energy rather than by heat. Specific impulses of ten thousand seconds or more are possible, depending on the amount of electrical power put into the fluid. Ion thrusters can be powered by solarvoltaic cells that convert sunlight directly into electricity, the same sort of solar cells that power satellites in orbit and pocket calculators here on the ground.

NASA's first *New Millennium* spacecraft, which will do a flyby of both an asteroid and a comet at the end of the century, will be propelled by a solar-electric-powered ion thruster that uses xenon gas as its working fluid.

The *plasma thruster* employs electromagnetic fields to accelerate an electrically conducting working fluid, such as a mixture of argon with a slight amount of cesium "seed." Physicists call a gas that has been ionized to the point where it easily conducts electricity a *plasma* (see sidebar). Plasma thrusters produce more thrust per weight than ion thrusters and are capable of specific impulses of ten thousand seconds or more.

Power Supply Limitations

Electrical rockets are limited by the weight (or, in space, the mass) of their electrical power systems. The more electrical power needed, the more massive the electric power generator must be. For most electric power systems, the mass of the generator tends to increase faster than its power output. Most of the systems considered for powering electrical rockets run in the range of about 45 watts per pound.

With that basic limitation on their primary energy source, whether it is a nuclear reactor or panels of solar cells, most electrical rocket systems have been small, low-thrust devices, limited to fractions of a pound of thrust. As we have seen, instead of burning all their propellants as quickly as possible the way chemical rockets do, electrical rockets can "burn" for days or weeks or even months, slowly accelerating all the time.

Their low thrusts, however, limit them to unmanned missions where travel times can be sacrificed for efficiency, until you get to the years-long deep space missions to the farther planets. Yet even microthrust rockets have their uses in space. While electrical

PLASMA: THE FOURTH STATE OF MATTER

We are familiar with solids, liquids and gases. Plasmas are a fourth state of matter.[3] A plasma is a gas that is *ionized*; that is, some or all of its atoms have been stripped of one or more of their orbital electrons. Thus a plasma consists of free electrons (which carry a negative electrical charge) and positively charged ions, which are the atoms that have lost electrons.

On the whole, the plasma is electrically neutral, since the negative charges of the electrons balance the positive charges of the ions. But a plasma can be moved, shaped, accelerated and otherwise influenced by electromagnetic forces; normal gases cannot be.

Plasmas are relatively rare on Earth. Lightning bolts create plasmas in the air, briefly. Fluorescent lights are weakly ionized plasmas. The Sun and all the stars are plasmas. So is the solar wind and many of the clouds of "gas" that float in interstellar space. In fact, most of the universe is plasma. It is only on small, cold, out-of-the-way places like Earth that such low-energy forms of matter such as gases, liquids and solids can exist!

rockets could never be used to boost spacecraft into orbit against the gravitational pull of Earth, once a spacecraft is in orbit they can be used for many purposes.

Electrical rockets are good for "station-keeping": providing the small bursts of thrust needed to keep a satellite or space station from drifting off its desired orbital position. When factories are established in orbit and mining bases set up on the Moon, uncrewed electrical rockets could be ideal for "pipeline" cargos of ores and other raw materials that would be mined from the Moon and transported to factories in Earth orbit.

There are other, more exotic forms of rockets that have been proposed by future-looking scientists and engineers. And even forms of space propulsion that do not require rockets at all. We will look at just one of them here, and save the other advanced ideas for a later chapter.

Solar Sails

An alternate form of "slow but steady" space transportation that uses no rockets at all, yet provides a specific impulse that is literally infinite, is the *solar sail*.

Light exerts pressure, although it is so small that delicate apparatus is needed merely to measure it in the laboratory. In space, though, sunlight is free and continuous. The pressure of light against a sail can accelerate a spacecraft in the vicinity of the Earth with a thrust of roughly 2.25×10^{-6} pound (0.00000225 pound) per square yard of sail.

Since no propellant is used, the solar sail's specific impulse is infinite. But to get any reasonable amount of acceleration from such a minuscule push, a sail of enormous dimensions must be used. The bigger the sail, however, the heavier it becomes and the more difficult to accelerate.

Solar sails are slow. It would take years for a sail of 2.152 million square feet (a square with sides of more than a quarter-mile) to reach Mars, for example, where chemical or nuclear rockets could make the same journey in months. The sail would have to be no thicker than a tenth of a mil (0.0001 inch). Sail designers believe that a sail of plastic such as Kapton, coated with aluminum to reflect sunlight, could be made as thin as four-hundredths of a mil (0.00004 inch).

Advanced thinkers such as the aptly named Robert Forward have proposed using powerful lasers to provide more light-push than the Sun does. Multi-gigawatt lasers in Earth orbit, for example, could provide an intense beam of energy to propel "lightsails" across the Solar System and even out toward the stars.

Match the Rocket to the Job

We can see that different rockets have different uses. The space shuttle serves as a good example, with its variety of rocket types.

There are the solid-rocket boosters that give millions of pounds of thrust but have low specific impulse; their job is to help lift the shuttle "stack" off the ground. Period. Once lit, they burn until they have exhausted their propellants and then are parachuted into the ocean, where they are recovered, reloaded and eventually used again.

The shuttle orbiter's main engines use liquid propellants, cryogenic hydrogen and oxygen. The three SSMEs can be throttled up and down, shut off completely and then restarted, if necessary. Their thrust is only a fraction of the SRBs', but their specific impulse is about as good as a chemical rocket can produce. Just before it reaches orbit, the orbiter's SSMEs have used all their propellants and that giant "egg" of the external propellant tank is dropped away.

It breaks apart and burns up as it reenters the atmosphere, the only part of the shuttle that is not reusable.

The shuttle orbiter also has two smaller liquid rockets, called the *orbital maneuvering system* (OMS), to help it maneuver in orbit and to slow it down when it is ready to de-orbit and return to Earth. They produce only 6000 pounds of thrust apiece, but this is sufficient to maneuver the shuttle orbiter when it is in orbit and essentially weightless. The OMS rockets are in the orbiter's tail section, just above the SSMEs (see figure 3).

The OMS rockets use monomethylhydrazine (MMH), a hydrocarbon-based fuel, and nitrogen peroxide as the oxidizer. The propellants can stay in their tanks for the duration of the shuttle's mission; they are neither cryogenic nor terribly corrosive. The OMS rockets can be turned on and off, as needed, until they run out of propellants.

The orbiter also has a *reaction control system* (RCS) for finer, more delicate maneuvers in orbit, where even gentler touches of thrust must be used. Like the OMS, the reaction control rockets use MMH and nitrogen peroxide, but the RCS engines produce only nine hundred pounds of thrust each. There are thirty-eight primary RCS engines, spotted around the orbiter, and six even smaller *vernier* RCS engines, which produce twenty-five pounds of thrust each.

Mass Ratio

Lifting a spacecraft up from the surface of the Earth requires a massive amount of thrust. The total takeoff weight of the fully loaded space shuttle, for example, is roughly 1500 tons. Of this, no more than 25 tons is payload, assuming a 160-nautical-mile orbit after a launch due east. Astronautical engineers call the ratio of payload weight to the total weight of the entire craft its *mass ratio*. The shuttle's mass ratio is thus about 0.016, or 1.6 percent.

The useful payload that the shuttle delivers into orbit is about 1.6 percent of its total takeoff weight. Compare this to a cargo-carrying Boeing 747-200C, which weighs 416.5 tons fully loaded and carries 114.25 tons of cargo, a payload ratio of better than 27 percent.

The gigantic Saturn V, tall as a 36-story skyscraper, flawlessly lifted all the Apollo astronauts and their spacecraft on their Moon missions. It weighed 3000 tons fully loaded. For the same due-east

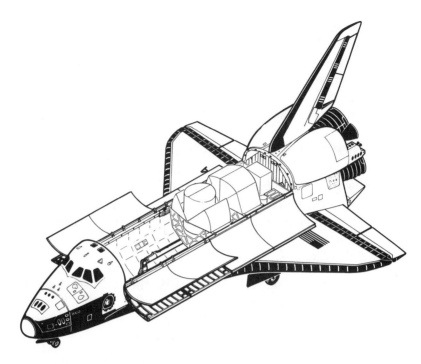

FIGURE 3 Drawing of the Space Shuttle *Orbiter.*
One orbital maneuvering system rocket (OMS) is visible at the rear, near the larger nozzles of the shuttle main engines (SMEs). Reaction control system (RCS) and smaller vernier RCS thrusters are shown on the nose and in the projection of the tail can. (Courtesy NASA)

launch and 160-nautical-mile orbit as we calculated for the shuttle, Saturn V could deliver 182 tons into low Earth orbit. Thus its mass ratio was 0.060, or 6 percent—nearly four times better than the shuttle's but still woefully less than your family car or a commercial airliner.

Of course, most of the space shuttle is reusable, while the entire Saturn V was expendable. In 1995, it would cost $1.2 billion to launch a Saturn V, assuming a rate of two launches per year, while it costs $500 million per shuttle launch, assuming five to seven launches per year. Still, the cost of putting a pound into orbit works out to be $3,297 per pound for Saturn V vs. $10,000 per pound for the shuttle (again, in 1995 dollars).

Compared to other forms of transportation, rockets seem terribly inefficient and expensive at best. Yet they are the only way we know of to boost people and payloads into space. Clearly, to make spaceflight less expensive, we need more efficient rocket systems—or something else. In later chapters we will look at some of the new rocket vehicles that are now being developed. And at alternative ideas that are still in the realm of theory, but perfectly fair material for a science fiction writer to use.

THE WRITER'S PERSPECTIVE

Most of the details given in this chapter are good examples of material that should be left out of any story you write.

Why? Well, think of the dog Snoopy in the "Peanuts" comic strip. Once Snoopy was writing a novel, perched precariously on his doghouse roof and pecking away at a typewriter. He wrote something like this:

> "I love you," he said. "My love is taller than the highest mountain, which is Mt. Everest, at a height of 29,028 feet. My love for you is deeper than the deepest ocean, which is the Marianas Trench, at a depth of 31,681 feet."

Then Snoopy looked up from his typewriter and muttered, "My hero is an awful bore."

Do not bore your readers with technical details that do not move the story forward.

You have to know the facts in order to write a convincing, well-crafted story that is internally consistent. But the reader does not have to know every tiny detail. There is nothing deadlier to good fiction than to have the writer trot out every little piece of research that went into the story. It is as if the writer is saying, "See all the hard work I've done? I hope you appreciate it!"

Rockets for a Mars Mission

Let me give you a practical example of what I mean. In my novel *Mars*, I spent months of research on every detail of the spacecraft that would carry my explorers to the planet Mars. If you read *Mars*, however, you will find that I never mentioned the type of rocket engines used to propel the spacecraft. I know what those engines are. The reader did not need to know, and I did not want to slow the pace of the story to describe such technical details.

On the other hand, if the story had required that something go wrong with the rocket engines, then I would have provided a good deal of detail about them.

If it's not important to the story's forward momentum, leave it out. You may have sweated for months to figure out every inch of plumbing in your spaceship's hydrazine/fluorine rocket system. Fine. Don't bore the reader with those details. Show that the rocket works—or fails to work. But spare your readers all the engineering drawings that you've made.

◆ ◆ ◆

[1] *Cryogenic* means "very cold," from the Greek *kryos* (cold) and *genis* (producing). Thus, the field of cryogenics deals with very low temperatures.

[2] Heavy atomic nuclei, such as those of thorium and uranium, spontaneously break down over time to lighter elements. This radioactive decay, as physicists call it, releases heat. And ionizing radiation.

[3] The ancient Greek philosophers believed there were four elements—earth, water, air and fire. A science fiction story could be written based upon this being a distorted memory of a once high-technology civilization.

CHAPTER 3

In Orbit

We set sail on this new sea because there is new knowledge to be gained, and new rights to be won, and they must be won and used for the progress of all people.

John F. Kennedy

TECHNICAL FACTORS

The first step is the most difficult one. It takes a lot of thrust to lift a spacecraft off the ground.

Once a spacecraft has established itself in orbit, however, it enters a whole new environment.

Weightlessness

A funny thing happens when you go into orbit. All weight seems to disappear. Everything in orbit is in a condition of zero gravity. Actually, it's not precisely zero *g*. There is some microscopic force present due to the gravitational attraction of the spacecraft's own mass. Physicists call the condition to be found in orbit *microgravity*, but for all intents and purposes—except for the most delicate experiments—it's zero *g*.

It all goes back to Newton's First Law of Motion. You recall that Sir Isaac found that a body in motion tends to remain moving in a straight line unless some outside force acts upon it.

OK. Time for a thought experiment, the kind that Albert Einstein called *gedanken*.

Picture yourself standing at second base in a baseball field with a ball in your hand. Toss the baseball lightly toward the center-field fence. What happens? The ball leaves your hand, travels a bit toward center field, and then drops to the ground.

Two forces have acted on the baseball: the force you gave it from

WHERE DOES SPACE BEGIN?

There is no hard-and-fast boundary between Earth and space. The upper reaches of our atmosphere thin out very gradually; even at 175 miles' altitude there are some fifteen billion atoms and molecules per square inch; enough of an atmosphere to cause some drag on an orbiting satellite.[1]

The U.S. Air Force awards astronaut's wings to any pilot who has flown higher than fifty miles.

For practical purposes we might say that space begins where a satellite can remain in orbit for several weeks before being dragged down by atmospheric friction. That is roughly 100 miles up. But don't look for a boundary line!

your throw and the force of gravity. Your muscles push the ball out across the field; gravity pulls it toward the center of the Earth.

Throw the ball harder—put more energy into it—and it travels farther before gravity pulls it to the ground. Imagine a superhuman throw, so strong that you clear the center-field fence. Still, after a while, gravity inevitably pulls the ball to the ground.

Now imagine a throw so powerful that its force is equal to the force of Earth's gravity. The ball "wants" to keep travelling in a straight line, on and on forever, but gravity keeps pulling it down toward the center of the Earth. Since the ball's momentum now equals the force of the Earth's gravity, the ball goes completely around the Earth. It is falling, because gravity is always pulling on it. But its forward momentum is now so strong that it no longer hits the Earth; it circles around it.

The ball is in orbit. Our thought experiment ignored the friction-induced drag that the air would impose on the ball. In the real world, that aerodynamic friction is important; it can slow a low-flying satellite and drag it down to a fiery crash.

To illustrate the two forces acting on a satellite, picture yourself whirling a weight on the end of a string. The force of the motion you have given the weight (called *centrifugal force*) is trying to fling that weight on a straight line outward. But the string keeps it tethered to your hand. So the weight moves in a circle around your head. For a satellite, the "string" is the force of gravity, while the force that wants to move it in a straight line outward toward infinity is the momentum imparted by the rocket booster's thrust.

Whether it's a baseball or a space station, an object must be moving at a speed of at least five miles per second to establish itself in orbit around the Earth: 5 mps is *orbital velocity* for our planet. Slower than that and it will fall back to Earth. Five mps equals 18,000 miles per hour.

You can see that the object to be orbited must be moving on a trajectory that roughly follows the Earth's curvature. Fire it straight up and even though it may reach 5 mps it will soon slow down and come hurtling back to Earth. The launching rocket, then, must not only impart orbital speed to the spacecraft, it must orient the spacecraft horizontally so that it will actually enter an orbit around the Earth.

Rockets take off vertically because that produces the least stress on the structure and gets the "bird" above the thickest, most drag-inducing layers of the atmosphere as fast as possible. But once at altitude, they tilt over so that they can release their satellites more or less horizontally.

And once in orbit you experience zero gravity, or weightlessness. You have not moved beyond Earth's gravity; if Earth were *not* exerting its gravitational pull, you would go flying off toward infinity. You feel weightless because your forward velocity neatly balances Earth's gravitational pull.

Physical Effects of Weightlessness

If you have ever been on a high-speed elevator when it starts to descend, you've had a moment of weightlessness. That sinking feeling you get when the elevator starts to drop is akin to the physical sensation of zero gravity.

Astronaut William R. Pogue, who spent eighty-four days in orbit aboard Skylab, describes the physical sensations of weightlessness from a firsthand point of view:

> The first thing you notice when you go into space is an absence of pressure on your body. You may feel light-headed or giddy. After half an hour or so, your face may feel flushed and you might feel a throbbing in your neck. As you move about, you will notice a strong sensation of spinning or tumbling every time you turn or nod your head. This makes some people uncomfortable or nauseated. You will also have a very

"full feeling" or stuffiness in your head. You may also get a bad headache after a few hours, and this too may make you feel sick to your stomach.

Most of these symptoms will go away in a few days. The head congestion or stuffiness may bother you off and on during your entire time in space. Throughout the space flight, you will feel a powerful sensation of tumbling or spinning every time you move your head too fast.

What is happening is that your body, which has been working under the influence of gravity all your life, suddenly finds itself weightless. All the fluids inside your body now weigh nothing. No longer restrained by gravity, they begin to shift because of the internal bodily pressures that are still present.

As your internal fluids shift, your waist slims somewhat and your legs become noticeably thinner. Pogue and his fellow astronauts called the phenomenon "bird legs." Your face gets puffier, too. The headache that Pogue mentioned is caused by fluids in your sinuses that cannot drain away, since gravity is no longer pulling them downward. There are no postnasal drips in orbit.

You grow a couple of inches taller! This is because your spine—which has been compressed slightly by the pull of Earth's one g—now expands, lengthens. Pogue reported that the tailor-made space suits the first astronauts wore all became too short in their sleeves, because of the spine-lengthening effect. The astronauts' hands felt cramped in their gloves as a result.

Space Sickness, or SAS

All of these sudden changes inside you cause some discomfort. For years, science fiction writers have written about "space sickness." NASA calls it "space adaptation syndrome" (SAS), a typically colorless title that is actually more descriptive of what is really happening. Your body is adapting to weightlessness. "Space sickness" is not like motion sickness or mal de mer.

Weightlessness has also been called "free-fall." You actually are falling, remember, but your fall will never end as long as you are in orbit. The balance mechanism of your inner ear is sending panic messages to your brain, while your eyes and other senses are telling your brain that you are snug and safe inside the spacecraft. That confusion of sensory signals adds to the miseries of SAS. After

WEIGHT VS. MASS

We are accustomed to dealing with how much things weigh because we live in Earth's gravity. In orbit everything is essentially weightless—but objects still possess mass.

Mass is the measure of how much material an object has. Weight is the measure of how much that material is pulled upon by another body. In our everyday world, we measure how much an object is pulled upon by the body of our planet Earth and call that the object's weight.

Since we have always equated mass with weight in our terrestrial experience, we use the same units for both. A piece of equipment—let's say a large telescope—that weighs 10 tons on Earth weighs virtually nothing in orbit. But it still has a mass of 10 tons. You may be able to push it with your fingertips, but it will respond very slowly, and if it bangs into you it will crush you just as effectively as it would on Earth.

To put it another way, you might weigh nothing in space, but you might still need to diet. Your mass will still be the same as it was on Earth.

a few hours (or, at worst, a few days), you adapt and stop feeling woozy.

Some spacefarers do upchuck during their first few hours in weightlessness. Senator Jake Garn, who was invited on a shuttle mission in 1985, apparently set world records for vomiting.

Once the body adapts to the zero-*g* environment, however, a feeling almost of euphoria sets in. You can float on air, literally! Videos of astronauts doing weightless acrobatics in the cavernous Skylab or in the closer confines of the space shuttle's mid-deck area show how much sheer fun it is to be in zero *g*.

Adapting to Zero *g*—and Then . . .

Since you weigh nothing, your muscles don't have to work as hard as they did on Earth. For space flights of more than a few days' duration, your muscles will begin to atrophy, go soft, unless you exercise strenuously. This includes your heart, which is essentially a muscle. Moreover, your bones reduce the amount of calcium they produce. On Earth that calcium keeps your bones strong. Under weightless conditions your bones no longer feel the stress of gravity, so they stop (or greatly slow) their calcium production.

Nothing really bad is happening—as long as you remain weightless. Your body is adapting to its environment. The problem comes when you return to Earth. Russian cosmonauts who have been aboard their space stations for many months need a few weeks to readapt to a full *g*. Some of them could not even stand up when they first returned to Earth.

Astronaut Pogue again, talking about his return after eighty-four days aboard Skylab:

> Everything felt heavy, including our own bodies. I picked up a three-pound camera just after splashdown, and it felt like it weighed fifteen or twenty pounds. . . . We were able to walk, but were a bit unsteady at first. . . . In weightlessness [we] had become used to releasing objects and having them float nearby until needed again. . . . I almost dropped a glass of water on the bathroom floor the first morning after return.

Just as the body adapts to weightlessness, it re-adapts to terrestrial gravity, in time. It helps to exercise as much as possible while in orbit to keep muscle tone.

Artificial Gravity

The Apollo missions to the Moon took less than a week, so the physiological effects of weightlessness did not present a great problem to the astronauts. But when humans go to Mars, the journey will take many months. If the Mars-bound spacecraft are in a state of zero *g* all that time, the explorers may have physical problems when they try to stand on the surface of Mars, even though Martian gravity is only about one-third that of Earth.

A similar problem will confront the men and women who live and work aboard space stations in Earth orbit. If they remain in orbit for months at a time, they may face physical problems—or at least a period of reconditioning—when they return to Earth.

For this reason, spacecraft and space stations may be designed to provide artificial gravity. This can be done by spinning the vehicle. Inside a space station, for example, the centrifugal force generated by spinning would feel like gravity. It would have the same physiological effects as gravity.

The spin rate could be set to produce the same force as a full

Earthly *g*, or it could be set at some lower rate. But the structure must be large enough so that it can spin slowly; otherwise the occupants could become dizzy. If the structure is too small, your feet will be spinning noticeably faster than your head—which would probably feel worse than weightlessness!

The exact dimensions of a spinning space station have not yet been determined; not enough is known yet about the human body's tolerance to spin forces. Yet it seems clear that spin rates of at least a few minutes will be desirable, which means that spinning space stations will have to be hundreds of yards across: Picture a bicycle tire with a diameter equal to the length of a football field.

In *2001: A Space Odyssey*, a Stanley Kubrick/Arthur Clarke film, one of the sequences showed a very large space station built like a wheel. It spun enough to give the people inside a comfortable feeling of normal terrestrial gravity.

Jobs That Satellites Do

Most of the satellites in orbit around the Earth are uncrewed, of course. They are remotely controlled machines sent into space to perform many different tasks:

Communications satellites relay telephone, television, radio and other forms of electronic communications around the world. *Telstar*, *Syncom* and *Westar* are among the satellites that relay commercial television broadcasts around the world. Russian communications satellites are usually named *Molniya*, while several other nations have launched communications satellites of their own.

Relatively poor nations such as India and Indonesia use communications satellites because a satellite is considerably less expensive than stringing cables or setting up microwave relay towers across the countryside.

Weather satellites observe the world's weather and make detailed meteorological measurements. Over the years they have saved millions of lives and trillions of dollars in property damage by spotting and tracking storms, thereby allowing forecasters to warn people in the storms' paths. *TIROS* (Television and InfraRed Observation Satellite) was the first dedicated weather satellite, launched in 1960. Today, a series of American *GOES* satellites covers the western hemisphere, while Europe's *Meteosat*, India's *Insat* and Japan's *GMS* observe weather conditions in the eastern hemisphere.

Navigation satellites provide precise positioning information to planes and ships. *Global Positioning Satellite* systems (*GPS*) beam such data to miniaturized, hand-sized receivers that individuals can use in their cars, pleasure boats or even on camping treks.

Earth resources satellites use a variety of sensors to identify and measure topological and geological features. The U.S. *Landsat*, for example, has provided forecasts of global wheat crops, spotted ancient ruins for archeologists, and discovered fault lines in the Earth's crust that indicate oil and mineral deposits.

Oceanographic satellites observe the Earth's seas. Much like the *Landsat* types, oceanographic satellites use a variety of sensors to map ocean currents, temperatures and other conditions.

Astronomical satellites take advantage of the fact that their instruments are above the obscuring layers of the Earth's atmosphere. Astronomical satellites can detect ultraviolet, X-ray and gamma-ray wavelengths that are always blocked from Earth-based instruments. The Hubble Space Telescope is able to peer deeper into the cosmos than any ground-based telescope and has sent an incalculable wealth of information about the planets of our Solar System, the stars, and the most distant galaxies and quasars.

Satellites such as the *Orbiting Solar Observatories* (*OSO*) have studied the Sun. The space probe *Ulysses* was sent into a trajectory that looped over the Sun's north and south poles, acquiring data that could not be obtained from Earth orbit.

The *COBE* (*Cosmic Background Explorer*) satellite has measured the very faint microwave radiation that is apparently the "echo" of the universe's very beginning (see chapter 12).

Military satellites are also used to relay communications, observe the weather, and perform surveillance of land, sea and air. In addition, the *Vela* series of satellites has monitored both the Earth and space for evidence of clandestine nuclear bomb tests. *Vela* satellites have also provided invaluable information about the levels of dangerous radiation in space and have even discovered gamma-ray "bursters" that have excited astronomers and cosmologists. (Again, more on this in chapter 12.)

Military surveillance satellites are also used for early warning of ballistic missile attacks. While, thankfully, there have been no large-scale missile attacks despite the forty-year-long Cold War and its nuclear arms race, early-warning satellites did spot Scud missiles fired by Iraq in the 1990-1991 Gulf War and provided targeting information for American Patriot defensive missiles.

As we will see in chapter 14, the original concept of the Strategic Defense Initiative (SDI, or "Star Wars," as the media dubbed it) was based on placing satellites in orbit that would be armed with sensors and weapons that could destroy ballistic missiles in flight.

GEO, LEO and Other Orbits

For each type of task that a satellite does there is a preferred type of orbit. Most satellite orbits fall into one of two broad categories: GEO and LEO.

GEO stands for *geosynchronous* (or *geostationary*) *Earth orbit*. This is the twenty-four-hour orbit, sometimes called the Clarke Orbit, after Arthur C. Clarke, who proposed in 1945 placing communications satellites in such orbits.

At an altitude of 22,300 miles above the equator, a satellite will revolve around the Earth in the same twenty-four-hour period that the Earth turns on its axis. This means that the satellite will appear to remain stationary above a point on the equator. Thus communications antennas can be "locked onto" the satellite; the antennas do not have to track it all across the sky.

The commsats that relay TV broadcasts around the world hang up there in GEO.[2] Weather satellites are also placed in GEO, where they can see almost half the world. So are certain "spy" satellites, orbited by various intelligence and military organizations.

Most satellites are placed in LEO: *low Earth orbit*, which means anywhere from sixty miles' up to about three hundred miles' altitude. The reason is obvious enough. The closer the satellite, the more clearly it can see the ground. Or the sea. Satellites sent aloft to look back at the Earth are usually sent to LEO.

The region between three hundred miles' altitude and GEO is usually referred to as *medium earth orbit*. Relatively few satellites are placed in MEO.

Although the major commsats ride in GEO, a new breed of communications satellites is being placed in low orbits. Smaller and cheaper, these LEO commsats are being orbited to relay cellular telephone messages and data around the world. Private companies such as Motorola and Orbital Sciences Corp. are building networks of such satellites for cellular phone service. Before the end of this century, cellular phones will be able to reach anywhere on Earth, at any time. (More on this in chapter 5.)

Orbital Inclinations

An orbit exactly above the equator is said to have an *inclination* of zero. A polar orbit has an inclination of ninety degrees. Obviously, the term inclination refers to the angle of the satellite's orbit to the plane of the equator.

As we have seen, commsats are placed in GEO; they orbit above the equator. They have to. Any deviation from their equatorial orbit will throw them out of the twenty-four-hour synchronicity that they require.

If you want to observe the Earth's surface, though, a polar orbit makes a lot of sense. At an altitude of a few hundred miles, a two-hour-long orbit that sweeps from north pole to south (or the other way around) will cover every square inch of the Earth's surface twice a day. This is because the Earth turns beneath the satellite's orbit.

A satellite launched due south into a polar orbit from the Vandenberg Air Force Base, for example, will start its first orbit close to 120° west longitude. The satellite will remain in its orbit continuously circling the Earth from pole to pole every two hours. The planet revolves beneath it, though, so that the ground track beneath the satellite sweeps 30° farther west on every individual orbit. After twelve hours the satellite is back over the longitude of Vandenberg AFB.

Earth Boosting

Most satellites are placed in orbits that are neither equatorial nor polar but somewhere in between. Such orbits are a compromise among many competing requirements, including the fact that the Earth's own spin can either help or hinder attempts to get a satellite into orbit.

Our planet is spinning from west to east at a rate of close to 1000 mph along the equator. If you launch a satellite in an easterly direction, you gain some of that velocity for free. That means the rocket starts off with at least a part of the Earth's velocity, depending on how far from the equator the launch pad is. The rocket's engines do not have to work so hard; alternatively, your booster can carry more payload for the same amount of rocket thrust.

If you want to launch in a westerly direction, however, your rocket engines will have to *add* thrust to overcome the Earth's motion, which now works against you. Launching into polar orbits, due north or due south, means you gain nothing from the Earth's spin.

Thus, almost all launches are aimed eastward, except polar launches, which carry smaller payloads, given the same rocket thrust.

Orbital Eccentricities

Orbits also have eccentricities. That is, they are not all perfectly circular.

If a satellite is placed into an orbit at exactly 5 mps, its orbit will be circular (neglecting air drag). If the satellite's velocity is below 5 mps, its orbit will intersect with the Earth's surface. Splash! Or more likely, the satellite will burn up from the heat of the friction it generates as it plunges into the atmosphere at hypersonic speed.

Give the satellite a velocity above that critical 5 mps, though, and its orbit will be elliptical, not circular. The degree of difference from a perfect circle is called the orbit's *eccentricity*.

The highest point in the satellite's orbit is called the *apogee*, from the Greek roots *apo*, meaning away, and *gee*, for Earth. The lowest point in the orbit is the *perigee*; Greek again, meaning "near the Earth."

When speaking of spacecraft that are put into interplanetary trajectories, which are really orbits around the Sun, the terms become *aphelion* and *perihelion*.

Five miles per second is the minimum speed a satellite needs to orbit the Earth. If it goes faster than 7 mps, however, it escapes Earth altogether and heads out into the Solar System: 7 mps is "escape velocity."

The higher above the Earth a satellite is, the slower it is moving. You can see this from the fact that a satellite just skimming the fringes of our atmosphere at a scant 150 miles up orbits around the Earth in about ninety minutes, while a geostationary satellite at 22,300 miles' altitude takes 24 hours to complete one orbit. And our natural Moon, at a distance of some 240,000 miles, needs about 27.3 days to complete its orbit around the Earth.

Sometimes a satellite is deliberately launched into a very eccentric orbit, with an apogee much higher than its perigee. Intelligence gathering "spy" satellites, for example, can be placed in orbits where the apogee is over the area to be watched. The high apogee gives the satellite a longer "dwell time" over the region of interest. The satellite will move more slowly at its apogee, then speed up as it approaches the Earth to whip past its perigee and start climbing again.

Such orbits are usually a compromise between dwell time and the sensitivity of the satellite's cameras and other sensors. You want the longest dwell time possible over the region of interest, but you cannot put the satellite apogee so high that its cameras and sensors will not have the resolution—the ability to see fine details—that you desire.

Adjusting the Orbit

Often the rocket booster does not insert the satellite exactly into the orbit that its controllers want. Or the booster can only carry the satellite into a low orbit, when the controllers want a higher one. That is why most satellites carry small rocket motors of one type or another, either to boost them to higher orbits or to correct the orbit they start with.

For example, the space shuttle cannot get to GEO. It was designed strictly for LEO operations, with a maximum altitude capability well below five hundred miles. Yet the shuttle has launched many commsats that are now in GEO. Each of those satellites had its own propulsion system that carried it up to GEO after being released from the shuttle orbiter's cargo bay in LEO.

The mathematics of orbital mechanics is well known and quite exact. In fact, it dates back to Isaac Newton's work. *Transfer orbits* can be plotted with great accuracy, and as long as the rocket thrusters work properly, satellites can be maneuvered from one orbit to another with pinpoint precision. We will discuss transfer orbits a bit more in chapter 9.

Satellites also carry small *attitude control thrusters* to keep them pointing in the direction they should and for station-keeping. A commsat up in GEO, for example, would be useless if its antennas did not point toward the ground, or if it drifted out of its "slot" in GEO and the antennas on the ground no longer pointed at it.

And satellites do jiggle around up there. Perturbations in a satellite's orbit are caused by slight irregularities in the Earth's gravitational field (such as those caused by our planet's equatorial bulge, for example), by tidal pulls of the Moon and Sun, and even tiny gravitational tugs from the distant planets.

The attitude control thrusters on most satellites are simply cold-gas jets that squirt a relatively inert gas such as nitrogen on command from the ground controllers. No need to burn chemical propellants; the thrust required is minuscule. But a $50 million commsat can go out of business when its gas supply is exhausted. Good reason to send repairmen up to GEO some day.

Delta v

Whenever an orbiting spacecraft has to change its orbit, it has to use rocket thrust. There is no other way to maneuver in the vacuum of space. Rocket thrust must be used to change the spacecraft's speed and direction of motion.

Engineers use the term δv, from the Greek lowercase *delta* (the symbol used to denote change) and v for velocity. Note that *velocity* means not merely speed, but speed plus direction, or the rate of change of an object's motion.

The thrust, and therefore the amount of propellant, needed to move from one orbit to another is expressed in delta v. It is quite a practical term. For example, a communications satellite released in LEO by the space shuttle must get to GEO. By calculating the change in velocity that must be imparted to the commsat, the engineers can find out how much thrust is needed, how big a rocket engine is needed for the task, and how much propellant it must carry.

Similar calculations are done for launching a lunar or planetary probe from Earth orbit toward its ultimate destination. As we will see in chapter 5, when the time comes when space miners want to get to an asteroid, one of their primary considerations will be, "How much delta vee do we need to reach the rock?"

Reentry and Landing

Getting into space is only half the fun. Getting back to Earth means that your spacecraft must reenter the atmosphere and reach the ground (or water) without burning up like a shooting star.

An orbiting spacecraft is moving at a speed of 5 mps or more. Spacecraft returning from the Moon or an interplanetary mission return at speeds of 7 mps or better, unless they use rocket braking to slow to orbital velocity.

It would be very nice if a spacecraft could slow itself to a safe, comfortable speed of Mach 2 or 3 (two or three times the speed of sound, about the speed of high-performance fighter jets) before reentering the atmosphere. But that would require more rocket propellant than any spacecraft can reasonably carry. Instead, engineers have learned how to use the atmosphere itself as a braking medium.

The space shuttle's orbiter, for example, fires its OMS engines to brake out of orbit and dip back into the atmosphere. Air friction slows the orbiter as it approaches its landing site. It starts into the atmosphere with a hypersonic speed, above Mach 20, crosses the Pacific Ocean in less than half an hour, and is "merely" flying slightly above Mach 1 when it starts its approach for landing, either at Edwards Air Force Base in California or Kennedy Space Center in Florida.

The orbiter's main engines have long since used all their propellants, and its OCS and RCS rockets don't have enough thrust to matter. Once it reenters the atmosphere, the shuttle orbiter becomes a 99-ton glider. Its astronaut pilot has to make a good landing the first time; there can be no "go around" for another try.

The friction that slows the orbiter also generates enormous heat. Temperatures of 2280°F have been measured during the orbiter's blazing reentry. During the few minutes of most intensive heating, the spacecraft is surrounded by a glowing sheath of plasma that blocks radio signals. This is the most dramatic point in a reentry, when the crew is out of contact with ground control.

To prevent that heat from destroying the spacecraft, the orbiter's underside and nose are covered with a heat shield that consists of thousands of brick-sized ceramic tiles. They radiate about 95 percent of the reentry heat away from the craft, while slowly absorbing the remaining 5 percent. The residual heat is radiated away after the orbiter lands. Those tiles are *hot* when the craft touches down on the runway. Less than 1 percent of the total heat load generated during reentry actually reaches the metal skin of the orbiter's structure.

Those heat shield tiles are fantastic stuff. I have held one in my hand while a smiling-technician played a blowtorch across it. My palm did not even get warm.

Earlier spacecraft, such as the Apollo command modules, used a different kind of heat shield. The Apollo heat shields were made of *ablative* material. The heat shield material actually boiled away—ablated—during reentry, carrying the heat off with it. Ballistic missile warheads have ablative heat shields. Obviously, ablative heat shields cannot be used more than once, while the shuttle's radiative tiles are used over and over again.

The shuttle's tiles are glued onto the orbiter by hand, a rather laborious process. On early shuttle flights some of them came loose and fell off during the thunderous rattling of liftoff. Fortunately, only a few fell off, not enough to cause a problem during reentry.

The epoxy used to glue the tiles onto the orbiter "sets" in a vacuum, so after a few dozen tiles have been glued on, the factory workers place a vacuum bag around the area and pump out the air until the epoxy firms up. It would be more efficient, actually, to put on the tiles while the shuttle is in orbit! The vacuum of LEO is better than the one produced on the Rockwell factory floor.

Future heat shields will depend on better materials that will be able to absorb or reject heat even more efficiently than the shuttle's ceramic tiles.

THE WRITER'S PERSPECTIVE

This chapter has been intended to give you a basic understanding of the factors involved in orbital mechanics and the physiological effects of weightlessness.

We have skipped the mathematical details, but you can find them easily enough in any competent book on astronautics. If you are interested in details, *The Cambridge Encyclopedia of Space* is a good place to start. Even better, in some ways, is Arthur Clarke's seminal *Interplanetary Flight*. First published in 1950, this little gem of a book contains all the basics of orbital mechanics and rocketry.

Astronaut William R. Pogue's delightful book, *How Do You Go to the Bathroom in Space?* presents a wealth of detail on what it's like to live and work in orbit.

Function Determines Orbit

As you can see, not only do satellites perform many different functions, but their individual functions determine what kind of an orbit they should have.

Think about GEO. To remain in a geosynchronous orbit a satellite must be moving above the equator (another way of saying that is that the satellite must be in the equatorial plane of the Earth). That orbit has a large but limited number of sites available for commsats. Each commsat needs a certain amount of elbow room, otherwise the communications beams from one satellite will interfere with the signals from another.

Therefore, commsats are assigned to GEO "slots" through international agreements. This makes GEO a valuable piece of territory, even though it is nothing more than (mostly) empty space.

Is GEO a National Territory?

That is grist for a science fiction writer's mill. My novelette "Sam's War" is based on the idea that the nations lying along the equator claim that the geosynchronous orbit is part of their national territory. In fact, there was exactly such a claim made in the United Nations in the 1970s by a band of Third World nations that called itself the Group of 77. None of the spacefaring nations paid the slightest attention to their claim, because the Group of 77's members were powerless to enforce it. But in "Sam's War" the equatorial nations are prepared to back their claim with force.

"Sam's War" is a humorous story; its protagonist is Sam Gunn, a roguish, womanizing, unscrupulous entrepreneur who is constantly making and losing fortunes in space. But many other kinds of stories could be written about claims to GEO—or other parts of the universe. (We will look at the legal aspects of space travel in chapter 13.)

Space Junk

Sam Gunn was also involved in another story that deals with a different problem in orbital space. The LEO region is accumulating a lot of junk. Bits and pieces of rocket boosters, chips of paint, even equipment accidentally lost by astronauts during EVA space walks is floating around in LEO. Most of the litter eventually spirals into the atmosphere and burns up, but new junk is constantly being added by new space missions.

The more active we are in space, the more debris we will be leaving in LEO. This can be dangerous. The space shuttle has been hit more than once by flying debris; one nearly microscopic flake of paint starred the orbiter cockpit's windshield. The Russian space station Mir, in orbit since 1986, has been hit several times.

NASA is looking at ways to remove the litter in orbit. That led me to write a Sam Gunn story titled "Vacuum Cleaner," in which Sam hatches a scheme to clean up the vacuum of LEO—not without making a profit, of course.

Sex in Weightlessness

As far as I know, my short story "Zero Gee" was the first to deal with the possibilities of sex in the weightlessness of orbit. The story was specific but not graphic.

Sex is a normal part of human behavior and thus should be considered as legitimate story material, if you can write about it without: (a) offending your readers or (b) looking foolish. If *you* are embarrassed by the subject, then don't try to write about it.

Mixed crews of men and women have flown on the space shuttle and the space station Mir. To date, no one has admitted to making love in orbit. But it's only a matter of time.

Several of my Sam Gunn stories deal with Sam's dream of building a honeymoon hotel in orbit. His motto for his sex palace in the sky: "If you like water beds, you'll love zero gee."

Even in stories that are not specifically about sex, as long as you are writing about normal men and women you will have to consider their mating urges, which will continue to exist in orbit, on the Moon, Mars, or the farthest reaches of the universe. In fact, the sexual tensions of a mixed crew on a long and dangerous mission to Mars formed a powerful subplot in my novel *Mars*.

The point is that the more you know about what is happening in space and the environment to be found there, the more story ideas will occur to you. New writers constantly worry about where they can find story ideas. Experienced writers know that ideas are everywhere—but like the salesman says in Meredith Willson's *The Music Man*, "You've got to know the territory."

[1] That may sound like a lot of particles, but there are about 360 billion *billion* atoms and molecules in our air at sea level, under normal conditions. That's some 24 billion times denser than the wisps of atmosphere at the 175-mile level, which can be considered a very good vacuum.

[2] Spell "commsat" with two *m*'s. *Comsat* is the legal trade name of the Communications Satellite Corp., and they get very irked when a writer calls a communications satellite a one-*m* "comsat."

CHAPTER 4

Living and Working in Space

They cannot scare me with their empty spaces
Between stars—on stars where no human race is.

Robert Frost, "Desert Places"

TECHNICAL FACTORS

To date, only a couple of hundred men and women have lived and worked in space. Most of them have flown on the U.S. space shuttle, and their space missions have lasted only a few days.

As of August 1995, a total of 323 men and women have flown in space: 204 Americans, 80 Russians, 7 Germans, 5 Frenchmen, 3 Japanese, 3 Canadians, 2 Britons, 2 Bulgarians, and 1 each from Afghanistan, Austria, Belgium, Cuba, the former Czechoslovakia, Hungary, India, Italy, Mexico, Mongolia, the Netherlands, Poland, Romania, Saudi Arabia, Switzerland, Syria and Vietnam.

The endurance record for living in space belongs to cosmonaut Valeriy Polyakov, who stayed aboard the Russian space station, Mir, for 438 days. He returned to Earth on March 22, 1995, shattering the previous record of 366 days set in 1988 by cosmonauts Vladimir Titov and Nusa Manarov, also aboard Mir.

Space—The Bad News

It would be difficult to imagine an environment less hospitable to life than the conditions to be found in space. To begin with, there is no air to breathe. Orbital space is a vacuum emptier than the best vacuums used in industrial processes on Earth.

That does not mean that space is completely empty, however.

As we have seen, at 175 miles' altitude the density of the Earth's atmosphere has thinned to some twenty-four billion times less than its density at sea level.

The unit of measurement for vacuum is the *torr*, named after Evangelista Torricelli, who invented the barometer in 1643. On Earth, standard air pressure at sea level is 760 torr. Vacuums of one ten-thousandth of a torr (10^4 torr) are used in terrestrial industrial processes. In *cislunar* space—the region between LEO and the Moon—the vacuum ranges from about 10^7 torr in LEO to 10^{12} torr at the Moon's surface: a hundred million times lower than the vacuum used in terrestrial factories and laboratories.

As we go outward, past the Moon, the vacuum of space becomes even thinner. Interplanetary space has a density of perhaps ten atomic particles per cubic inch. Beyond the Solar System, in interstellar space, the density of particles is at least ten times lower.

The Solar Wind

Not only is space a vacuum, but it is drenched with lethal radiation and bombarded by celestial buckshot.

An ethereal wind blows across the Solar System, a wind of subatomic particles driven off the Sun's blazing corona, where temperatures exceed a million degrees. This solar wind consists almost entirely of electrons and protons, basic subatomic particles. The solar wind usually passes Earth's vicinity at a velocity of some 250 miles per hour, although during episodes of violent flares on the Sun the wind can reach a "hurricane strength" of more than a thousand miles per hour.

By ordinary terrestrial standards the solar wind is a vacuum of about ten particles per cubic inch. If you could stand naked in cislunar space your skin would not feel any wind at all. Yet those particles carry tremendous energy on the atomic level, especially the protons, which are nearly 2000 times more massive than the electrons. You wouldn't feel the solar wind, but it would fry you in moments with its lethal radiation.

The Geomagnetosphere

The Earth creates a shock wave in the solar wind, somewhat like the bow wave of a boat as it cuts through water (see figure 4). But the shock wave in the solar wind is not made by the solid body of our planet; it is made by the Earth's magnetic field. Our planet is a large dipole magnet, with its magnetic poles near the geographic north and south poles. It is this *geomagnetic field* that makes compass needles point roughly north.

Planetary astronomers call the magnetic field that surrounds a planet its *magnetosphere*. The Earth's magnetosphere is called the *geomagnetosphere*. The solar wind presses on our geomagnetosphere, flattening it on the sunward side and stretching out the night side into an enormous "tail" that reaches past the orbit of the Moon.

The Weather in Space

When the Sun is quiet and there are few sunspots or solar flares, the "upwind," the daylight side of the geomagnetosphere extends to about ten Earth radii above the Earth's surface (one Earth radius equals 3959 miles). A shock wave stands out slightly in front of the main body of the magnetosphere, at about fourteen Earth radii. During powerful disturbances on the Sun, when the solar wind blows hard, the magnetosphere can be flattened down to as close as eight radii.

Solar flares are sudden bursts of energy that can release as much energy as a hundred million *billion* tons of exploding TNT (10^{11} megatons) in a few seconds: more energy than the whole world consumes in fifty thousand years.

The electromagnetic radiation from a flare—visible light, radio energy, ultraviolet and X-rays—reaches the Earth with the speed of light, in about eight minutes. This is the warning of danger. Close behind (a few minutes to a few hours) comes the first wave of extremely energetic protons and electrons, travelling at "relativistic" speeds; that is, close to the speed of light.[1]

The energy in these particles is measured in *electron volts* (ev). One electron volt is a minuscule bit of energy; it would take 5 million ev to light a 50-watt bulb. But protons with energies of 20 to 40 million electron volts (Mev) can easily penetrate a quarter-inch of lead, and particles from solar flares with energies of more than 15,000 *billion* electron volts—15,000 Bev or 15 giga-electron-volts (Gev)—have reached the Earth.

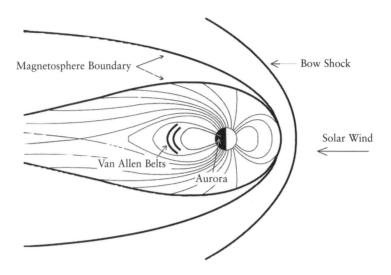

FIGURE 4 The Geomagnetosphere.
Van Allen belts of radiation are regions where energetic protons and electrons from the solar wind are captured by the magnetic field. The auroras occur where particles from the belt excite gases high in the Earth's atmosphere.

And the most violent effects of the solar flare are yet to come.

The flare has ejected a great puff of very energetic plasma into interplanetary space; it expands as it moves outward from the Sun, growing to dimensions far larger than the Earth. When it hits the geomagnetosphere it rattles the entire geomagnetic field, causing a *magnetic storm*.

The auroras at the north and south poles flare dramatically, and "northern lights" (aurora borealis) are seen far south of their usual haunts.[2] The *ionosphere*—layers of ionized particles that begin some fifty miles up—runs amok, gaining and losing ionized particles in a wildly unpredictable fashion that makes a shambles of long-range radio transmissions normally reflected off its ionized layers. Within a few days the ionosphere settles down. The auroras stop flaring. Cislunar space returns to normal. Until the next solar flare.

But any astronauts caught unprotected by shielding during such a solar storm would be quickly killed by the intense radiation levels of those energetic protons. Fortunately, as we shall soon see, the

RADIATION IN SPACE

The word "radiation" is used in two ways, and it is important to understand the distinction between them.

Electromagnetic radiation is light, in its many forms. Visible light is only one small slice of the broad electromagnetic spectrum, the part that our eyes have adapted to sense. Radio waves are electromagnetic radiation, too—"light" that we can't see. So are microwaves, infrared and ultraviolet light, X-rays and gamma rays.

The kind of radiation that can cause physical damage to the human body is called *ionizing* radiation. That is because such radiation can ionize atoms within your body, strip electrons off those atoms, which causes harmful physiological effects. X-rays and gamma rays can harm you that way, so in addition to being forms of electromagnetic radiation they are also dangerous forms of ionizing radiation.

Other forms of ionizing radiation come from energetic subatomic particles, such as the protons accelerated to Bev and Gev levels in a solar flare. These invisible bullets can kill unprotected humans in space.

Earth's own magnetosphere offers a good measure of protection for astronauts in LEO.

Cosmic Rays

Another source of ionizing radiation in space are the so-called *cosmic rays*, which are not rays at all but subatomic particles. Unlike solar protons, cosmic particles can be the stripped nuclei of much heavier elements, including iron and other heavy metals, although bare protons make up their vast majority. Cosmic particles are the most energetic things we have observed in the universe: Bev energies are commonplace, and energies of 100 million Gev have been seen.

Apparently cosmic rays are created in supernovas, the titanic explosions that very massive stars undergo at the end of their lifespans (see chapter 10). In 1995, the Japanese-U.S. scientific satellite ASCA (Advanced Satellite for Cosmology and Astrophysics) detected the X-ray signature of high-energy cosmic rays in the remains of supernova SN 1006. The star-wrecking fury of the supernova explosions acts as a particle accelerator, firing out subatomic particles at tremendous energies.

Such energetic particles can penetrate miles of solid ground, and cosmic radiation showers the surface of our world constantly. However, most of the cosmic radiation that reaches the ground is not the original particles from space. The "primary" cosmic particles almost always run into an atom or molecule in the Earth's atmosphere and cause a shattering collision that produces a shower of "secondary" particles. It is these secondaries, for the most part, that reach the ground.

Extremely energetic primary cosmic particles can be a major danger to space travellers, causing genetic mutations and cell damage, even though the infall of such particles, while constant, is fairly thin. Here on Earth, half a dozen secondary cosmic particles strike your body every minute of your life. They may cause mutations, and they probably cause some cancers, but they have not killed anyone directly—that we know of.

Earth's Umbrella

Fortunately for us on the ground—and for people in LEO—our planet has a natural radiation shield, an umbrella that protects us against most of the dangers of solar flares: the geomagnetic field.

The earliest satellites discovered that the magnetosphere contains regions where electrically charged particles are trapped in the geomagnetic field. The particles come from the solar wind, solar flares and cosmic rays. They are caught in the geomagnetic field, spiralling back and forth along the magnetic field lines.

These regions were named the *Van Allen radiation belts,* after James A. Van Allen, the physicist whose instruments aboard the first American satellite, Explorer 1, discovered them in 1958.

The lower Van Allen belt is centered about 1800 miles above the magnetic equator and consists mainly of energetic protons. Some 9000 miles up, the outer belt contains very energetic electrons. Both belts curve downward around the geomagnetic poles and dip into the atmosphere. They tend to dump some of their particles into the air in those regions, where the energetic particles excite the molecules and atoms of the atmosphere. The northern and southern auroras are nothing less than gigantic fluorescent displays, like neon lamps, powered by the particles from the Van Allen belts that excite the gases in our atmosphere and make them glow.

The belts do not have hard and fast boundaries. Charged sub-atomic particles can be found below, above and in between the heaviest regions of the belts. But notice that the geomagnetic field absorbs and traps most of the incoming particles from the solar wind and solar flares. The belts are part of our protective umbrella.

Space stations and other satellites in LEO orbit below the belts. Commsats in GEO orbit above the main regions of trapped particles, although there is still enough ionizing radiation at that altitude to make permanent human stations in GEO unlikely, unless they are "armored" against such radiation.

Travelling Beyond the "Umbrella"

The Apollo missions to the Moon left the protection of our geomagnetosphere's umbrella far behind them. If a solar flare had erupted during an Apollo mission the astronauts may well have been killed. James Michener used this possibility in his novel *Space*.

Although solar flares are not entirely predictable, they do tend to occur when there is lots of sunspot activity on the Sun. NASA was able to time the Apollo flights at periods when flares were unlikely.

But missions to Mars and the other planets will take months, not the few days of the Apollo flights. Interplanetary missions will undoubtedly run into solar storms. They will need some form of protection against the high levels of radiation. As we will see in chapter 8, "storm cellars" will be an important part of deep-space missions.

Meteoroids

There are objects far bigger than subatomic particles zipping through orbital space, as a glance at the Moon will show. Meteoroids, ranging in size from grains of dust to mountainous boulders big enough to wipe out the dinosaurs, fall to Earth at speeds of 25,000 mph (7 mps) or more.

Astronomers estimate that about 100 tons of meteoroids fall into the Earth each year. That is a considerable amount of matter. Most of the meteoroids are no bigger than dust grains, although even a dust grain can cause a damaging impact when it is moving at 7 mps.

That is why space suits, spacecraft and space stations must have at least a thin outer layer of protection, to stop this hail of meteoric

METEORS, METEOROIDS AND METEORITES

When you see the streak of a "falling star" flash across the night sky, that is called a *meteor*, after an ancient Greek root meaning, roughly, "something in the air." The thing that causes that streak is a chunk of matter, which astronomers calls *meteoroid*. Most meteoroids burn up in the atmosphere, but some of the larger ones make it through their blazing flight to reach the Earth's surface. When a meteoroid reaches the ground, it is called a *meteorite*.

So a meteoroid is the solid body (although it may be only as large as a dust mote), a meteor is the blaze it makes when it enters Earth's air and begins to burn from atmospheric friction, and a meteorite is what's left of the body if it survives to reach the ground.

Meteoroids begin to burn up at about 60 miles' altitude, where the air becomes thick enough to generate significant atmospheric friction.

musketry from penetrating beyond the outermost shell.

Meteoroids are apparently the leftovers from the earliest days of the Solar System, when the planets and their moons were growing to their present sizes by pulling together smaller bodies in a process called *accretion*. The face of the Moon shows that there was a massive meteoritic bombardment there; Mars, Venus, Mercury and even the moons of the outer planets show similar evidence of meteoritic bombardment.

The heaviest phase of this bombardment ended more than three billion years ago, but there are still a good deal of "leftovers" flying through the Solar System. As we have seen, about one hundred tons' worth come close enough to Earth each year to be pulled in by our gravitational attraction.

Here on Earth, the weathering action of sea and wind have erased most of the meteor strikes. But there are several *astroblemes*—scars of meteoroid hits—scattered around the globe. Probably the most famous is the Barringer Meteor Crater in Arizona.

Killer Meteoroids. Paleontologists are largely agreed that a meteoroid about fifteen miles wide hit the Earth near what is now the

Yucatan peninsula at the end of the Cretaceous Era, about sixty-five million years ago. Its impact drove so much dust and debris into the atmosphere that it blocked sunlight for months and caused the death of three-quarters of all species of life on land, sea and air—including the dinosaurs.

There are plenty of meteoroids of similar size roaming through the Solar System. Or larger.

Some astronomers have urged that NASA and other space agencies begin a "meteor watch" to find and track meteoroids that might be on their way to causing *our* extinction.

This has been a fruitful concept for many science fiction writers. In "The Hammer of God," Arthur C. Clarke described how the asteroid Kali is diverted (just in time, as you might expect) from impact with Earth. Larry Niven and Jerry Pournelle also dealt with this theme in their best-selling *Lucifer's Hammer*.

Space Stations

A space station, as we will use the term in this book, is a structure that is placed in orbit for the purpose of housing human beings who have gone into space to work. The purpose of a space station is to allow men and women to work in orbit. Think of it as a workshop in space, an outpost on the frontier—the frontier that begins 100 miles over your head.

Even though the space environment is fraught with danger, humans have already begun to work in space. Space stations will allow them to live in orbit for months, or years, or as long as they want to.

By the 1940s, just before the beginning of the Space Age, when dreamers such as science fiction writers and a few farsighted (and derided) engineers talked about their visions for our future in space, one of the first steps they planned was to build a space station in LEO.

The idea was that a space station would be a base in orbit, from which we could:

1. Learn how to live and work in the strange new environment of space;
2. Begin to study the conditions in space;
3. Conduct scientific research under the conditions of weightlessness;

4. Assemble spacecraft that could take us to the Moon, planets, and eventually to the stars;
5. Use the conditions of weightlessness, high vacuum, and free solar energy for manufacturing, chemical, and other industrial/commercial purposes.

Two things happened in the real world to demolish that plan. First, the swift progress in electronics allowed engineers to build uncrewed satellites that began the exploration of orbital space. No need to send human beings to do the job.

Starting with *Sputnik I* in 1957, the conditions in space were studied mainly by robot satellites. As we have seen, the first American satellite, *Explorer 1* (launched on January 31, 1958), discovered the Van Allen radiation belts.

The Space Race

But more shattering to the plan of building space stations on the orbital frontier was the politics of the 1960s Space Race. The U.S. and U.S.S.R. were bitter Cold War enemies in those days, and one of their battlegrounds was in space.

The Soviet Union stunned the Western world with a long string of "firsts" in space: the first artificial satellite (1957), the first spacecraft to photograph the far side of the Moon (1959), the first spacecraft sent on an interplanetary mission (1961), the first man in space (1961), the first woman in space (1963), the first EVA space walk (1965).

The American government was concerned for two reasons. First, the Soviet government was using its successes in space to show the world that Communism could outdo the West in the highest of high technologies. Thus, the U.S.S.R. made enormous gains in the international competition for influence and power.

Underlying that prestige was the deadly serious matter of ballistic missiles. The Soviets had taken the lead in building ICBMs (intercontinental ballistic missiles) that could carry multi-megaton hydrogen bombs across half the world in thirty-some minutes. The United States quickly began to build its own fleet of missiles and arm them with hydrogen bombs.

The rocket boosters that were used for the early space missions were all modified ICBMs. Thus the Soviet triumphs in space were also showing to everyone that the U.S.S.R. had rockets that could drop H-bombs on any city in the world.

President Kennedy decided to "leapfrog" the Soviets in space. The U.S. would send astronauts to the Moon and do it in less than ten years. The Soviets officially claimed that they were not racing the Americans to the Moon, but Kremlin documents made public after the collapse of the U.S.S.R. in 1991 showed that they were bending every effort to get cosmonauts to the Moon first.

With the intense political pressure to be first to the Moon, the American project Apollo dropped all plans for building a space station. Apollo missions flew straight to the Moon from Cape Canaveral.

No space station. And when the Apollo program ended in 1972, there was still no American space station.

Salyuts and Skylab
The Soviets, however, had placed the world's first space station into orbit in 1971. Called Salyut, it was the first of seven space stations that remained in orbit for a year or more, then were deliberately de-orbited and crashed back into the ocean.

Some of the Salyuts were dedicated to military operations, mainly experiments on Earth-observation surveillance and development of electrical power systems for laser and particle-beam weaponry. The others were civilian missions devoted to science and industrial experiments. The Salyuts usually were manned by two to four cosmonauts who stayed aboard for a few months and then were replaced by another crew.

Meanwhile, back in the United States, the Apollo program had been cancelled by Washington after six successful landings on the Moon. NASA's plans to go ahead with lunar exploration and building bases on the Moon were wiped out by political shortsightedness. Yet there was still a good deal of Apollo hardware left on hand, including several of the giant Saturn-family rocket boosters.

NASA developed a plan to convert one of the upper stages of a Saturn to a space station and launch it into orbit with the lower Saturn stages. Then, other Saturns would be used to launch three crews of three astronauts each.

Good plan, but it started with a near disaster and ended with an absolute catastrophe.

Launched on May 14, 1973, Skylab was damaged as it flew into orbit, damaged so badly that it was feared the space station would be unusable. One of its solar-cell panels was ripped away, the other jammed so that it would not open, and part of the vehicle's thermal shield (to keep its interior cool in sunshine) was torn off.

Astronauts as Repairmen. Brilliant improvisation by NASA engineers and inspired repair work by the first team of astronauts to visit the station patched up Skylab well enough to make it not merely usable, but almost as capable as it would have been if there had been no damage at all.

Three teams of astronauts worked aboard Skylab for 28, 56 and 84 days, respectively. They conducted medical experiments on their own physical adaptation to weightlessness, as well as scientific observations of the Sun and the Earth. Then, after the third astronaut team departed in February 1974, Skylab was left alone.

Ground controllers moved the space station to a higher orbit to wait until 1979, when the space shuttle was expected to be flying. The plan was for the shuttle to carry new astronaut teams to Skylab.

The shuttle's development was delayed so much that its first orbital flight did not take place until 1981. In the meantime, unexpectedly high levels of solar radiation heated Earth's atmosphere so much that it expanded enough to begin to drag Skylab out of its orbit. And NASA had no rocket booster to even try a rescue mission.

Death of Skylab. The eighty-two-ton space station was dragged down to its destruction by atmospheric friction on July 11, 1980. Most of it burned up in the atmosphere or fell into the Indian Ocean, but parts of Skylab hit a sparsely populated region of western Australia. There were no casualties, except to NASA's hopes to return to Skylab and use it again.

Both C.M. Kornbluth, in the story "The Rocket of 1955," and Robert A. Heinlein, in many of his "Future History" stories, speculated that there would be a hiatus between the first spate of successful space launches and the major use of space. They were not so much predicting as making an analogy to the period between Columbus' first voyages and the permanent British and French settlements in North America in the early 1600s. Some historians refer to this period as "The Empty Century," although Spanish *conquistadores* spent those "empty" years creating an empire for Spain in what is now Latin America.

A VISIT TO SKYLAB

You can visit Skylab. NASA's backup for Skylab now resides in the Air and Space Museum in Washington, DC. It is the real thing, not a mock-up or a simulation. It would have been launched into orbit if the original Skylab could not have been repaired. You can walk through the station and see for yourself what it is like.

Mir, the First Permanent Space Station

The Russians, meanwhile, kept plugging ahead with their Salyut space stations. Then, in 1986, they orbited a newer, bigger space station that they called Mir. In Russian, "mir" means both peace and home. The Russians announced that Mir was intended to be a permanent station that would be occupied continuously.

The day when every human being lived on the surface of the Earth had ended. Since it was first placed in orbit, there have been at least two cosmonauts living aboard Mir virtually every day. The Russians have added several sections to the original structure: two Kvant modules, for astronomical observations; a module called Kristall, for industrial experiments in microgravity; and two Spektr modules (the second added in June 1995) for studies of the Earth's atmosphere, biomedical and pharmaceutical experiments.

Mir has been visited by "guest cosmonauts" from other countries. In 1995 astronaut Norman Thagard became the first American to visit Mir. He remained aboard for four months—incidentally breaking the record of 84 days for American space flight, set by the third and final Skylab crew.

Mir is a "permanent" space station only in a relative sense. It has been in orbit for more than ten years, much longer than even most unmanned spacecraft have functioned. Yet its equipment has shown signs of age and wear. While some of the equipment can be repaired or replaced, eventually Mir will be abandoned and perhaps deliberately de-orbited and crashed into the ocean, as the earlier Salyuts were.

(On the other hand, an enterprising soul might want to bring Mir back to Earth intact and make a museum exhibit out of it. How would such an entrepreneur go about the task?)

Very patiently, the Russians have extended the duration of their space station crews' stays in orbit. As we have seen, several cosmonauts have remained aboard for more than a year at a time. The Soviet Union collapsed, but the Russian space program continued. One cosmonaut team was launched by the U.S.S.R., but returned to the new Confederation of Independent States; while they were in orbit the U.S.S.R. was abolished. Several science fiction authors have written stories about how the world might change while space travellers are off on missions to the distant stars (see, for example, L. Ron Hubbard's "Return to Tomorrow"). No one expected such swift political changes while a space station's crew was in orbit!

There is some reason to believe that the Russians want to extend their space-endurance flights to two full years. That is the approximate length of time that a mission to Mars would take.

A Home in Orbit

To live aboard a space station, human crews need everything they need to live on Earth: food, water, air to breathe, protection from the environment. They do not need gravity, as we have seen. The human body adapts to weightlessness very nicely, although physical problems can arise when a weightless-adapted person returns to Earth.

A space station, then, must be a self-contained little world. It must provide all the necessities of life, or its crew will swiftly perish.

So far, no space station has been built to be truly independent of Earth. Mir receives regular supplies of food, air, water and other goods from the ground. Uncrewed resupply spacecraft dock with the space station, and the cosmonauts welcome them like the citizens of western frontier towns once welcomed the Wells Fargo wagon.

Skylab was sent aloft with all the supplies its three sets of crews would need. But if the American space station had survived long enough to be used again, astronaut crews would have had to re-stock it with air, food and water.

Electrical Power. Space stations also need electrical power. Air-circulating fans, food storage freezers, microwave ovens, water pumps, sensors, communications gear, control systems—everything aboard a space station requires electricity.

Fortunately, sunshine is not only free in orbit but more intense than it is here on the ground, because the sunlight is not filtered by the Earth's atmosphere. Solarvoltaic cells—similar to the solar cells that power pocket calculators—provide electrical power for satellites and space stations in Earth orbit.

As we saw in the discussion about electrical rockets (chapter 2), the best power systems for spacecraft, including nuclear systems, can produce about 45 watts per pound. Current solar panels deliver roughly 20 watts per pound of structure, but they can continue to deliver that electrical power as long as the Sun shines and panels are not damaged or degraded.

Sunshine provides about 130 watts of energy per square foot in LEO, which means that to produce a kilowatt of electrical power (ignoring losses) you need a solar panel of about 7.7 square feet, which amounts to a square that is a bit less than 2.8 feet on each side.

The Mir space station produces about 10 kilowatts from its solar panels. The international space station that the U.S., Russia, Japan and Europe are building will need 110 kilowatts when it starts full-scale operations in 2001. This power will be provided by several panels of solar cells, although there are plans to add "solar dynamic" power systems later.

Solar dynamic power systems use solar energy to heat a working fluid (probably water) that spins a turbine, which in turn runs an electric power generator.

The space shuttle gets its electrical power from *fuel cells*, where the chemical energy from combining hydrogen and oxygen (slowly!) yields not only electrical power but water as well. Fuel cells are quiet, reliable and efficient, but they must be fed the fuels they need continuously. That is why their use is restricted to short missions, such as the shuttle flies. On a space station, fuel cells might serve as emergency power units (EPUs), backing up the main power system.

While solar panels work well enough in cislunar space, as we move farther from the Sun we must either build bigger solar arrays or go to alternative energy systems, such as nuclear. Beyond the orbit of Mars, solar panels become impractical—unless you "invent" much more efficient solar cells.

Radiators. Alongside the broad "wings" of solar panels, a space station needs another type of winglike structure: radiators to get rid of the waste heat.

Human bodies and all the equipment inside the space station generate heat. That heat must be taken away from the station or the temperature inside will become intolerably dangerous to both the equipment and the people.

In space, the only way to get rid of waste heat is by radiating it away. Conduction and convection, which carry heat in solids and fluids on Earth, do not work in the vacuum of space. That vacuum acts as an insulator and will not carry heat the way solids and fluids do. But heat energy—in the form of infrared radiation—can be radiated into space just as effectively as heat from the radiator in a home can warm a room. More effectively, in fact.

Skylab and the Russian Mir both use winglike panels for radiators. Heat from inside the space station is piped to the panels, where it radiates away into the near-absolute-zero vacuum of space. On the space shuttle, the orbiter's cargo bay hatch doors are lined with radiators. That is why the shuttle *must* fly with its cargo bay hatch open while it is in orbit.

All future space stations and spacecraft will need radiators, unless someone discovers some principles of physics that we don't know about today.

Closed-Cycle Life Support. Since space stations—including the international station that the U.S., Russia, Europe and Japan are developing—orbit only a few minutes' flight from Earth, it is relatively easy to resupply them.

Their life support systems are called "open cycle." That means that the systems are not totally independent; they need fresh supplies from time to time.

Here on Earth we have a *closed cycle* life support system. Nobody has to bring new air or food or water to us; our planet's natural recycling processes provide fresh air, clean water and more food for all the plant and animal life across the globe. That's our planetary ecology.

But Earth is a whole planet. Its recycling processes need lots of room and plenty of time. For example, it takes the better part of a year to "recycle" seed, sunshine, water and fertilizer into a new food crop.

Even the largest space station would be minuscule, compared to a planet. Might it be possible, though, to develop a closed-cycle life support system for a space station? Would we be able to recycle the air, food and water within the station so that it is completely independent of outside help?

The Need for Recycling. One human being breathes in about two pounds of oxygen each day and exhales two pounds of carbon dioxide. Aboard Skylab, NASA engineers provided some twenty pounds of water for each man-day, for drinking, cooking and washing. None of it was recycled, although Skylab did have a condensing heat exchanger to remove excess humidity from the air. This consisted of cold metal plates; the water vapor in the air condensed into droplets when it passed over them. The water was then piped into a wastewater tank. It was not recycled or reused.

Nuclear submarines, which remain submerged for ninety-day-long patrols, are equipped with systems that remove carbon dioxide from the air and desalt ocean water for drinking. The Mir space station has equipment to recycle air and water, although the systems are not entirely closed-loop; resupply spacecraft bring additional air and water from time to time.

When we decide to send human explorers to Mars or even farther, their spacecraft will need closed-cycle life support systems. Or at the very least, they will need systems to recycle air and water. It would be a designer's nightmare to try to fly all the tons of air and water that a human crew would need for a two-year mission to Mars.

It should be possible, also, to grow food crops aboard a space station or an interplanetary spacecraft. For many years experimenters have used *hydroponics* to grow crops without soil. The plants are cultivated in baths of high-nutrient liquid. Researchers at NASA's Ames Research Center in California have produced crop yields ten times more abundant than typical "dirt" farming, using hydroponics and intense lights that remain on twenty-four hours a day. Thus a relatively small area aboard a space station might be able to produce enough food to feed the crew.

The International Space Station

At present, the United States is working with Russia, the European Space Agency (ESA) and Japan to build an international space station, named Alpha as of this writing, but its name and design have changed many times in the past and might well change again.

Alpha's first segment will be a modified Salyut with enough

propulsion power to serve as a "tugboat" that can bring other segments together and even boost components or the entire station assembly to a higher orbit, if necessary. The space tug is called the FGB, after a Russian acronym meaning "functional energy block." It is slated to be launched in 1997, although launch schedules are notoriously prone to slippage.

The station's core will be an improved "second-generation" Mir-type Russian module, to be launched in 1997. American modules will be added to it, and the station will be visited by several teams of astronauts and cosmonauts. European and Japanese modules will then be added, and the station will be completed and "open for business" in late 2001. From that point onward, Alpha will be continuously crewed by six people.

NASA expects that it will take nineteen shuttle flights and twelve flights of Russian boosters to complete the construction of the station.

From Fighter Jocks to Tourists to . . .

The first men to go into space (and they were all men, at first) were "fighter jocks." The earliest astronauts and cosmonauts were all recruited from the ranks of jet pilots. Almost all of them were military officers, although the first man to set foot on the Moon, Neil Armstrong, was a civilian test pilot. And the next-to-the-last man on the Moon, Harrison H. Schmitt, was a civilian geologist who later became a U.S. Senator for New Mexico.

With the advent of the space shuttle, men and women who were not pilots of any kind could fly into space. NASA calls them *mission specialists* or *payload specialists*. Strictly speaking, they are not astronauts, not in the sense of being the person who flies the spacecraft. They are crew members, but not pilots.

As space flight becomes more commonplace, cheaper and safer, other kinds of people will begin to go into space: news reporters, filmmakers, even tourists.

NASA's first attempt to fly an "ordinary citizen" (not a member of Congress) aboard the space shuttle ended in disaster on January 28, 1986, when the *Challenger* blew up, killing schoolteacher Christa McAuliffe and the six other crew members.

Eventually space travel will be open to anyone who can afford it. More than that, living in the relatively benign low-gravity environment of the Moon, or even the zero-*g* environment of orbit, may prolong the lives of persons who would be helplessly bedridden on Earth.

It might turn out that the old Biblical adage about the meek inheriting the Earth is slightly wrong. The meek (or at least the infirm) may go into space to live full, rich, active lives instead of remaining frail and useless in the full gravity of Earth.

Space Suits

Whether the characters you write about are rocket jocks or geriatric cripples, they will need space suits if they are going into space.

A space suit is nothing less than a miniature spacecraft built for one person to occupy (although the character Rhysling sang about "A Spacesuit Built for Two" in Robert A. Heinlein's short story "The Green Hills of Earth"). It has to provide protection against the vacuum of space, air (or oxygen) to breathe, and heating or cooling to keep you at a safe and comfortable temperature.

Strictly speaking, space suits do not come with propulsion systems, although NASA has developed a Manned Maneuvering Unit (MMU), which looks somewhat like a chair without legs. The MMU allows astronauts to fly independently from the space shuttle without a safety tether.

The basic idea of a space suit is to keep a livable environment around you while you are outside your spacecraft or space station. The suit has to be tough enough to keep the air in and the vacuum of space out and to protect its wearer against radiation and strikes from microscopic bits of space dust or human debris. If the suit leaks or is punctured, its wearer quickly dies from decompression. The eyes may not pop out of your head, and your body probably won't explode (that is the stuff of sensationalist fiction), but your blood could boil away while you're dying of asphyxiation.

However, humans can survive in a vacuum for several seconds. This was an important plot element used by Arthur C. Clarke in both *Earthlight* and *2001: A Space Odyssey*. Perhaps some day daredevil (or foolhardy) space travellers will indulge in "vacuum breathing" contests!

Space suits are not designed for long-time occupancy. The best current models are safe only for ten to twelve hours, although future improvements may extend that to a full day or more.

NASA's astronauts wear a water-cooled undergarment beneath their space suits. Cool water is circulated through the one-piece "long johns" to carry body heat away. Temperature is regulated by adjusting the rate of water flow. This is somewhat like the "still-suits" used by the desert-dwellers of Frank Herbert's novel *Dune*. The idea is to prevent the body from overheating.

It may seem strange to worry about overheating in the vacuum of space, where the temperature outside your space suit is hundreds of degrees below zero, but exactly because the space suit is airtight (it had better be!) it is very difficult to get accumulated heat out of the suit. And the human body is a heat engine, converting food into energy and giving off heat as a waste product.

To date, space suits do not use radiators to get rid of excess heat. It is easier to cool the occupant's body than to add a large and clumsy radiator surface to the suit.

Going from the undergarment outward, a space suit has many layers of materials, starting with a softly pliable heat-resistant layer, then an airtight layer of neoprene-coated nylon (neoprene is a rubberlike substance), several layers of insulating materials, and finally an outer protective layer that is fire resistant and strong enough to absorb hits from microscopic meteoroids.

No space suit is complete without a helmet with a transparent visor (usually made of a plastic such as Lexan), gloves and boots.

Depending on the equipment loaded onto them and the amount of oxygen to be carried, a space suit can weigh from 40 to 200 pounds. Since they have been used in the zero-*g* of orbit or the low-gravity conditions on the Moon, though, no one has had a problem with the weight (or, more properly, with the mass) of their space suit.

The gloves have always been a problem. It is difficult to do fine work with gloves on, and space-suit gloves have to be thicker and bulkier than those used on Earth. If there is one item of equipment that virtually every astronaut who has been on EVA complains about, it is the gloves.

Future Space Suits
The fundamental problem of space suits is that they must maintain an air pressure of at least several pounds on the inside while facing essentially zero pressure (vacuum) on the outside.

Fabric suits tend to balloon, and this makes it difficult to move the arms and legs. And fingers. This is why the earliest space suits used pure oxygen atmospheres; it is possible to breathe pure oxygen at pressures of only a few pounds per square inch. On Earth, normal sea-level air pressure is 14.7 psi. The higher the suit's internal pressure, the more it balloons and the stiffer its limbs become. A fabric suit using 14.7 psi would balloon so much that its wearer would find it just about impossible to bend the arms, legs and fingers.

Hard suits, made of metal or stiff shells of composite plastics, are possible, but the wearer must still be able to bend at the elbows, knees, wrists, ankles, shoulders and hips. One possible solution is to equip the suits with miniature servomotors that can amplify the wearer's muscular movements and provide the strength to make the suit's joints flexible enough for easy use.

Small servomotor systems might also be used with the gloves, to amplify the astronaut's gripping strength. But they might make the gloves even clumsier to use. Clever design solutions are needed.

THE WRITER'S PERSPECTIVE

Living in space gives us a rich and exciting new world to write about. In fact, it returns to the writer a theme that has just about disappeared from modern fiction: the struggle of human beings against nature.

With today's technological civilization, very few people still challenge nature. Jack London, writing a century ago, could produce stories of high adventure about men struggling to survive in the frozen waste of the Yukon. His short story "To Build a Fire" is a classic of one man's battle against nature. But if London were alive today, he would find that his desperate protagonist would undoubtedly be equipped with modern thermal clothing, a handheld radio, a lightweight but tough and durable tent, packaged foods, and a global positioning system that could tell him exactly where he was by getting geodetic information from orbiting satellites. Not all that much of a challenge.

If London were writing today he would very likely be writing science fiction stories about living, working, surviving in the strange and hostile environment of space.

Who Are the Decision-Makers?

The drama of space has one foot planted on Earth, however. Nothing happens in space without very dramatic debates and decisions being made in the highest circles of government and corporate industry. The Space Race of the 1960s took place in Washington and Moscow as well as in cislunar space.

Those men and women who make the decisions that underlie any program of action can be very important characters for your stories. Find the decision-makers!

Of course, if you are writing about a future time when human settlements have existed in space for generations or centuries, then your story may not need any scenes on Earth at all. But still there will be the decision-makers—political and corporate—to be dealt with. No adventure can even begin until someone has agreed to pay the bills.

Astronaut Bill Pogue and I co-authored *The Trikon Deception*, a novel that is set on a space station built by an international consortium of private companies. The Trikon station is a center for very advanced, very sensitive biological research. The scientists aboard the station are trying to genetically engineer microbes that will be able to eat up toxic wastes and convert them into harmless materials that can safely be released back into the environment.

Of course, not *all* the scientists are pursuing that noble goal. And even those who are have conflicts with one another. These conflicts are aggravated by the fact that they are all living in cramped quarters, with very little personal privacy, under weightless conditions. The environment of the space station—which Pogue knew intimately from his eighty-four days aboard Skylab—provided new and different problems for the characters, problems that they would not have faced in a similar laboratory on the ground.

The Excitement of the Frontier

Since the essence of fiction is to put interesting characters into agonizing dilemmas, the orbital frontier presents a grand opportunity for writers. Use the factors of weightlessness, crowded living conditions, confinement inside a thin metal shell with nothing outside but deadly vacuum, hard radiation, and the constant infall of meteoroids. It beats writing about the suburbs of New York!

As part of the research we did for *The Trikon Deception*, we studied reports from science teams that have wintered at Antarctic research stations. Always try to find a "baseline" of actual human experience from which to build your fictional situation. Scientists spend three months or more in the cold and dark at the bottom of the world, locked inside their buildings, getting on each other's nerves, trying to do the work they have come there to do without worrying too much about the cold, hostile environment beyond their walls.

John W. Campbell, Jr., captured the feeling of such a research station in his story "Who Goes There?" which was twice made into motion pictures. The first attempt, the 1951 black-and-white *The Thing*, also successfully captured the mood of such an isolated research station.

On the other hand, you don't have to belabor the details of the space environment to produce memorable fiction. Ray Bradbury's haunting short story "Kaleidoscope" is about the crew of a spaceship that has exploded, hurling the space-suited crewmen in different directions. Hardly any scientific basis at all, yet under Bradbury's masterful hand the story is unforgettable.

◆ ◆ ◆

[1] The speed of light is 186,282.3959 miles per second. According to Einstein's special relativity, this is a universal speed limit, and nothing can travel faster than light. All experiments done to date have verified this, although there are some theoretical possibilities around it, which will be discussed in chapters 10 and 11.

[2] The "southern lights" (aurora australis) are seen far to the north of their usual displays, of course.

CHAPTER 5

Space
Industries

"Chance of a lifetime, nuts! This is the greatest chance in all of history. It's raining soup; grab yourself a bucket!"

Robert A. Heinlein, *The Man Who Sold the Moon*

TECHNICAL FACTORS

On the front page of the October 10, 1995 issue of *The Wall Street Journal*, staff reporter Jeff Cole wrote:

> There is a new space race under way, one as risky and competitive as the U.S. government's $25 billion program that put a man on the moon more than two decades ago. This time, though, the risk is being borne by industry. The mission: to profit by transmitting voices, images and information to any spot on Earth.

Communications Satellites

In 1945 Arthur C. Clarke, then an obscure young engineer and space enthusiast, pointed out that the geostationary twenty-four-hour orbit made an ideal location for communications satellites, since at that altitude the commsat would hover over one spot on the equator all the time. Not only could a satellite "cover" almost half the world, it would remain fixed in one spot over the equator, so that ground-based antennas could lock onto it without needing to track it all over the sky.

Since 1962, when AT&T's first *Telstar* satellite went into orbit, satellite communications has grown into a multibillion-dollar world-wide industry. We are so accustomed to global television that we take commsats for granted. Yet this industry has developed almost entirely through private enterprise, pioneered by major corporations such as AT&T and Hughes Electronics. International consortiums such as Intelsat and Inmarsat have arisen, and international agreements decide which nations can have "slots" along the limited geosynchronous orbit in which to place commsats.

Intelsat, the International Telecommunications Satellite Organization, provides two-thirds of all the international telephone, telex and television services to nearly two hundred nations. Inmarsat, the International Maritime Satellite Organization, operates commsats above the Atlantic, Pacific and Indian oceans, providing communications for ships and oil rigs. In addition to telephone, telex, data and fax services, Inmarsat provides emergency communications, distress and rescue services.

Those GEO slots are extremely valuable, and nations vie for positions in which to place new satellites or replace old ones that have gone defunct. Commercial broadcasters have paid tens of millions of dollars for a single transponder (transmitter/receiver) on a new commsat, which typically carry a dozen or more transponders aboard them.

And, as *The Wall Street Journal* reported, a hearty competition is already underway to produce a new type of commsat: small, low-orbit relay satellites that will turn cellular telephones into global instruments that can carry voice and data from anywhere on Earth to any other spot on Earth.

Instead of placing large, complex satellites with many transponders on them into GEO, this new breed of commsats features whole fleets of small but highly sophisticated satellites in LEO or MEO. Motorola's Iridium system, for example, will consist of sixty-six LEO commsats when it is complete. No place on Earth will be without two or three such satellites overhead. Calls from cellular phones will be picked up by a satellite and routed from commsat to commsat to their destinations almost at the speed of light.

By the turn of the century, cellular telephones will be able to call anyone, anywhere on Earth, at any time of the day or night, thanks to this new breed of small, smart, low-altitude satellites.

Most of the commercial (nongovernment) space launches to date have placed commsats in GEO. Private launch companies are already starting to place the new LEO commsats in orbit. While commsats are still the major customer for launch services, new markets are opening for various kinds of observation and reconnaissance satellites, industrial experiments in low gravity, energy production from space, even space advertising and tourism.

Global Positioning Satellites

During the Desert Storm phase of the 1990-1991 Gulf War, U.S.-led forces were able to outflank the Iraqis by making a wide "left hook" maneuver around the entrenched Iraqi defenses. Iraqi generals were stunned that American heavy armor columns could find their way across the trackless, barren desert, where bedouins themselves got lost. The Americans had a secret weapon: *Global Positioning Satellite* systems (*GPS*) provided the American tanks with pinpoint navigational information.

GPS also guide submarines on patrol beneath the seas and planes in flight. Now *GPS* equipment, no bigger than the palm of your hand, is available commercially for campers, hikers, boaters, mountain climbers—anyone. Trucking companies use the technology to keep track of their fleets of trucks. Railroad companies keep track of their rolling stock through satellite-relayed signals.

Geographic Information Systems

A new market is opening in the field of geographic information systems (GIS), a market that has been estimated at $3 to $5 billion annually, thanks largely to new high-speed systems allowing near real-time processing of satellite remote-sensing data, and the rapidly growing ability to transmit such space imagery to small desktop computers.

Earth Satellite Co.,[1] of Rockville, Maryland, and other firms are selling geographical information, which includes mapping, searching for natural resources, detecting lightning strikes, weather observation, and other surveillance and observation tasks. In the not-too-distant future, satellites will routinely help the media to gather news.

The Earth Observation Satellite Co. (Eosat) Corp., of Lanham, Maryland, is offering satellite data to real estate agents. High-resolution satellite imagery shows prospective home-buyers all the homes available for sale in a neighborhood, as well as the location and distance of schools, shopping and public transportation.

By the end of 1995 as many as one million users globally are expected to be involved in the use of GIS-type data. These new capabilities will be supplied by the French Spot Image, Eosat (using Landsat data), and future satellite operations such as Canada's Radarsat.

Just as cable and satellite television has led to "pay-per-view" home services, the satellite remote-sensing and GIS sector are beginning to offer similar private access capabilities made possible by the same "information highway" technology.

A key factor in the mushrooming GIS market is the significant reduction in the cost of data processing and software. Systems that a few years ago cost $500,000 can now be purchased for $2,000. This drop in cost, coupled with the new information technology, is creating ever-increasing demand for GIS services. The important fact for science fiction writers to recognize is that the price of gadgetry goes down with time; what cost a fortune a few years ago can now be bought by children with their allowance money.

Digital satellite imagery is even finding uses in legal applications. South Florida Water Management District officials are using Spot Image satellite data—which can resolve features as small as ⅟₄₀ of an acre (a square 33 feet on a side)—to identify land-use violations in their 16,641-square-mile jurisdiction. In a case involving illegal drainage of a wetlands area, comprehensively documented by satellite, the defendant repaired the environmental damage and paid a $650,000 fine. Comparable helicopter and ground-based surveillance would be too costly and time-consuming for the agency to use effectively.

The New Space Entrepreneurs

Private enterprise sometimes results in strange bedfellows. Sea Launch Investors, headed by the retired former chairman of the U.S. Joint Chiefs of Staff, Adm. Thomas H. Moorer, is working with the retired former head of the Soviet navy to convert two hundred or more submarine-launched ballistic missiles into space boosters.

Sea Launch Investors is looking at the SS-N-23 Shtil missiles for suborbital microgravity missions and other uses. The Shtil-3 could place a 1470-pound payload into a 124-mile orbit or put 900 pounds into a 495-mile orbit.

More about Russian boosters later.

While some of the major aerospace corporations, such as

Lockheed Martin and McDonnell Douglas, are becoming heavily involved in commercial space operations, new companies such as Orbital Sciences Corp. and EER Systems are carving their own niches in space industries.

Orbital Sciences Corp. (OSC) is perhaps the leader among these new companies devoted to space technologies. OSC developed the Pegasus booster, a winged rocket launched from a converted jet airliner. It has produced the Transfer Orbital Stage (TOS), an upper-stage rocket system, and the medium-sized Taurus booster.

OSC is marketing spaceflight services for small science missions using an ultralight, low-cost satellite "bus" developed for the company's own commsat network. The MicroLab Orbital Experiments Service will offer frequent flight opportunities to experimenters for a fixed price of less than $10 million. The 100-pound satellites will be launched by Pegasus.

This service offers university and laboratory researchers a "turn-key" operation where the customer provides the instruments, sensors or other small payloads, which OSC integrates with its satellite "bus"; and then launches, operates, and collects data for 12 to 24 months. Typically a mission would be launched within a year of contract signing.

In contrast to the gigantic projects and decades-long time frames of NASA and other governments' space programs, OSC has pioneered the "small (and swift) is beautiful" concept in spacecraft and launchers, concentrating on systems that can be designed, built, tested and put into operation in a matter of a few years at most.

OSC is the major player in ORBCOMM, a global communications network based on small, low-altitude satellites. Here the competition is strong. Motorola is leading a competing international consortium in the Iridium program, which is also aimed at global cellular phone service. The first two ORBCOMM satellites were successfully orbited in 1995.

And OSC is in the observation and surveillance business, too, with its subsidiary Orbital Imaging Corporation. Under contract from NASA's Marshall Space Flight Center, Orbital Imaging will provide atmospheric research data from its first MicroLab satellite. MicroLab I will detect lightning strikes worldwide, part of an effort to help understand and predict major storms. The satellite will also carry additional experiments related to atmospheric effects on the radio signals from the *GPS* network.

Space—The Good News

Communications and observation are not the only advantages space offers to industry. The very same factors that make orbital space so hostile to human life make it very useful for many manufacturing processes.

Hard vacuum, weightlessness, solar radiation, even the meteoroids in space represent incalculably valuable assets for industries in orbit. G. Harry Stine was among the first writers to point out the advantages of orbital space for industrial operations in his nonfiction book *The Third Industrial Revolution*.

Solar Energy

Solar energy can be converted into electricity with solarvoltaic cells. It is free and constant as long as the space factory is not in the shadow of the Earth, whereas solar energy on Earth is restricted by clouds and night. Thus space factories will either be placed in high orbits, where they are always in sunlight, or carry some form of energy storage system—such as batteries or fuel cells—to provide electrical power while they are masked from the Sun by the bulk of our planet.

Sunlight can also be used directly as heat. Simple mirrors can focus sunlight to attain temperatures of thousands of degrees. All the smelting, metalworking, chemical processing, boiling and heating done in terrestrial factories can be done in orbit without the need for fuel, or the pollution usually associated with furnaces. The space factory's "furnace" is the Sun, some 93 million miles away.

Vacuum Cryogenics

Space factories can attain very low temperatures as well. In the vacuum of space, objects in sunlight get very warm, but objects in shadow can become cryogenically cold. Simply by shielding a container from sunlight (and reflected Earthlight) the container could be cooled to cryogenic temperatures—again, without expending any fuel or energy. The container could be as large as you need it to be: the size of the space shuttle's external tank, for example. Or even larger.

Because vacuum is an excellent thermal insulator (the secret of the Thermos bottle), a space factory could be melting steel ingots in one place and only a few yards away could simultaneously be liquefying oxygen or hydrogen.

In sunshine it's hot; in shadow it's cold. Space factories can manipulate temperatures up and down the scale from thousands of degrees to almost absolute zero merely by arranging the amount of sunlight or shade. Without bringing an ounce of fuel up from Earth's surface. Without the pollution that comes from burning fuels. Virtually free energy means freedom from a heavy and continuous expense, as well as freedom from the pollution products that inevitably accompany factories on Earth.

Hard Vacuum

On Earth, it takes a lot of effort and money to make nothing—vacuum. So many industrial processes require vacuum chambers at some stage of their operation that a considerable part of the cost of electronics, pharmaceuticals, metals and other industrial products stems from the need to pump air out of a chamber and produce a vacuum.

As we have already seen, vacuums of 10^{-4} torr are used on Earth in metallurgical processes. (Normal atmospheric pressure is 760 torr.) The pharmaceutical and food industries also use such vacuums to freeze-dry medicines, antibiotics, blood plasma and foodstuffs. Vacuum down to one-millionth of a torr (10^{-6}) is used for insulating cryogenic liquids, electrical insulation, vacuum tubes, film coatings and electron welding.

In LEO the vacuum is ten times better, some 10^{-7} torr. And it's free. No need to expend energy to pump air out. Moreover, an even rarer vacuum can be produced by putting up a shield in front of the spacecraft or space station as it orbits around the Earth. The shield serves as a sort of umbrella, bumping aside the rare molecules of gas as the spacecraft flies in orbit. Behind the shield, a vacuum of 10^{-14} torr could be produced, a hundred million times better than most industrial and research facilities use on Earth.

NASA has flown such a Wake Shield Facility, attached to the shuttle's remote manipulator arm. Experimenters hope to use such shields to protect space facilities that manufacture semiconductors and other vacuum-sensitive products.

Vacuum is *clean*. Contamination is always a problem in manufacturing, chemical processing, and especially in producing pharmaceuticals. The vacuum of space is not only free of external pollution sources, but contaminants *inside* the materials being processed can be removed very easily. Metals, for example, usually have a certain amount of residual gases trapped inside them from the smelting process. In the vacuum of space such gases seep out of the metal's crystal structure and boil off into space. This process is called *degasing* or *outgasing*.

Metallurgical researchers have estimated that it will be possible to make steel alloys in space, for example, that are ten times stronger, pound for pound, than anything produced on Earth— because the contaminants within the alloys have outgased.

Low Gravity
Not only does the vacuum of space offer an ultraclean environment, the nearly zero-gravity conditions in orbit allow containerless processing.

Think of mixing a salad dressing on Earth. You want the ingredients to mix thoroughly, but no matter how hard you stir the bowl, the heavier ingredients sink to the bottom. The same problem exists in laboratories and factories on Earth. Whether it's a salad bowl, a centrifuge, a test tube, a blast furnace, the heavier ingredients tend to sink to the bottom.

And there will always be microscopic bits of the container mixed in, too. While this may not matter for your salad dressing, in products that require the highest degrees of purity, such as pharmaceuticals, contamination from the container can be a problem.

In orbit all this changes for the better. The heavier elements do not sink to the bottom of the container because all the ingredients are effectively weightless: the olive oil "weighs" the same as the vinegar—zero.

And you don't even need a container! Under zero-*g* conditions liquids form themselves into spheres and just hang there, no matter whether they are ice-cold droplets of fruit juice or giant balls of molten metals. Containerless processing, combined with the cleanliness of hard vacuum, can lead to ultrapure manufacturing and chemical processing.

Space Manufacturing Experiments
One of the long-term dreams of space pioneers such as G. Harry Stine has been to use the microgravity environment and free solar energy of space to develop orbital manufacturing industries. Researchers at several universities and corporations are taking the first steps in that direction.

While materials-processing experiments have been carried out on the space shuttle and the Mir space station, such government facilities are too expensive, and their waiting lists too long, for most researchers. Low-cost boosters that can be available quickly, such as those developed by OSC and other launch-services companies, are the key to opening up the orbital manufacturing frontier.

Pharmaceutical products, crystals of various kinds, and even cast iron smelting are being investigated. Biocryst, a new company spun off from the University of Alabama in Birmingham, is studying the biomedical applications of microgravity research.

Space Tourism

What about tourism in space? In 1983, a Seattle-based company—Space Travel Inc.—announced it would build a passenger compartment that would fit into the space shuttle's cargo bay and take paying tourists for rides in orbit. That goal proved impossible, mainly for safety reasons: The passengers would not be able to get out of the sealed compartment in an emergency.

In 1986 the company moved from Seattle to Washington, DC, changed its name to Spacehab Inc., and hired former NASA administrator James Beggs to be its chairman. Spacehab now builds a pressurized experiment module—"a sort of walk-in closet in space"—that flies in the shuttle's cargo bay and contains fifty-some lockers that can be rented by experimenters for $1.8 million per flight.

Will tourists fly in space? Eventually. NASA and the Space Transportation Association (a private, nonprofit think tank) are studying the possibilities. A study already conducted in Japan concluded that space tourism could be a $10 billion per year industry within twenty years.

Solar Power Satellites

One dream that is very much alive—in Japan, at least—is the concept of the Solar Power Satellite: building miles-long space platforms that use solar cells to convert sunlight into electricity and then beam their gigawatts of power to receiving stations on Earth.

Riding in GEO, gigantic SPSs could deliver gigawatts of electrical energy to Earth with no air pollution from burning fossil fuels, no radioactive wastes from fission fuels. The "powerplant" is the Sun.

Miles-long arrays of solar cells would convert the unfiltered sun-

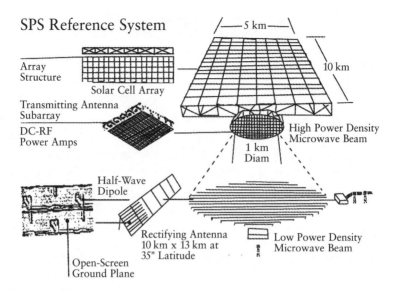

FIGURE 5 Solar Power Satellite system design used by NASA and Department of Energy in the 1970s to study the SPS concept. SPS satellite (upper right) transmits microwave power beam to receiving antenna "farm" (lower right). Figures at left show details of solar cell construction, transmitting antenna and receiving antennas. (Courtesy NASA)

light of GEO to electricity. This would then be converted into microwaves and beamed to special receiving antenna (rectenna) farms on Earth. The microwave beam would be kept very diffuse, so birds flying through it would not harmed, and the rectenna farms would be sited far from populated areas (see figure 5).

Solar Power Satellites could not only provide clean electrical power to Earth, they could also beam power to spacecraft, orbital stations and space habitats elsewhere in the Solar System.

Invented in 1968 by Dr. Peter Glaser of Arthur D. Little Inc., SPS has been studied by NASA and the Department of Energy and quietly buried in a mountainous pile of reports.

Not so in Japan. In February 1993 Japan's Institute of Space and Astronautical Science conducted the first experiment in space in which microwave power was beamed from one spacecraft to another. The power level was only 900 watts, and the experiment took less than a minute.

But that was the first step in Japan's Sunsat program, which includes a project called SPS 2000, aimed at building an experimental Solar Power Satellite capable of beaming ten megawatts of electrical power to the ground.

The global electrical power market will exceed one trillion dollars per year early in the next century. Whoever can supply a significant portion of that energy from space stands a good chance of attaining enormous wealth—and political clout. In Japan, where private corporations and the national government are intimately intertwined, the Sunsat program is part of a carefully planned long-range program to achieve the kind of energy independence that the U.S. government has talked about from time to time but done little to achieve.

Raw Materials for Space Industries

When the first SPS is built, the raw materials for its construction may well come from the Moon or the asteroids. Why haul up raw materials from the bottom of Earth's gravity well if they can be found elsewhere?

If there is one thing that space exploration has already shown us, it is that the Solar System is incredibly rich in natural resources. Not only is clean, reliable and plentiful energy from sunlight available, but the raw materials for industrial operations exist in space in quantities larger than the whole planet Earth can provide.

The samples of rock and soil returned from the Moon by the Apollo astronauts show that the topmost layers of the Moon's surface are rich in oxygen, aluminum, silicon, iron, titanium and many other metals and minerals that can be vitally useful in space construction and industry.

The meteoroids that pose a danger to spacecraft and spacefarers are also a source of raw materials for space industries.

Here we are not interested in the dust-mote-sized meteoroids but in the larger chunks of rock and metal that are floating through the Solar System.

Planetoids or Asteroids. Shortly after midnight on January 1, 1801, a Sicilian astronomer, Giuseppe Piazzi, discovered the first asteroid. The rest of Europe was celebrating the New Year, but Piazzi was a pious monk as well as a dedicated astronomer. What he saw in his telescope had the orbit of a planet, yet was so small that he saw nothing more than a pinpoint of light. Piazzi called it a planetoid, meaning a small planet, and named it Ceres, after the patron goddess of Sicily (an unusually pagan thing for a Catholic monk to do).

Before the year was over several other planetoids were discovered. By 1802, William Herschel—discoverer of the giant planet Uranus—coined the term "asteroid," meaning "little star." Technically, planetoid is more correct, but Herschel was more famous, and these minor planets are most frequently called asteroids even today.

Ceres, a ball of rock about 560 miles across, is the largest of the asteroids. More than five thousand asteroids have since been discovered, ranging in size from Ceres to tiny irregular chunks only a few miles long. There are most likely millions more, too small to imaged from Earth.

On October 29, 1991, the robotic *Galileo* space probe, on its way to the planet Jupiter, was steered by remote command from Earth to within ten thousand miles of the asteroid Gaspra. *Galileo*'s cameras took the first close-up photographs of an asteroid. Gaspra is about 12 miles on its longest axis, roughly the size of Manhattan Island. Almost two years later, on August 28, 1993, *Galileo*'s cameras snapped asteroid Ida and found that this 32-mile-wide asteroid was accompanied by a tiny chunk of rock less than a mile across— an asteroid with its own "moon" orbiting around it.

Most of the asteroids orbit between Mars and Jupiter, more than 150 million miles from Earth. That region has been called the Asteroid Belt. But at least forty are on orbits that cross the Earth's orbit. These are called the Apollo group.

Astronomers believe that the asteroids in the Belt represent the "makings" of a planet that never came together because of the gravitational interference of the giant planet Jupiter. The meteors that flash into our sky are most likely the same kind of thing: leftovers from the earliest days of the Solar System's creation. Some of them, at least, must be refugees from the Belt, ejected by the gravitational disturbances of Jupiter.

Some meteors apparently come from comets, however. The well-known meteor showers that periodically flash into our night skies are the remains of comets, still travelling on the comet's orbit around the Sun.

Gold Mines in the Sky. Meteorites come in two basic types: rocky and metallic. The asteroids are composed of the same materials. Thus the asteroids have all the metals and minerals that space industries require. If—and when—we can mine the asteroids, space factories will not need to bring raw materials up from Earth.

Since the asteroids are very small bodies, their gravitational fields are negligible. It will take little energy (which translates to money) to land on them or get off them again. Compared to hauling cargo up from the surface of the Earth, mining the asteroids should be cheap and easy—once you get to them.

The Apollo asteroids pass through Earth's orbit. No need to travel past the orbit of Mars to reach them, although space miners will have to match their velocities to the speed and direction of the individual asteroids. Such maneuvering will require large delta vees, and therefore significant amounts of rocket thrust.

Asteroids have been called "mountains floating free in space." Like mountains on Earth, the asteroids contain untold treasures of metals and minerals: gold, silver, platinum, iron, nickel, copper, manganese, carbon, potassium, silicon, phosphorus, rare earths, even water and organic chemicals.

In "To Bring in the Steel," Donald M. Kingsbury describes the long process of moving an asteroid into Earth orbit:

> There was no dawn on the asteroid called Pittsburgh. The spaceship that had brought them out to the Belt was leeched to the rock's surface like a great space bird of prey, its huge sunward facing mirror keeping the planetoid in darkness, its talons grasping its victim, its beak devouring her substance. The mirror soaked up energy which had been lasered 400 million kilometers across the solar system from a power station circling the sun well inside Mercury's orbit, energy which, out here in this dark energy desert was used to smelt four tons of rock per second, to refine it, and to deliver three tons of waste per second to the vaporizers, where ionized slag was accelerated to eight kilometers per second and blasted out forward along the line of orbit, day after day, year after year, in thundering flame. Twelve years the beast would spiral inward. When the ship finally reached Earth its claws would be clutching the digested remains of its victim, something like

300 million tons of refined metal. Most of it had already been sold to the Japanese.

Asteroids by the Trillions? We have seen only the largest of the asteroids, the big fellows that show up on our Earth-bound telescopes. Planetologist Clark R. Chapman has estimated that for each asteroid we have identified, there must be ten others one-third its size. And so on, down to "Literally trillions of uncharted boulders the size of a basketball or larger," he says.

A single rocky asteroid of the type astronomers call a *carbonaceous chondrite*,[2] no larger than one hundred yards long (the size of a football field), could contain some ten tons of gold—as an impurity. The real value of the asteroid would be the organic chemicals it contained: carbon compounds and water-bearing rocks called hydrates.

A single 100-yard-wide asteroid of the metallic type would contain nearly four million tons of high-grade nickel steel, more than half the annual steel production of the United States. From one smallish asteroid.

The Apollo, Earth-crossing asteroids are mainly of the carbonaceous chondritic type. To get to the nickel-iron asteroids, we will most likely have to travel at least to the outer fringes of the Asteroid Belt.

Better Boosters

All of these hopes and plans are critically dependent on the cost of getting payloads into orbit. If the space frontier is going to blossom, it will require better, cheaper, and more reliable access to orbit than we now have.

It is difficult to get reliable figures for how much it costs to put a pound of payload in orbit, but the *lowest* numbers published are all well above $1000 per pound. That means a ticket for me to go to LEO would cost me considerably more than $175,000 (if I lose a couple of pounds). Clearly, cheaper fares are needed before space tourism—or even space industries in general—can thrive.

Private companies are pushing hard in this crucial area of launch services. As we will see in chapter 8, perhaps the most exciting possibility is McDonnell Douglas' Delta Clipper program. Still in its very earliest stage of development, the Delta Clipper offers the hope of reducing the cost of going into orbit to $100 per pound or even less.

If the Delta Clipper and other advanced ideas can be brought to useful fruition, flights to space may become as commonplace as commercial airline flights and as inexpensive as a round-the-world cruise. We will examine these possibilities in chapter 8.

In the meantime, American space launch companies find themselves locked in a global competition with the government-subsidized launch services of Russia, China and other nations. A few years ago the U.S. government formally complained that China was subsidizing the launch costs of its Long March booster so heavily that they were competing unfairly, marketing the Long March at artificially low prices to squeeze American and other competitors out of the business of selling launch services.

Yet capitalism has a strange way of making partners out of competitors. Lockheed Martin, for example, is marketing both the veteran Atlas booster, which began its career as the first American ICBM,[3] plus the workhorse Russian Proton boosters for heavy-lift missions—as well as designing and building its own fleet of small and medium-lift boosters for the commercial market.

The Russian Energya is today's heavyweight champ among rocket boosters, with a lift capability similar to the Saturn V. There are no commercial applications in sight for Energya—yet. But if and when Japan begins to build its first Solar Power Satellite, Energya may become their primary booster.

From OSC's Pegasus to Russia's Energya, space entrepreneurs now have a broad range of rocket boosters available for payloads of any size. When and if the Delta Clipper starts flying into orbit, the costs of working in space should come down dramatically, and the profits go up.

At present the leader in the commercial space launch business is the European Space Agency's *Arianespace*, a French-based company whose supporting members include government agencies and aerospace corporations from more than a dozen European nations.

Arianespace has developed the Ariane family of rocket boosters, which are launched from French Guiana, on the Atlantic coast of South America. Ariane boosters have launched more commercial satellites than any other launch system in the world.

Where Is the Money Coming From?

It takes a heavy investment to do anything in space. And the risk is enormous: Even the most reliable rocket boosters frequently fail, blowing hundreds of millions of dollars to smithereens. Spacecraft occasionally malfunction, too, turning multimillion-dollar hardware into useless orbiting junk.

So who is going to take such huge risks with such staggering amounts of money? Anyone who thinks the profit potential is worth the risk.

Already, today, private investors are sinking billions of dollars into space enterprises.

For example:

In late 1994, Iridium, Inc., the consortium led by Motorola Corporation, completed its first phase of equity financing, raising $1.573 billion to build its global cellular telecommunications system. The consortium will seek bank loans for the rest of the $3.4 billion it needs to begin service in 1998.

Earlier in 1994, Loral Corp. announced that it had raised more than $275 million of the projected $1.8 billion it needs to deploy its 44-satellite Globalstar system, which will offer services similar to Motorola's Iridium.

Meanwhile, Teledesic Corp. requested FCC approval for a $9-billion commsat system dedicated to serving remote areas in the U.S. and the rest of the world. Teledesic's proposed system would employ 840 satellites plus 84 spares in 435-mile-high near-polar orbits.

These are not futurists' fanciful projections. These programs are as real as the pages of *The Wall Street Journal.*

Estimates of Markets
Billions of investor dollars are available because there are multibillions in profits to be had.

According to an assessment of world markets made in 1994 by Euroconsult, a private think tank based in Paris, new space-based communication programs will produce a $95-115 billion global market for satellites, ground stations and launch services by 2004.

Euroconsult's 440-page World Space Market Survey sees three primary elements of the satellite communications market through 2004:

• *New spacecraft development* will generate a market totalling $14.4-17.4 billion, an overall 6.5 percent increase from projections made in 1992.

• *Launch services:* $14.5 billion to orbit 217 communications spacecraft. Although 33 of these satellites will be military, private companies may be contracted to launch at least some of them.

In addition, another 14 meteorology satellites should be launched through 2004, generating another $900 million in launch service business, Euroconsult found.

• *Ground segment:* Commsat ground stations and receivers will grow into a $65-83 billion global market.

In 1994, sales and exports for U.S., European and Japanese markets in all space sectors totalled about $35 billion per year, the report said. A considerable global market, but only a third of what the space communications market *alone* will be generating in ten years. No wonder investors are starting to look skyward.

The simple fact is that now, today, you can buy stock in companies that do their business in space. Private investors are already sinking billions into space-based businesses. And there will be more to come.

Financing Tomorrow's Space Industries
What about the really big developments, like building bases on the Moon or constructing mammoth Solar Power Satellites to beam electrical energy cleanly to Earth?

Investors generally take four factors into consideration before they sink their money into a new venture.

1. How much money is needed? In space, the order of magnitude is usually in the billions. As we have already seen, this is not—by itself—a deterrent to investment in space industries.

2. What are the risks? Again, many investors have decided that the risks are bearable. As space technology continues to mature and become more reliable, the risk factor will go down even more *for well-known operations* such as communications and surveillance satellites. The risks for huge orbital construction projects or lunar bases are bound to be considerably larger, of course.

3. How much profit can the investor expect to reap? Once again, the well-known and understood operations offer a well-known and understood profit factor. Pioneering ventures may hit a jackpot, but there are usually so many unknowns that it is difficult to make a reliable forecast of profits. As the great science fiction editor John W. Campbell said, "Pioneering boils down to inventing new ways

to get killed." You can get killed financially, too, at the frontier.

4. How long will it take to start making a profit? How long must the investor's money be tied up in the project before the profits start to come in? This is the major stumbling block in large, long-range programs such as Solar Power Satellites, lunar bases or other deep-space programs.

It would take hundreds of billions of dollars to do anything that grand in space. And it would take many years, perhaps decades, before any profit could be expected.

Yet there may be a way to get private investors to put up the money even for these massive, long-term construction projects in space, a way that has already been used successfully, almost a hundred years ago.

Early in the twentieth century the U.S. government and private entrepreneurs successfully worked together to build the massive hydroelectric power dams of the western United States. The same funding technique can be used to finance development of a lunar base or a Solar Power Satellite.

Today we take those big power dams for granted. But a hundred years ago they were on the cutting edge of engineering technology. And they were too big a risk for private investors to handle by themselves. Several tried and went broke doing it.

But when the dams were built, they were not funded by the federal government the way Washington finances NASA or other government projects, taking tax dollars from the treasury to directly fund the development.

The dams were financed by long-term, low-interest federal loans. Loans, not grants. For example, Hoover Dam (originally named Boulder Dam) was financed by a fifty-year loan at 4 percent interest. Hoover Dam paid off its loan in 1986, fifty years after it first started selling electricity to customers in the Southwest.

Solar Power Satellites could likewise be financed by federal loans or by federal guarantees for commercial lenders, much the same way that Washington helped bail out Chrysler Corporation in 1979 and Lockheed a few years later.

Over the long term, the federal treasury would show a profit. And so would the private firms that build and operate the powersats.

The same financing arrangements could be used to construct lunar bases or other space developments—providing they offer the hope of profitable long-term operations.

Thus, even the largest space projects could be financed and developed by cooperative arrangements between government and private industry. Without draining the federal budget.

THE WRITER'S PERSPECTIVE

Space is no longer restricted to government programs or scientific research efforts. Private enterprise has arrived.

Entrepreneurs, by their very nature, have to be inventive. As long as there is the possibility of making profits in space, entrepreneurs will find—or create—the means to get private business into this new frontier. If there truly is gold in them th'ar hills, private enterprise will start digging, even if it means offering "burials" in orbit.

Which makes space entrepreneurs exciting characters on which to base science fiction stories. Heinlein's Delos D. Harriman, in *The Man Who Sold the Moon*, is a marvelous prototype. I have written numerous stories about roguish Sam Gunn, and two novels about Dan Randolph, a space entrepreneur who is slightly less of a rogue (but only slightly).

The redoubtable Patrick Henry, in his "Liberty or Death" speech, said, "I know of no way of judging the future but by the past."

Science fiction writers must look into the future. The best way to do that is to understand the past—and the present. Space travel began with government programs that were aimed at military power, national prestige and scientific exploration. In that order.

That era is not finished; perhaps it never will be. But private enterprise is moving ahead in space; greedy, competitive capitalists are doing their damnedest to get rich from space operations. Some of them will become the Rockefellers and Gateses of the twenty-first century. Most of them will go broke and die in obscurity.

For example, the American Rocket Company, of California, went into bankruptcy in 1995. Founded in 1985, Amroc was trying to develop hybrid rocket engines, rockets that use a combination of liquid and solid fuels. Despite building and testing about one hundred hybrid engines, their one attempt to fly a hybrid-powered vehicle, in 1989, was a failure.

Even large corporations are not immune to failures. Lockheed Martin's first flight test of its LLV-1 commercial booster on August 15, 1995, ended in a deliberate destruct three minutes after launch when the rocket vehicle went out of control. Both of OSC's first two attempts to fly a larger version of its Pegasus booster—Pegasus XL—failed, although its third flight was successful.

Whether the entrepreneurs go boom or bust, whether they make multibillions of dollars or end up in bankruptcy court, they can all be great story material.

A New Era?

From what our space explorations have already shown, the Solar System contains more true wealth in the form of energy and raw materials than the entire Earth can provide. A new era may be at hand, an era in which the human race's ancient problems of poverty and hunger might very well be erased forever.

All through history, people and nations have been driven by the politics of scarcity. There has never been enough wealth for everyone to be well fed, well housed and well educated. Even today, in the richest nation in the history of the world, large segments of our population live in poverty and ignorance.

Most of our current organizations—governments, religions, etc.—are based upon a scarcity of resources, energy and education. Most societies create strong central control organizations that attempt to dole out these limited resources "fairly."

The incredible riches of space offer a new hope, a new era in which the politics of abundance will replace the politics of scarcity. The major problems of the coming century may well be these: (1) How do we get our hands on the wealth that space offers; and (2) once we've got it, how will it be shared with the rest of humankind?

Think about that. There is a cornucopia of story material in the possibilities of this new era of abundance. The whole mind-set of the human experience is about to be changed. Who will gain from space wealth? Who will be hurt? If you begin mining the asteroids, what will happen to the price of metals on the commodities market? How will this affect metals-exporting Third World nations? Or metals-consuming industrial nations?

The changes go farther, deeper. If and when we begin to draw the bulk of our natural resources from space, we can stop digging up the Earth. Stop the strip-mining and the logging and all the other resource harvesting that damages our environment. When we get clean energy from Solar Power Satellites and nuclear fusion we can stop using petroleum and coal and natural gas. And uranium.

Space industries can turn our home world into a clean, green place to live. Earth can become a first-class residential center; industry will move into space.

Who will go into space to run the factories? Who will remain on Earth? Will cities still exist? Will new cities grow in orbit from the kernels of space stations?

Let the facts of today guide your thinking about tomorrow. But do not put blinders on your vision of the future. Challenge your own basic assumptions. As space technology bestows the riches of the Solar System on the human race, human societies will change. What we take for granted today in our relationships of family, community, nation and race will inevitably be changed.

Just as Europe and the whole world was fundamentally changed once Columbus reached the New World, just as the Declaration of Independence and rock-and-roll both resulted from migrations— free or forced—across the Atlantic, just so will the exploration and industrialization of space change us and our society.

Change is the heart of science fiction.

◆ ◆ ◆

[1] EarthSat's former president is the well-known science fiction author Charles Sheffield. He now is a member of the company's board of directors.

[2] *Carbonaceous* means that the asteroid contains a good deal of carbon compounds. *Chondrite* means the asteroid is composed of *chondrules*, small spheres about the size of a pea.

[3] Intercontinental Ballistic Missile. Atlas' first payloads were hydrogen bombs. Atlas was also the booster for John Glenn's first American orbital flight in 1962 and all the subsequent Mercury astronaut missions.

CHAPTER 6

Space Habitats

Mankind will not remain on the Earth forever, but in the pursuit of light and space, we will, timidly at first, overcome the limits of the atmosphere and then conquer all the area around the Sun.

Konstantin Edvardovich Tsiolkovskii

TECHNICAL FACTORS

For the purpose of discussion, we have defined space stations as structures in Earth orbit where people can work for weeks or months at a time. The purpose of a space station, as given in chapter 4, is to serve as an outpost on the orbital frontier where people can perform tasks that benefit from the station's location in orbit: workshops in orbit.

A space *habitat*, as we will use the term in this book, is a place where people go to live. A city in space. A condominium in the sky. Most residents of space habitats will have jobs, employment in the habitat itself. They will be living in the habitat for the long haul, not merely a few months or even a couple of years. The residents of a space habitat are *home*; they live there.

Space habitats have two other features that distinguish them from space stations. They do not have to be in LEO. And they are much bigger than a space station.

In the beginning, they were called space *colonies*, but that is a word with an unpleasant burden of history. Earlier generations spoke of colonies on the Moon or Mars, and the "conquest" of space, as if we were about to repeat the bloody European conquest of the native Americans.

"Colony" is not the correct word to describe what we are talking about. We are not setting up a colony in a foreign land; we are building habitats in empty space where humans will be able to live in an Earth-like environment.

Planetary Chauvinism

Although stories about flights to the Moon have been written since Plato's time, until the 1970s science fiction writers largely ignored the possibilities of constructing mammoth habitats in space, where nothing but emptiness exists today. They tacitly assumed that the first permanent human settlements off-Earth would be on—or under—the surface of the Moon or one of the planets.

Tsiolkovskii wrote about establishing permanent habitats in cislunar space, but hardly anyone paid attention. Certainly the idea did not become a hot topic in the science fiction field.

Until the early 1970s.

In the autumn of 1969, two months after *Apollo 11* landed on the Sea of Tranquility and at the height of the anti-Vietnam-War unrest on college campuses across the United States, Professor Gerard K. O'Neill was preparing to teach the freshman course in physics at Princeton University. In an attempt to get the students more interested in the work, O'Neill prepared a list of informal challenges for them to think about. The first one was: "Is a planetary surface the right place for an expanding technological civilization?"

He never got to ask the next question.

His students took off with that problem and literally invented what was soon called the L-5 space habitat concept. (Actually, it was called a space colony back then, even at the height of the Vietnam War.)

The idea was to build gigantic habitats between the Earth and the Moon, big enough to house thousands or even millions of permanent residents in a completely Earth-like environment. The concept caught the imagination of people everywhere and received enormous publicity in media as diverse as *Physics Today* (the journal of the American Institute of Physics), *Time* magazine, and the *60 Minutes* television show.

Why hadn't science fiction writers thought of it first? "Planetary chauvinism," was Isaac Asimov's rueful answer to that question. The writers had always assumed that human settlements would be built on the Moon, Mars and other planets.

In his story, "Down and Out on Ellfive Prime," Dean Ing described such a habitat:

The colony hung below them, a vast shining melon the length of the new Hudson River Bridge and nearly a kilometer thick. Another of its three mirror strips, anchored near the opposite South end cap of Ellfive Prime and spread like curved petals toward the sun, hurtled silently past the view port. . . . Prime was the second industrial colony in space, dedicated in 2007. These days it's a natural choice for a retirement community.

L-5 and the Geography of Space

The term L-5 goes back to the work of Comte Joseph-Louis Lagrange, an Italian-French astronomer and mathematician of the eighteenth century. He found that there are certain points between any two astronomical bodies where the gravitational forces from those two bodies (such as the Earth and the Moon) tend to balance one another.

There are five such *Lagrange points* between the Earth and the Moon (see figure 6). The L-1, L-2 and L-3 positions lie on a line connecting the center of masses of the Earth and the Moon. L-1 lies between the Earth and Moon, approximately 36,000 miles above the Moon's surface. L-2 is a slightly farther distance above the Moon's far side. L-3 is at the point on the Moon's orbit precisely on the opposite side of Earth from the Moon itself. These three Lagrange points are not gravitationally stable; any object drifting away from the point will experience a force moving it farther away. These points are not generally considered useful for space habitats.

However, the two other Lagrange points, L-4 and L-5, are gravitationally stable. They lie on the Moon's orbit, 60° on either side of the Moon's position.

The L-4 and L-5 positions can be thought of as two invisible harbors that travel around the Earth, always remaining equidistant from both the Earth and the Moon, about 240,000 miles away. Place an object in the L-4 or L-5 region and it will stay there indefinitely, orbiting around the Earth just as the Moon does. It would drift slightly back and forth in the region, but it would not move far.

Lagrange points exist for any two-body system in which one of the bodies is at least twenty-five times more massive than the other. The planet Jupiter orbits around the Sun, which is more than ninety times more massive than Jupiter. Collections of asteroids have been seen at the L-4 and L-5 positions on Jupiter's twelve-year-long orbit.

Earth-Moon Lagrange Points

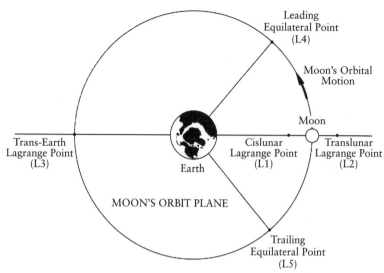

FIGURE 6 Libration Points in the Earth-Moon System (not to scale). All five Lagrange points lie in the plane of the Moon's orbit around the Earth.

Called the *Trojan asteroids*, they are tethered to those areas just as a space habitat would remain in the L-5 or L-4 position of the Earth-Moon system.

Gravity Wells

Arthur C. Clarke first popularized the idea of thinking about a planet's gravity field as a deep, steep well that you must climb out of if you want to reach orbit. When you boost up from Earth's surface to go into orbit, your rocket vehicle does the same amount of work that it would take to climb straight up nearly four thousand miles (the size of the Earth's radius).

Professor O'Neill asked, why climb out of Earth's four thousand-mile-deep gravity well merely to sit yourself down at the bottom of some other world's gravity well? Instead of building settlements on other worlds, why not build them in empty space?

A base on the Moon, for example, would exist in the Moon's gravity well, which is one-sixth Earth's. There is no way around that. Lunar habitats would also tend to be small and cramped, especially if they have to be dug underground into the lunar rock (see chapter 7).

Settlements on Mars or any other planet or moon would also have to dig themselves in or take their chances with conditions on the surface. Each would be in a constantly hostile, alien environment. And it would take a considerable amount of rocket propellant to lift off from the surface again.

The L-5 concept neatly sidesteps those problems. Built in empty space, the habitat is designed from the outset to provide an Earthly environment. The habitat would have to be *big*, miles across. But a habitat ten miles long can be spun, so that it will have a completely Earth-like feel of gravity inside it and still have virtually zero *g* on the outside.

A ten-mile-long habitat could comfortably house a million people, yet still its mass would be so low that its gravitational field would be negligible. Hardly any propellent need be spent in landing or taking off from such a habitat. By spinning it, the residents inside the habitat would have a fully Earth-like feeling of gravity in most of the habitat's interior.

Picture a ten-mile-long cylinder, its inner surface landscaped with hills and little streams running through grassy fields.

I described such a habitat in my novel *Colony*[1]:

> She knew that Island One was a huge cylinder hanging in space. She knew that she was standing inside a long, broad, man-made tube. Numbers from her background briefings played through her head. . . . But the numbers were meaningless. It was all too big, too open, too vast. This was a *world*, a rich, verdant land of beauty and peace that defied every attempt to measure and define it. . . .
>
> Evelyn could feel herself trembling. *There's no horizon!* The land curved up. It reached upward, dizzyingly, sweeping higher and higher. She lifted her head and saw through the bluish, cloud-flecked sky that there was more land above her, straight overhead. An inside-out world. She swayed.

Because the habitat is spinning, its inhabitants feel an Earthly one *g* as long as they are on the inner surface of the landscaped cylinder. But when they move up along the endcaps of the cylinder they feel the "gravity" fading away. If they go to the cylinder's centerline, the axis around which it is spinning, they will be essentially at zero *g*. They could literally float on air—although if they drift very far away from the centerline of the cylinder they will plummet to the "ground," just as Icarus did in the Greek myth.

Shirtsleeve Environment

By building habitats at the L-4 or L-5 locations instead of on the surface of another world, it is possible to create environments that are totally Earth-like, even with normal terrestrial gravity.

The interior of such habitats could be landscaped to suit the desires of its residents: streams and hills and trees, or lush tropical growth, or even the austere vistas of arid desert lands. The air temperature and humidity would be closely monitored and controlled.

The habitat's energy would come from gigantic panels of solar cells—although nuclear power plants would be more compact and could be stationed entirely outside the habitat structure for safety and ease of maintenance.

The construction materials for the habitat could come almost entirely from ores scooped off the Moon's surface. We saw in chapter 5 that lunar soil contains silicon, oxygen, aluminum, iron and many other raw materials. It is deficient in nitrogen and hydrogen— two elements very important for life support. These will probably have to be lifted up from Earth. Or found elsewhere.

Many different designs for space habitats have been studied. The earliest were huge cylinders, as long as Manhattan Island and four miles in diameter. Other designs looked like doughnuts or spheres; one was even dubbed "Sunflower."

Self-Sufficiency

The interiors of these habitats, whether they are cylinders, toruses or some other shape, will be as completely Earth-like inside as possible, and dotted with little towns and villages. Grass, trees and flowers will be plentiful.

Of course, living inside a giant cylinder or torus will be different from living on the surface of a large planetary sphere. When you look up, you see more land, towns, woods, streams, meadows— all hanging overhead, a few miles away. In my novel *Colony*, the inhabitants of a space habitat even started to "draw" constellations out of the patterns of nighttime lights they saw overhead, much the same as the ancient peoples who created the constellations in the starry night sky of Earth.

A space habitat will be as self-sufficient as possible. It can have farms to raise its own food, and the farms can be placed in separate modules outside the main habitat, where they can be kept at optimum conditions for the crops being grown. A farm for tropical fruits, for example, would be kept at a higher temperature and humidity—and a different day/night cycle—than a farm for wheat or corn.

Life support will be helped by all the greenery; just as on Earth, green plants will take carbon dioxide out of the air and put fresh oxygen into it. No one yet knows how large an ecology has to be before it is self-sustaining; chances are even the biggest habitats will still rely mainly on the same kinds of artificial (mechanical or perhaps bioengineered) life support systems for recycling air and water that the smaller space stations will use.

Factories, as well as farms, will be placed in separate structures outside the main habitat, where each individual module can maintain its own special environment. Factory modules would be studded with mirrors for focusing sunlight to create high-temperature heat, while nearby there might be solar parasols to create the shadow needed for cryogenic work.

In the same orbit as the Moon, the habitats would be in sunlight constantly, except for a few hours of eclipse each year, at the spring and autumn equinoxes, so solar energy should be plentiful and reliable. Giant windows in the habitats could be shuttered to produce day/night cycles similar to Earth's.

Gravity

The main habitat would be spun so that a centrifugal force equal to one Earth g is felt inside. Or a different gravity level, if desired. Perhaps slightly less than one g would be optimal: It would feel almost exactly like Earth, yet the inhabitants would undoubtedly feel sprightlier, more agile, than on Earth. Small rockets on the outer shell of the habitat would start the structure spinning; in the frictionless vacuum at the Moon's orbit, that should suffice for an indefinitely long time.

While the residents would feel a completely normal "gravity" and walk through their habitat in shirtsleeve comfort, just outside the structure there would be zero-g landing docks for spacecraft. And the habitat's exports of manufactured goods, foods, medicines or whatever could be launched Earthward—or to the Moon or distant planets—with just the barest of nudges.

The habitat will be constantly bathed in the harsh radiation from the Sun and cosmic rays, so it will need a protective mantle of rocky rubble from the Moon's surface. From the outside the habitat may look like a large and lumpy asteroid—peculiarly studded with antennas, mirrors and other structures.

Beyond L-5

Space habitats do not have to stay tethered to the Earth-Moon system. Given enough propulsion power, they could roam the Solar System. Or even beyond.

Probably a city-sized habitat housing a million people or more will not go roving beyond the L-5 point. But smaller habitats, housing a few dozen families, might become the gypsies of outer space. Specialized habitats for prospectors and miners could go out to the Asteroid Belt, take in megatons of ores, and refine and smelt them on the journey back to the Earth-Moon region. They would be somewhat like the whaling ships of old that went out for years at a time and came home laden with precious whale oil—if they came home at all.

Such roving habitats would have to be completely self-sufficient, with totally closed-loop life support systems. There will be no restaurants or repair shops beyond cislunar space for the first rovers. They will have to be totally self-reliant, except for electronic communications links with Earth.

THE WRITER'S PERSPECTIVE

When thinking about space habitats as a subject (or background) for fiction, the writer faces two intriguing questions:

1. Who would leave Earth to live in a space habitat?
2. Why would anyone build a space habitat?

The two questions are intertwined, of course. O'Neill himself originally proposed space habitats as an answer to Earth's problem of unchecked population growth; to ease the crowding on Earth, move people up to habitats at L-5. A few simple calculations quickly showed, however, that the cost of lifting millions of people into space would break the back of any nation's treasury. And those people would continue breeding. They would produce a population explosion in space. Far from solving the problem, "exporting" people aggravates the so-called population bomb.

Then O'Neill hit on the idea that space habitats could have an economic rationale: They would be the manufacturing centers for Solar Power Satellites. The habitats would get rich selling space-generated electrical energy to a power-hungry Earth. But that scenario seemed to put the cart before the horse. Who would put up the money to build the habitats *before* the SPSs were making profits? And construction workers do not need such habitats, nor would most of them want to live off-Earth permanently.

So the twin questions remain: Who would put up the money to build L-5-type space habitats, and who would agree to live in them for the rest of their lives (or some major portion thereof)?

When I wrote my novel *Colony* I tackled those two interlinked questions. In fact, they were the driving forces behind the plot.

Incidentally, I placed the first space habitat in my novel at the L-4 position rather than L-5, for an esthetic reason. From L-4 you see part of the Moon's far side, the side that is always turned away from Earth. The view includes the entire Mare Orientale region, a spectacular 560-mile-wide "bull's-eye" of mountain ringwalls centered on a 375-mile-wide crater. From the L-5 position the Moon offers a far less scenic vista, although you can see the crater Tsiolkovskii on the far side.

Space habitats, whether they remain within the cislunar region or go sailing out through the Solar System or even beyond, will transform the human race into a truly spacefaring species. This brings us once more to the question of why people would build such habitats.

The Biological Imperative

The ultimate reason for our expansion into space, it seems to us, is biological. Humankind is moving into space in response to a biological urge that is built into our genes.

Each species of plant or animal exists within an *ecological niche*: a set of conditions that allows the species to live, grow, thrive, reproduce. Every species tends to increase its numbers until it fills its ecological niche. Then it begins to mutate, change, so that it can spread into other ecological niches. Living species try to fill every ecological niche they can reach.

The human species, with its intelligence and its technology, has reached the point where we can expand into new ecological niches without mutating. We do not change to adapt to new ecological conditions; we use our technology—from clothing to computers—to carry our own ecology into the new niche. We do not adapt to the conditions of vacuum and hard radiation, we build space suits and space habitats to protect us while we breathe the same way we did on Earth.

(But you could write fascinating science fiction stories in which people use advanced understandings of biology and biochemistry to create new species of humans who can live unaided in alien environments. Frederik Pohl's *Man Plus* is a fine example of this concept.)

Thus, we are expanding into space. It is a new ecological niche for us, and like any biological species, we are in the process of trying to fill it.

Think of what this means to the future of our kind. Space habitats will allow significant numbers of humans to live, work and reproduce entirely off-Earth. Such self-sufficient habitats will no longer need to link themselves to the planet of our origin.

Space habitats will allow the human race—or at least, some of its members—to detach their destinies from the fate of the Earth. Our home world could be destroyed by war or ecological collapse or some other form of catastrophe. The space habitats will survive, even if all human life is wiped out on Earth.

That is the ultimate reason for building space habitats. They will be the shelters for the ultimate survivalists. There is a rich vein of material for stories in considering who would be farsighted (or fanatical) enough to build a space habitat for such a reason.

Picture a future where space habitats cluster in cislunar space, each one housing its own particular environment and ecology, while others move outward toward the Asteroid Belt or the farther reaches of the Solar System or even out to the stars themselves. Like gleaming jewels linked by an invisible web of communications waves, space habitats will spread across the void, carrying the human race to its ultimate destiny, taking us, in the words of Robert Frost:

> To the land vaguely realizing westward,
> But still unstoried, unenhanced,
> Such as she was, such as she would become.

♦ ♦ ♦

[1] The title, alas, was chosen by the publisher, not me. My original title for the novel was *Island One*.

CHAPTER 7

The Moon

Reaching the Moon by three-man vessels in one long bound from Earth is like casting a thin thread across space. The main effort, in the coming decades, will be to strengthen this thread; to make it a cord, a cable, and, finally, a broad highway.

Isaac Asimov, *The Beginning and the End*

TECHNICAL FACTORS

Time to think about distances in space. We have blithely talked about placing space habitats equidistant between the Earth and Moon, and even sending them out beyond the fringes of the Solar System.

The Moon's average distance from Earth is roughly 240,000 miles. The numbers don't mean much because they are too big for our easy comprehension. So do this:

Take a piece of paper or cardboard and cut out a circle one foot in diameter. That will represent the Earth. Cut out another circle three inches wide; that represents the Moon, which is just about one-quarter the size of the Earth. Now connect the two circles with a piece of string. It will have to be a *long* piece of string, because you will need 30 feet to correctly represent the distance between the Earth and the Moon. On a scale where one foot equals 8000 miles, the Moon is 30 feet from the Earth.

Pace out the distance. Stretch that string taut and take a good look at how far the two objects are from one another. And that is our nearest natural neighbor in space.

More Thrust Means Less Time

Still, the Apollo astronauts travelled that 240,000-mile distance in a few days, and they were coasting most of the way. A high-energy boost could get you to the Moon in a day or less—if you were prepared to spend the rocket propellants (and money) to accelerate more and coast less.

For example, if you go to the Moon on "economy fare," using the least acceleration (and hence, the least rocket propellant) possible, you would barely attain escape velocity from Earth, which is just under 7 miles per second. Once you achieve that velocity you shut off the rocket engines (or they burn out of propellants) and coast the rest of the way Moonward. One-way flight time is 116 hours, or four days plus a bit under 20 hours.

Increase your burnout velocity to 7.5 miles per second, though, and you cut the trip time to the Moon to about 19 hours. At 9.5 mps the one-way trip takes only 10 hours. You can cut the time to six hours if you goose your burnout velocity to just a tad over 13 mps.

You need not increase your ship's acceleration, or the *g* forces you feel; merely let the rocket engines burn longer. Future trips to the Moon will offer a variety of fares based on the amount of time you want to spend getting there.

Landing

Landing a spacecraft on an airless body such as the Moon is completely different from landing an airplane or the space shuttle orbiter. Lunar landings are done under rocket thrust; the spacecraft is gently lowered on its tail until it touches its landing pads on the ground at a speed very close to zero.

Apply too much thrust too soon, and the spacecraft could run out of propellant while still high above the ground. Too little thrust and the landing will be hard, maybe a crash.

Landings can be automated, although Neil Armstrong had to take over for the malfunctioning computer of *Apollo 11*'s *Eagle* lunar module and land the bird manually. When Armstrong reported, "Houston, Tranquility Base here. The *Eagle* has landed," the response from mission control was, "You got a lotta guys turning blue here."

Low Gravity, No Air, Huge Temperature Swings

Two important factors about the Moon are that it is so small that its surface gravity is only one-sixth that of Earth, and it is airless.

An object that weighs 100 pounds on Earth would weigh a bit less than 17 pounds on the Moon. Remember, though, that its *mass*

> ## NO "DARK SIDE"
> There is no "dark side" of the Moon.
>
> The Moon rotates. Its "day" is 27 days, 7 hours, 27 minutes long. That is the same period as its orbit around the Earth, so that a lunar "day" is exactly the same length as an Earth month.
>
> The Moon's rotation is "locked" by Earth's gravity pull so that the Moon always keeps its same side facing the Earth. The other side is never seen from Earth. But both sides receive the same amount of sunlight; each side of the Moon is in daylight approximately fourteen Earth days and then in darkness for the same length of time. There is no perpetually dark side.

remains the same. It will still smash your toes if you drop it, although it will fall more slowly and give you more time to get out of the way.

The term "airless" is a relative one. There is a tenuous atmosphere on the Moon, a *very* tenuous atmosphere made up of gases that seep out of the Moon's interior and even rarer gas from the inflowing solar wind. By terrestrial standards the Moon's atmosphere is a wonderful vacuum, some 10^{-12} torr.

Because there is no appreciable atmosphere to moderate the heat of the Sun, temperatures on the lunar surface can swing from 270°F at local noon to -240°F in the darkness of the two-week-long lunar night. Surface temperature can swing by hundreds of degrees merely by stepping from sunlight into shadow, or vice versa.

As we saw in chapter 5, the same environmental conditions that make orbital space dangerous to human life also offer powerful advantages for industrial development.

Much the same can be said of the Moon. The low gravity and airlessness of the Moon—combined with its natural resources—make the Moon an ideal place for producing the raw materials that space industries will need. The Moon will be a mining center, and its first useful product will undoubtedly be oxygen.

Surface Features
Before discussing the practical industrial and commercial uses of the Moon, we should briefly look at this strange new world.

	Moon	Earth
Diameter:	2160 miles	7918 miles
Mass:	0.0123	1.00
Density:	3.34 × water	5.11 × water
Surface gravity:	0.17	1.00
Orbital velocity:	0.99 miles/sec	4.90 miles/sec
Escape velocity:	1.48 miles/sec	6.94 miles/sec
Length of day:	27 days, 7 hours, 27 minutes	23 hours, 56 minutes
Mean distance from Earth:	238,331 miles	——
Atmosphere:	none (almost)	nitrogen, oxygen, water vapor, carbon dioxide, inert gases
Highest surface temperature:	270°F	136°F
Lowest surface temperature:	-240°F	-129°F
Magnetic field:	negligible	0.5 gauss

TABLE 2 Physical Facts, Moon Vs. Earth.

The Moon's surface is composed of four main types of features: mountains, regolith, craters and maria.

Mountains

Although they have not been weathered by wind or rain, which does not exist on the airless Moon, the lunar mountains have been worn down, sandpapered by the constant infall of meteoric particles that reach the ground undisturbed by the virtually nonexistent atmosphere.

Thermal erosion also occurs: Eons of alternate baking in daylight and freezing at night crack the rock and help to wear it down. There is also continuous minor seismic activity; moonquakes occur most frequently when Earth and Moon are closest and thus appear to be triggered mainly by Earth's strong gravitational pull. The quakes are so minor that most of them can only be detected by special seismic equipment.

Thus there are no sharp peaks on the Moon; billions of years of meteoric sandblasting have smoothed the mountains, rounded their crests, made them look old and slumped and worn.

Most of the Moon's mountain chains are named after mountain systems on Earth: the Apennines, the Carpathians, the Alps, etc. The Leibnitz chain, near the south pole, probably has several peaks taller than Mt. Everest.

Regolith

The surface layer of the Moon is called the *regolith*. The temptation is to call it soil, but soil implies living things such as worms and beetles and plant life. The Moon's "soil" is utterly devoid of water and of life. Hence the geologists' term, regolith.

The lunar regolith consists of rocky debris originally ejected from volcanic explosions and the impact of large meteorites. Over the eons since these violent events occurred, much of the rock has been pulverized into a fine powder by the constant infall of smaller meteorites, ranging in size down to dust particles. The intense heating of the fourteen-day-long lunar day and equally intense cold of the fourteen-day-long night have also helped to turn the original rocks into powder.

Soft as beach sand on the surface, the regolith quickly hardens to rocklike consistency with depth. The regolith averages a few feet deep in the lunar plains but can be considerably deeper in the mountainous uplands. Beneath the regolith lies the rocky crust of the Moon. The regolith's surface is strewn with rocks and pockmarked by craters of all sizes.

Craters

Craters can range in size from tiny pinpricks to gigantic structures such as Bailly, in the southwest corner of the Moon's near side (which always faces the Earth), 183 miles across. A crater that size on Earth would stretch from New York City to Baltimore.

Major lunar craters are usually named after famous scientists or philosophers, such as Copernicus, Archimedes, Kepler and Plato.

Most of the craters were created by the impact of meteorites, although some are probably the result of volcanism that took place billions of years ago, when the Moon's interior was still hot.

Some of the largest lunar craters, such as Plato and Aristarchus, are often called *walled plains*, in part because they lack the central mountain peak of the large true craters.

Several large craters are the centers of bright *rays* of material
streaking outward across the lunar surface. Most notable among
these are Tycho, Copernicus and Kepler. The rays are composed of
rocks and pulverized material ejected when the crater was formed,
presumably by meteoritic impact. Thus the rayed craters are undoubtedly younger than most other surface features.

Maria

Mare is the Latin word for "sea"; the plural is *maria* (pronounced
MAH-ree-a). Thought from ancient times to be bodies of water, the
maria are the dark areas of the Moon's face that can be easily seen
by the unaided eye. Telescopic observations eventually showed that
these "seas" are waterless. Even so, the maria have been given
fanciful names such as the Sea of Rains, the Ocean of Storms and
the Sea of Tranquility.

The maria are large flat plains of basaltic rock that were originally
molten lava. Many of the maria have concentrations of massive
material beneath them. These *mascons* were discovered when the
earliest artificial satellites placed in orbit about the Moon showed
slight disturbances in their orbital paths. Mare Imbrium (Sea of
Rains), Mare Crisium (Sea of Crises), Mare Orientale (Eastern Sea)
and several others are the sites of mascons.

The mascons may be the remains of large, dense meteoroids
that created the maria when they hit and now lie buried deep beneath the lunar surface.

Oxygen Yes; Water No

Like the Earth, the Moon is roughly 50 percent oxygen. Like the
Earth, most of this oxygen is chemically locked up in the rocks of
the surface and interior.

While different types of surface rocks and strata on the Moon
have differing chemical compositions, the *overall* chemical composition of the Moon is given in table 3.

You can see from the table that the Moon is rich in oxygen,
silicon, iron, aluminum, calcium, magnesium and titanium. But
there is no water on the Moon.

At least, none has been found. The lunar rocks returned by our
Apollo astronauts were totally *anhydrous*, lacking in compounds
containing water molecules. In contrast, terrestrial rocks and even

SiO$_2$	= 43 percent
FeO	= 16 percent
AlO$_3$	= 13 percent
CaO	= 12 percent
MgO	= 8 percent
TiO$_2$	= 7 percent
other	= 1 percent

Si = silicon; O = oxygen; Fe = iron; Al = aluminum; Ca = calcium; Mg = magnesium; Ti = titanium.

TABLE 3 Composition of the Moon.

meteorites of the carbonaceous chondrite type contain water chemically linked to other elements.

The fact that no hydrates have been found in lunar rock samples may indicate that water has never existed on the Moon. Yet some hopeful souls theorize that pockets of ice may exist in "cold traps" in the polar regions, where there are areas permanently shaded from sunlight.

As we shall see, it might be possible—and necessary—to "manufacture" water on the Moon.

Lunar Industries

While there are good scientific reasons for establishing bases on the Moon (which we will discuss shortly), the most powerful incentive for a permanent human presence on the Moon is economic. The Moon can become the hub of the Solar System, first as a mining center, then as a site for manufacturing industries.

The evolution of lunar industries will most likely parallel the growth of major industrial cities on Earth. Pittsburgh, for example, began as a tiny fort in the forested wilderness of western Pennsylvania, but grew into a major city. Why? Because it was close to the important raw resources of coal and iron that led to steel-making, and it was located at the confluence of rivers that gave it easy access to those natural resources and to the cities where the markets for manufactured products existed.

As we have already seen, the Moon's regolith contains oxygen, silicon and metals that are valuable raw materials for space industries. And since the Moon's gravity is only one-sixth Earth's, and it is airless, it will be possible to launch those raw materials to space factories much more cheaply than they could be launched from Earth.

Mining on the Moon

Lunar mines will not be underground. In fact, we know practically nothing of the resources to be found beneath the lunar surface. All the natural resources we are talking about come from the sandy top layer of the regolith and the rocks strewn across its surface.

Open-pit mining will prevail. Bulldozers will scrape up the top foot or so of the regolith for processing plants to extract the valuable ores, including the oxygen that makes up roughly 50 percent of the Moon. The dozers will either have sealed, pressurized cabins or their operators will have to work in space suits.

In addition to the oxygen and ores, atoms of hydrogen and helium, blown onto the Moon's surface by the solar wind, lie trapped in the regolith's topmost layers. On Earth, solar wind particles are caught by the magnetosphere or absorbed in our thick atmosphere. On the Moon, these atomic particles from the Sun strike the lunar surface and stick—some of them, at least—in the upper layer of the regolith.

Hydrogen and helium represent precious natural resources. If they are abundant enough, they could make life on the Moon much easier, and much more profitable. More on them a little later.

Cheap Transportation

Since the Moon's gravity is so low, and there is negligible atmospheric friction, cargos can be launched off the Moon very inexpensively. In fact, it is possible to launch payloads off the Moon without using rockets. An electrical catapult, variously called a *rail gun* or a *mass driver*, can hurl cargo off the Moon cheaply and easily, as Arthur Clarke pointed out as far back as 1951 in his nonfiction book *The Exploration of Space*.

Electricity will be cheap on the Moon. The Sun shines fourteen days in a row, and the regolith has plenty of silicon. Use the silicon to make solarvoltaic cells and spread them across the ground in ever-expanding solar energy farms. Use the electricity generated to drive the catapult.

The catapult will be essentially a linear synchronous motor, a kind of electric motor that is laid out in a straight line. Electrical energy accelerates its cargo-carrying "buckets" to lunar escape velocity (1.48 mps). Not only is this better than four and a half times less than escape velocity from Earth (6.94 mps), the Moon's lack of atmosphere means there is no measurable air friction to hinder the catapult launches.

If the energy required to boost a payload is expressed in terms of kilowatt-hours, it takes about eleven thousand kilowatt-hours of energy to lift one ton of payload from Earth's surface to LEO. To lift a ton of payload from the Moon's surface to lunar *escape* velocity requires only eight hundred kilowatt-hours. When you factor in the atmospheric drag that must be overcome on Earth, the result is that payloads can be launched from the Moon to LEO about twenty-two times more cheaply than lifting them from Earth to LEO.

Notice that distance in space is not so important as the energy you need to travel that distance. The Moon is a quarter-million miles from Earth, yet it costs twenty-two times less to send cargo from the Moon to LEO than it does to lift the same mass a scant 100 miles or so from Earth.

The lunar mass driver will be at least a couple of miles long. The cargo-carrying "buckets" will be accelerated along its track by powerful electromagnets to more than 100 *g*: more than one hundred times the Earth's gravitational force. By comparison, the space shuttle pulls no more than 3 *g* during its launch. Clearly the mass driver will *not* be used for launching people.

Home-Grown Rockets

Humans will use rockets to get off the Moon's surface. Most likely they will be powered by aluminum and oxygen, both obtained from the lunar regolith. Aluminum/oxygen yields a specific impulse of only 270 seconds, but the propellants are easily available, and the gravitational field the rocket needs to overcome is only one-sixth that of Earth.

Specialized transportation systems will evolve. Travelling from the Earth to the Moon, you will most likely use a shuttlelike craft to go into LEO, transfer to a deep-space ship that goes from LEO to lunar orbit, and then transfer again to a lander that brings you to the lunar surface. Or perhaps the deep-space transfer craft will itself land on the Moon, since there is no atmosphere to worry about.

The transfer craft and lunar lander need not be aerodynamically streamlined because they operate in the vacuum of space and never enter Earth's atmosphere. They will be ungainly-looking collections of tankage, rocket engines, cargo modules and passenger quarters. The landers' legs will undoubtedly be spindly struts that look too weak to hold such a bulky mass, ending in oversized pads that can touch down gently on the sandy regolith.

A Possible Scenario

We can envision the growth of space industries as hinging crucially on the development of the Moon's natural resources.

Today we are witnessing the beginnings of industrial development in orbital space. The communications industry has been "in space" since the first commsats were launched in the 1960s. As we saw in chapter 5, observation satellites are generating a multibillion-dollar market in geographic and other types of space-based information systems. Industrial and chemical processing experiments have been done aboard the space shuttle and Mir space station, with more planned for the International Space Station Alpha, due to open for business in 2001.

Space factories will evolve in LEO. But if they are dependent on getting their raw materials from Earth, these orbital factories will be restricted to producing only those products that can be sold for very high prices: exotic alloys and pharmaceuticals that can bring in a profit despite the exorbitant costs of manufacturing in orbit.

But if a viable mining center is created on the Moon the cost of raw materials for the LEO factories goes down by more than a factor of twenty, as we have already seen. Orbital manufacturing can expand and prosper.

And so will lunar manufacturing. For the Moon's surface possesses most of the environmental conditions to be found in orbit, except for weightlessness, and has a couple of advantages that orbital factories lack.

The lunar surface has a better vacuum than LEO and free solar energy fourteen days of every month. The Moon has a fourteen-day-long night, true enough, but electrical power can still be supplied from sunlight either by building solar energy farms on the far side (which is in daylight when the Earth-facing side is in shadow) or by building enough electrical generating capacity and storage facilities to carry through the night. Electricity can be stored in batteries or superconducting magnets, for example.

The greatest advantage of the Moon as a manufacturing location is that the raw materials are right there. No need to transport them back to LEO. Send the finished products Earthward; that is much cheaper than sending bulk cargos of raw materials.

Hydrogen and Helium

Particles of hydrogen and helium from the solar wind are imbedded in the lunar regolith. The hydrogen can be vital, literally. Combined with lunar oxygen, it can produce water. There is apparently no water on the Moon, but we know that there is plenty of oxygen. If the hydrogen in the regolith is abundant enough, lunar bases can become self-sufficient very quickly. If not, they will be dependent on importing hydrogen from Earth—or perhaps from asteroids or even comets, eventually.

No matter where the hydrogen comes from, water will undoubtedly be "manufactured" on the Moon. Perhaps hydrogen and lunar oxygen will be fed into fuel cells that generate electricity while producing water.

Helium is an inert gas used mainly to blow up balloons on Earth. But some forms of helium may be extremely valuable, especially the *isotope* called helium-3. Helium-3 can be the key to safe, abundant energy through the process of *nuclear fusion*.

If helium-3 can be easily extracted from the regolith, and there is enough of it to be useful, then the fuel for fusion power on Earth may be supplied by the Moon.

Science on the Moon

The profit motive is not the only incentive for going to the Moon. Scientists want to explore this barren world thoroughly and use its unique environment to study the universe—and the human animal, as well.

Among the scientific investigations that will undoubtedly be conducted on the Moon are these:

1. Studies of the origin of the Solar System
2. Astronomical observations of the Sun, planets and stars
3. Physics of the Sun/Earth/Moon and their interactions
4. Particle physics
5. Ultrapure chemistry research

ISOTOPES

There are more than 100 known chemical elements, ranging from hydrogen to elements heavier than uranium that do not exist naturally on Earth but are made in physics laboratories. Many of these elements come in different varieties, called *isotopes* (from the Greek, meaning "same place").

The number of protons in an atom's nucleus, which is the same as the number of electrons orbiting its nucleus, determines the chemical nature of an element. Most atoms also contain neutrons in their nuclei: neutral particles that are slightly heavier than protons. Differences in the number of neutrons make different isotopes of an element.

For example, hydrogen is the lightest element. Its nucleus consists of a single proton, orbited by a single electron. But for every 6500 "normal" hydrogen atoms on Earth there is one atom of *deuterium*, which contains one neutron in its nucleus in addition to the proton. The atom is still hydrogen: It still has a single proton and a single electron. It behaves chemically exactly as ordinary hydrogen does. But its mass is twice that of ordinary hydrogen. Deuterium is often called "heavy hydrogen," and it can be used to make "heavy water."

An even heavier isotope of hydrogen, tritium, has two neutrons in the nucleus. Tritium is vanishingly rare on Earth; its nucleus is unstable and decays into an electron and a helium-3 nucleus. On average, half of a given amount of tritium will break down in 12.5 years. This is what physicists call an isotope's *half-life*.

Helium, with a nucleus of two protons and two neutrons, is the next-heaviest element. Helium-3 is an isotope that has only one neutron in its nucleus in addition to the two protons.

6. Biological and medical sciences
7. The search for extraterrestrial intelligence (SETI)

Let us examine briefly just two of these areas: particle physics and SETI.

Listening for E.T.

For more than thirty years astronomers have been searching the stars with radio telescopes, seeking signals that might be sent out

NUCLEAR FUSION

The nuclear power generators we use today are based on nuclear *fission*. That is, heavy atomic nuclei, such as those of uranium or plutonium, are broken apart. The process releases energy.

Nuclear *fusion* also produces energy. In hydrogen fusion, nuclei of the lightest atom—hydrogen—are forced together to produce helium. And lots of energy. In an 8-ounce glass of ordinary water there is enough fusion fuel (the isotope of hydrogen called deuterium) to equal the energy in 500,000 barrels of petroleum! And all that energy comes from using only the 1 deuterium atom in every 6500 hydrogen atoms in the water—less than 1/100,00 of the water! The rest of the water is untouched.

The Sun runs on hydrogen fusion. The stars are fusion generators. On Earth, physicists have labored for half a century to make a controlled fusion reactor. So far, their only success has been in producing *un*controlled fusion devices: hydrogen bombs.

Fusion experiments have used mainly deuterium as the fuel: It is abundant in ordinary water. But there is a much easier fusion reaction, according to theory, that uses a mixture of deuterium and helium-3. Helium-3 is extremely rare on Earth, but there may be significant amounts of it imbedded in the regolith of the Moon.

by an intelligent extraterrestrial civilization. This program is called SETI: the search for extraterrestrial intelligence.

No intelligent signals have yet been found. There are billions of stars to search through, and their distances from us are tremendous. Even if intelligent aliens are beaming radio messages in our direction, their signals would undoubtedly be very faint and masked by the natural radio "noise" of the stars themselves—and the constant radio signals broadcast by our own civilization.

As far as radio-frequency noise is concerned, the far side of the Moon is the quietest location in the Solar System.

Some 2,155 miles of rock insulate the far side from the constant radio and TV chatter of Earth. During the fourteen-day-long lunar night, even the natural radio emissions of the Sun are blocked out.

When the planet Jupiter is not in the far side's night sky the radio emissions from the distant stars can be studied with as little interference as it is possible to attain anywhere in the Solar System.

On the Moon's far side astronomers will be able to search for very faint radio signals, far fainter than anything they could detect on Earth. And they will be able to build much larger radio telescopes—miles across, if they can afford it. The low lunar gravity will make the engineering easier, and the Moon's own natural resources can provide the raw materials.

Particle Physics

The Moon's surface is an ideal place to study cosmic "rays," the most energetic particles in the universe. Primary cosmic particles bombard the Moon's surface constantly, whereas on Earth the primaries are usually stopped by collisions with atoms of our atmosphere.

In addition, man-made particle accelerators could be built on the Moon's surface, perhaps "piggybacked" on the powerful magnets used to drive the mass accelerator.

Lunar Commsats

On Earth we place commsats in GEO. It is impossible to do the same for the Moon, because the synchronous orbit for the Moon is at the distance of the Earth! The orbits of lunar-synchronous commsats would be so perturbed by Earth's gravity that they would inevitably crash into the Earth.

Lunar commsats will have to be of the low-altitude type, which means that many of them will be needed to provide continuous coverage over the entire Moon all the time. However, the earliest bases on the Moon will probably be placed close to the lunar equator, because that region is the least costly to reach in terms of rocket propellant and therefore money. With this in mind, a few small commsats in low equatorial orbit might suffice for the first years of lunar development.

It should also be possible to place a commsat in the L-1 libration point. From that vantage point, thirty-six thousand miles above the lunar surface, the commsat could "see" the entire near side of the Moon. As we found in chapter 6, however, the L-1 point is not gravitationally stable. Therefore, a satellite hovering at L-1 would have to use small squirts of rocket thrust from time to time to remain on-station. It would occasionally have to be resupplied with propellants, of course.

A Walk on the Moon

Taking what we know of the Moon, including the information brought back by the Apollo astronauts, we can show what it would be like to walk on the lunar surface.

You would be encased in a space suit, of course, with a bulky life-support backpack. The suit will be cumbersome, unless it is made of some as-yet-unknown materials. On Earth, your suit and equipment might weigh two hundred pounds, but in the Moon's one-sixth gravity it will feel like a thirty-some-pound pack.

Your helmet visor will be heavily tinted to block out the glare of a Sun unfiltered by atmosphere. You may not be able to see all the stars blazing in the sky. But even though you are walking in day-light, there are plenty of stars up there in the deep, dark blackness of the airless sky. Cup your hands under your visor to block out the reflected light from the lunar surface, and you may be able to see some of the stars. During the lunar night, of course, so many thousands of stars will be visible that the familiar shapes of the constellations will be swamped and almost impossible to make out.

The first thing you notice about the Moon is that the horizon seems disturbingly close. And unlike the gentle vistas of Earth, the lunar horizon is a sharp line that abruptly divides the solid rocky world from the black depths of space.

The horizon *is* close. Since the Moon is only about one-quarter the size of the Earth, the horizon is only about half the distance it would be on Earth. And it is sharp because on the airless Moon there is no atmospheric haze to soften the distant views.

A harsh, unforgiving world, it seems at first. Astronaut Buzz Aldrin called it "magnificent desolation." Yet there is beauty on the Moon.

Although the Sun sets for some 350 hours at a stretch, there is seldom any true "night" on the Earth-facing side of the Moon. Our big blue home planet is always hanging in that sky, shining up to fifty times brighter than the full Moon on Earth, bright enough to read the fine print of a contract with ease. It is a breathtakingly beautiful sight, that big blue marble. Even its night side twinkles with the lights of cities and highways.

Sandpapered Rocks

The lunar surface is barren, true enough. Not a blade of grass or a drop of water. Nothing but rocks, from tiny pebbles to boulders the size of apartment buildings, and craters ranging from fingertip-sized holes in the ground to mammoth ringwalls hundreds of miles across. And bare rock mountains that soar miles high.

But look again. Despite its forbidding appearance, the lunar landscape is far gentler than you might expect. For billions of years this rocky surface has been sandpapered by the constant infall of meteoric dust that has smoothed every boulder and mountain peak. Large meteorite strikes have blasted out craters. Subsurface "volcanism," mere seepages of thin gases rather than terrestrial-type volcanoes, has caused some parts of the surface to slump into sinuous rilles and potholes.

When you step out across the lunar regolith your boots stir up clouds of dust that spread and fall slowly, lazily back to the ground. The Moon, with its gentle gravity, is a slow-motion world. If you trip and fall you can easily put out a gloved hand and push yourself back to your feet before your body hits the ground.

Dangerous Dust

The dust can be dangerous, though. Atomic particles from the solar wind and cosmic radiation strike the Moon's surface and create an electric field that tends to make dust cling electrostatically to space suits and equipment. If you are not careful, dust could clog the hinges of your suit or, worse, obscure vision through your visor. It may be necessary to electrically "ground" space suits and equipment, to get the dust off them. Hal Clement made this the basis of his story "Dust Rag."

While the surface of the regolith is dark, you notice that the footprints you leave behind you are much brighter. That is the true color of the regolith. The surface layer has been darkened by eons of hard radiation from the Sun and stars.

Dawn on the Moon is breathtaking. Without air to diffuse the Sun's light, the difference between night and day is virtually instantaneous. One moment you are in darkness, the next in full brilliant sunlight. Because the Moon rotates so slowly, you can keep pace with the day-night terminator line just by walking.

In some areas the ground literally sparkles at sunrise, as if millions of jewels were sprinkled across the landscape. This phosphorescent effect is the result of minerals in the soil reacting to the sudden light and heat of the Sun.

Meteor Hits

But you can't stay out on the surface too long. A space suit can carry only a limited supply of oxygen, and even inside the protective suit you are threatened by hard radiation and meteoroids.

The Moon is constantly bombarded by meteoroids. Even though most of them are no bigger than dust motes, over time they have worn down the mountains and eroded the craters. Astronomers have calculated that the chance of a person on the lunar surface being hit by a meteoroid big enough to penetrate the outer shell of a space suit is approximately one in ten trillion. Still, that infall of microscopic dust could damage a space suit eventually. And you don't want to be the one in ten trillion!

Radiation Exposure

Hard X-rays, gamma rays, energetic protons from the solar wind and cosmic "rays" all bathe the Moon's surface ceaselessly. Radiation exposure is measured in *rads*; a rad is defined as the energy released by radiation when it is absorbed by living tissue. One rad equals 100 ergs per gram, or less than $\frac{1}{10,000}$ of a calorie per ounce. This is an extremely small amount of energy, but even a small amount can have serious biological consequences.

On Earth, in the latitudes of the "lower forty-eight" United States, at sea level the mean radiation dose coming in from space is from 0.20 to 0.40 rads per year. On the Moon's surface the dose is from 13 to 25 rads per year, although a solar flare can drench the Moon with more than 1000 rads over a period as short as a few hours.

Space suits should provide enough protection against the normal lunar radiation environment, although when a solar flare strikes, everyone will have to go underground until it is over.

Underground Living

Although people will work on the Moon's surface, they will live underground. The best protection against the temperature swings, the hard radiation, and the constant rain of meteoritic infall is a few feet of dirt.

The first shelters for lunar explorers will undoubtedly be prefabricated modules, very much like the living quarters of a space station. They can be placed in trenches scooped out by a bulldozer and then covered with the rubble to a depth of a few feet.

Permanent bases will either be dug into the ground or, if they are built on the surface, covered with regolith dirt for protection. One way or another, lunar residents will be cave dwellers.

THE WRITER'S PERSPECTIVE

Before the space explorations that culminated in the Apollo landings, even the finest science fiction writers could only deal in generalities about what it would be like to live and work on the Moon. George Pal's 1950 motion picture *Destination Moon* was as technically accurate as possible.[1] Yet its depiction of spacecraft and the lunar surface is so faulty in the light of today's knowledge that it seems woefully artificial.

We now have a wealth of detail about the Moon. We have seen astronauts working—and playing—on its surface. This knowledge is priceless for writers, not merely because it allows us to write stories that are technically accurate. There is a far more important reason to treasure this kind of knowledge.

It allows us to *use* the physical conditions of the Moon as integral parts of our stories. Not merely convincing background, but vital components of the tales we tell. We can also use the known physical conditions to make the story more real, to engage the reader thoroughly in the world you are creating. In my short story "The Man Who Hated Gravity," there is a scene were the protagonist accidentally knocks a wine bottle off his dinner table. This happens on the Moon, though, so he has time enough to grab the bottle before it can hit the floor or even spill a drop. A trivial little scene, perhaps, but I think it helped to make the reader feel that these events were really happening. And to feel the *differentness* of living on the Moon.

That's what writing fiction is all about: making the reader feel that he or she is actually living in your story.

Think about living underground, about putting on a cumbersome space suit just so you can go out on the surface and escape the corridors and tunnels of your living quarters. Think about how romantic it is to watch the Earth, full and bright, in the dark lunar sky. Or how lonely you might feel, gazing that quarter-million miles back to the world of your birth.

Think about pouring yourself a glass of water in $\frac{1}{6} g$. It doesn't pour at the same angle as on Earth, you know.

Story ideas can grow from the physical environment of strange new worlds. In my novel *Test of Fire*, most of the Earth is devastated by an enormous solar flare that burns the entire day-side of our planet. Civilization is destroyed in the enormous ecological collapse. But the people living on the Moon, already dwelling underground, ride out the solar flare with hardly a bump. Except that the lunar settlers have always lived with the idea that they can get whatever supplies they need from Earth. Now they can't. In fact, Earth needs their help now.

We can no longer write about giant ants living underground on the Moon, as H.G. Wells did. We can no longer write about canal-building Martians, as Edgar Rice Burroughs did. Not science fiction stories, that is.

But we can write about the Moon and Mars and other parts of the Solar System with more knowledge, more detail, and more solid reality than our predecessors could.

And that is all to the good, I think.

♦ ♦ ♦

[1] The script was worked on by the dean of American science fiction writers, Robert A. Heinlein. The art work was done by the father of all space artists, Chesley Bonestell.

CHAPTER 8

Advanced Spacecraft

It is difficult to say what is impossible, for the dream of yesterday is the hope of today and the reality of tomorrow.

Robert Goddard

TECHNICAL FACTORS

As we saw in chapter 5, getting to LEO currently costs more than $1000 per pound. Most estimates have placed the cost as high as $10,000 per pound.

The figures are inexact, because there are several different kinds of launching service operations. Space launch organizations include government agencies such as NASA, semigovernmental outfits such as the European Space Agency's Arianespace, and private companies such as Lockheed Martin and Orbital Sciences Corp. As we saw in chapter 5, Russia, China and other government-run launching services subsidize their operations with taxpayers' money so that they can offer lower prices to customers.

Also, some estimates of launch costs include a share of the cost of developing the booster and maintaining the launching center; others do not.

Still, even the low-end figure of $1000 a pound is too high for practical industries to develop in orbit. Everyone agrees on that.

Missiles and Launch Centers

The first space boosters were converted from ballistic missiles. Both Russians and Americans launched satellites and people with rockets that had originally been designed to carry hydrogen bomb warheads. These were expendable rockets; they were used only once. When their various stages burned out they fell back to Earth.

That is why the two major U.S. space centers are on the seacoast. Launches from Kennedy Space Center at Cape Canaveral and Vandenberg Air Force Base in southern California are out over the water, where empty rocket stages can plunge into the sea without harming anyone.

Arianespace's launching center is at Kourou, on the Atlantic coast of French Guiana, only five degrees north of the equator. Land-bound Russia and its federated states have major launching facilities at Baikonur, in Kazakstan, and Plesetsk, north of Moscow. Neither is near the sea, but both are situated in barren, thinly populated regions.

Reusable Launch Vehicles

One way to bring down launch costs is to make as much of the launching vehicle as possible reusable.

NASA's space shuttle was the first step toward a fully reusable launching vehicle. The winged orbiter can be flown again and again. The solid rocket boosters are parachuted into the ocean once they have burned out and are recovered, refurbished and filled with propellants again. Only the "egg" of the external tank is thrown away; it breaks up upon reentry into the atmosphere, and its pieces either burn completely or fall into the sea.

Save the Eggs?

Some have suggested that the external tank could be carried all the way into orbit and parked in LEO, to be used as the shell for future space stations. Big as a twelve-room house, the external tank would have to be purged of residual hydrogen left inside it before its interior could be used by human beings. And carrying it all the way into orbit would mean that the orbiter's payload would have to be reduced somewhat.

Bill Pogue and I used shuttle external tanks as part of the industrial space station we created for *The Trikon Deception*. We attached two ETs to the Trikon station; they added a lot of extra room for very little cost.

By the way, although the shuttle orbiter is reused, it takes weeks or even months of refurbishing before it is ready for another mission. In particular, its main engines have to be removed and refurbished after each flight. This all adds to the shuttle's operating cost.

Air-Launched Vehicles

Suppose that instead of using a rocket booster as your launch vehicle's first stage, you used an airplane?

Orbital Sciences Corp.'s Pegasus launcher does just that. Pegasus flies up to thirty thousand feet or higher tucked under a Lockheed L-1011 jet transport plane. Then it is released and flies on its own rocket power into orbit. Pegasus is a small vehicle and can deliver only a few hundred pounds to LEO. But it has successfully launched many small satellites and is the main launching vehicle for OSC's network of LEO commsats that will relay communications around the world.

One of the original designs for NASA's space shuttle had the orbiter perched atop a four-engine jet airplane that would do essentially the job that the shuttle's solid rocket boosters now do. This design was rejected by Washington's politicians as being too expensive, so the SRBs were substituted. It was a failure of an SRB that caused the Challenger explosion and killed seven astronauts. So much for political decisions.

The British and Russians are both working on a HOTOL concept: horizontal takeoff and landing. This too is a system where the "first stage" is a jet plane and the winged orbiter lands on a runway, like an airplane or the shuttle orbiter.

SSTO: The Delta Clipper

The most exciting launch vehicle development program currently underway is the Delta Clipper of McDonnell Douglas. The Clipper is designed to go from the ground to LEO in one leap—single stage to orbit (SSTO)—and to be completely reusable.

The Delta Clipper is the brainchild of Maxwell Hunter, a leading aerospace engineer, thinker and maverick.

Hunter pointed out that space boosters were originally derived from ballistic missiles, which he calls "ammunition." They were designed to be used once and thrown away. Practical transportation systems, on the other hand, depend on vehicles that can not only be used over and over again, but need very little turnaround time between trips.

Hunter wants a space launcher that is operated like a commercial airliner, instead of "ammunition." That is, he wants a launcher that can be used over and over again, with minimal maintenance time between missions (a few days, at most) and a small maintenance and operation crew.

The real cost of space launches, Hunter insists, is neither the cost of the launch vehicle nor its propellants nor its crew. It is the "standing army" of technicians that are needed to maintain and operate the launch vehicle. The space shuttle, for example, has some ten thousand men and women working on it in between missions. Hunter wants to reduce that "army" to a few dozen people.

The result of Hunter's prodding is the DC-X, a one-third scale model of the ultimate Delta Clipper, built by McDonnell Douglas to demonstrate the main features of the SSTO principle.

Significantly, the Clipper development program was originally funded not by NASA, but by the Air Force's Strategic Defense Initiative Office (SDIO), the "Star Wars" people. If a "Star Wars" system is ever deployed in orbit to defend against ballistic missile attack, it will require hundreds of satellites, megatons of payload to be lifted into LEO or higher. SDIO was vitally interested in reducing the cost of reaching orbit, hence its backing of the SSTO concept.

NASA was accused of neglecting SSTO because it was a possible competitor against the shuttle for future funding. The way Washington politics has worked out, NASA has been handed the Delta Clipper program (whether they want it or not), and the Air Force has been eased out of the picture.

But not before the DC-X flew a successful series of unmanned test flights. They only went a few thousand feet up, but they demonstrated that the vehicle could take off vertically, hover, move sideways and land vertically, on its tail. And be "turned around" by a small ground crew for another flight very quickly.

DC-X is a cone-shaped vehicle, twenty-nine feet tall. While its structure is as modern as the latest advances in materials can make it, most of its components are "off-the-shelf" items, well known and reliable. It is propelled by four RL-10 hydrogen/oxygen rocket engines. Using multiple engines allows the vehicle to abort a flight and land safely if one or even two engines fail during liftoff.

Little DC-X even survived an accident in July 1994 that would have destroyed a more conventional rocket vehicle. Some hydrogen fuel leaked from a ground line and was ignited when the rocket engines lit off. The explosion tore off some of the vehicle's skin, but it flew and landed safely anyway.

Hunter and the Delta Clipper team firmly believe that, with modern lightweight structural materials and miniaturized electronics, it will be possible for the full-scale Delta Clipper to carry ten tons of payload to LEO at a cost of $100 per pound, although some aerospace engineers strongly disagree with their assessment. The dissenters claim that the spacecraft's structure cannot be made light enough to make single-stage-to-orbit flight possible. Only flight tests will tell which side is right, so we will have to wait for several years of testing before we find out.

The Clipper could operate unmanned, completely controlled from the ground; or it could carry passengers. All for $100 per pound. Or less.

The key is the lightweight structure. Burt Rutan, who designed the Voyager airplane that flew all the way around the world without refueling, is putting his knowledge of lightweight composite materials into the Clipper's development effort.

Skyhook

Suppose, instead of using a rocket booster, you could ride an elevator up to GEO? This fantastic idea was first put forth by Tsiolkovskii almost a century ago. It was the centerpiece of Arthur C. Clarke's novel, *The Fountains of Paradise.*

A 22,300-mile-high Skyhook tower that stretches from the ground all the way up to GEO is theoretically possible, although a couple of very sticky engineering problems stand in the way of its practicality today.

The theory is surprisingly simple. You start with a satellite in GEO. You drop a cable to the ground. To balance it you unreel another cable in the opposite direction, deeper into space. The centrifugal force that keeps the satellite in its orbit also keeps the cables rigid. Add electrical power and elevator cars and you can ride into space!

The practical problems, however, are severe. To begin with, that 22,300-mile-long cable will be so heavy it would crash from its own weight. *If* you could carry it up to GEO in the first place. And the end that reaches the ground is going to be subjected to all the wind and weather that our turbulent atmosphere can throw at it. That includes the powerful jet streams, up in the stratosphere.

And yet—perhaps the cable could be manufactured in orbit, from lunar or asteroidal materials. Perhaps we can learn how to make a cable that is stronger and yet light enough to do the job; zero-*g* manufacturing in orbital vacuum holds that promise.

Even if the Skyhook idea is impractical on Earth, it could work— even using today's known materials—on low-gravity worlds such as Mars or the moons of the outer planets. It would not work on our Moon because, as we have seen, the lunar-synchronous orbit is unstable due to the Earth's gravitational influence—unless, perhaps, we built the lunar skyhook on the Moon's far side, which always faces away from the Earth.

Some day we may ride in elevator cars at speeds of several thousand miles per hour up to GEO, at a cost of pennies per pound. After all, the energy will be supplied by electrical power stations on the ground.

In a variant of the Skyhook idea, the cable does not stretch all the way to the ground. It "merely" reaches into the stratosphere, a few miles above Earth's surface. The cable rotates, like the spoke of a wheel, so that it dips down into the stratosphere and then swings up, past GEO, and deeper into space before starting another downward swing.

Passengers and cargo would fly from the ground in a jet plane, make a rendezvous with the swinging cable, transfer onto it, and then ride into space on it. The plane would return to the ground, presumably loaded with passengers and cargo coming back from orbital space.

Astronauts can rendezvous with satellites in orbit, where both craft are moving at 5 mps or better. It should be possible to rendezvous with that swinging cable in the upper reaches of the stratosphere, above the jet streams, where the air is usually calm and stable.

It should be possible. Fliers, including astronauts, have an understated term for dangerous situations; they call them "interesting." The first rendezvous between a high-flying jet plane and that cable swinging down from GEO should be *very* interesting.

Mass Drivers

In chapter 7 we saw that an electric catapult could be used to boost cargo payloads off the Moon. That concept was the brainchild of Arthur C. Clarke, the visionary author who "invented" the communications satellite; he suggested in 1951 that electrically powered catapults would be a very efficient way to launch payloads off the Moon.

Some thirty years later, Gerard K. O'Neill of Princeton University developed Clarke's idea into the modern concept of the *mass driver*.

A mass driver, however, need not be attached to the Moon. It can float in space and be used as an orbital catapult or even as a spacecraft propulsion system. It is actually a rocket that fires solid pellets rather than hot gases to create thrust. Newton's Third Law works just as well for pebbles as it does for plasmas.

A typical design for a mass driver reaction engine (MDRE), as such systems are called, is a mass driver some three to six miles long that uses powerful superconducting magnets to accelerate pellets of about half an ounce. About three megawatts of electrical power are needed, provided either by nuclear or solar energy.

The pellets could come from lunar or asteroidal materials. They are accelerated to velocities of 17,600 miles per hour within one second or less. This would produce a thrust of some 126 pounds at a specific impulse of 816 seconds.

The MDRE would be most useful for moving heavy cargos from low orbits to higher ones. It could carry a 1700-ton payload from low earth orbit to geosynchronous orbit (22,300 miles up), expending 2100 tons of pellets along the way.

MDREs could also be used as interplanetary spacecraft that "eat" chunks of asteroids and spit them out to provide thrust. For long-term expeditions seeking raw materials among the Asteroid Belt, beyond the orbit of Mars, an MDRE might turn out to be more efficient than carrying propellants for the return trip all the way from Earth.

However, a question arises: What happens to all those pellets after they have been spat out by the MDRE? Those directed toward Earth would burn up in the atmosphere and provide man-made meteor showers, an interesting highlight for a science fiction tale.

But in deeper space they could create hazards to navigation!

Laser Propulsion

Laser propulsion may become the most efficient and economical way to travel in space.

The laser itself does not have to be lifted off the ground, so most of the mass of the propulsion system never leaves the earth. And since the laser beam can heat propellants to far higher temperatures than can be obtained by chemical burning, a laser-powered rocket can give specific impulses of 1000 to 2000 seconds.

A laser-driven rocket would carry hydrogen or possibly argon in its propellant tank, laced with a small amount of water, ammonia, or another compound that absorbs laser energy easily.

Lasers of thousands of megawatts' power would be needed to boost spacecraft from the ground. While multi-megawatt lasers are now being developed for military purposes, future developments could be applied to laser space propulsion systems. Laser-boosted spacecraft could carry payloads that are 50 percent of their total liftoff weight, rather than the 1.6 percent of today's space shuttle. Ground-based lasers could also be used to raise the altitude of satellites that have been lifted to low orbit by more conventional rocket boosters.

As we saw in chapter 2, huge lasers in orbit near the Earth could propel spacecraft through the far reaches of the Solar System, and even out toward other stars. Or such lasers might be placed in orbits closer to the Sun, where they could be powered by solar cells more efficiently.

The MHD Torch Ship

You recall from chapter 2 that most electrical rocket systems produce very low levels of thrust, even though their specific impulses can be as high as 10,000 sec. It may be possible to combine nuclear energy and electrical power to produce rocket engines of high thrust *and* high efficiency, by using magnetohydrodynamic (MHD) power generators.

MHD generators draw electrical power from the hot exhaust gas streaming from a rocket engine. Essentially, an MHD generator is a tube or channel through which the hot exhaust gas flows. Strictly speaking, the rocket exhaust is a weakly ionized plasma; it can be seeded with a small amount of easily ionized cesium or potassium to raise its electrical conductivity. Wrap a powerful magnet around the channel and put electrodes along its inner wall, and you have a working MHD generator.

If an MHD generator had been connected to the launch pad of the Saturn V boosters during the days of the Apollo program, for example, the electricity produced from the rocket exhaust gases could have lit the entire East Coast of the U.S.—for as long as the rocket engines were burning.

MHD generators thrive on hot, ionized gases; the hotter the better. They could take advantage of the full potential of nuclear power.

Solid-core nuclear reactors, such as those used in today's electrical utility power generators, are limited to temperatures below 6300°F because at higher temperatures their solid fissionable fuel elements begin to break down. A nuclear reactor that uses *gaseous* uranium, such as uranium hexaflouride (UF^6), can attain temperatures up to 14,000°F. A gas-core reactor can thus impart considerably more energy to the working fluid of a rocket system than a solid-core reactor.

But if the propellant is put directly through the reactor, the gaseous uranium will flow out of the rocket nozzle along with the working fluid. To keep from losing the uranium, the UF_6 is piped through a heat exchanger—where it transfers its heat energy to the propellant—and then is cycled back into the reactor core. The amount of heat that can be transferred to the working fluid is limited by the top temperatures that metal pipes, heat exchangers and radiators can stand. We seem to have hit the same stumbling block that limits the top temperatures of solid-core fission reactors: Solid materials can only take a certain amount of heat.

That is where the MHD part of the system comes in: MHD offers a way to add energy to a gas (a plasma, really) that is literally too hot to touch with anything solid.

The hot gaseous uranium flows continuously through a closed-loop system. As it leaves the reactor core it passes through an MHD generator that extracts some fifteen megawatts of electrical power from the stream. The gas expands and cools in the MHD generator and ceases fissioning. At this point it can go through the heat exchanger without damaging it. Then the uranium gas is condensed again and pumped back into the reactor core. Condensing it raises its temperature to the point where fission begins again.

So we have a two-step energy-transfer process. In the heat exchanger, the working fluid (hydrogen or an argon/cesium mixture) is heated to the hottest temperature that the metal walls can stand. The electrical energy from the MHD generator is then added to the plasma in the rocket chamber, so that the ionized gas comes out of the rocket nozzle at a velocity almost as great as if it had been passed directly through the core of the reactor (see figure 7).

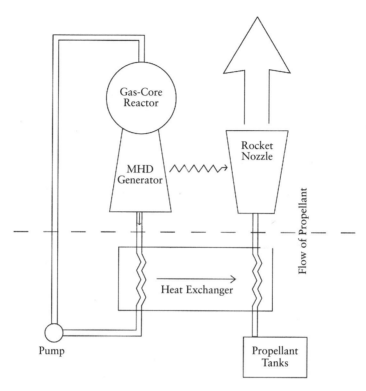

Nuclear-MHD Torch Drive
(Thermal energy transfer below dotted line–
electrical energy transfer above dotted line)

FIGURE 7 Schematic of a Nuclear-MHD Rocket System.
Heat energy from nuclear fission is imparted to the propellant in the heat
exchanger; electrical energy from the MHD generator is added in the rocket
nozzle. Gas-core reactor uses uranium hexafluoride, which goes through the
heat exchanger and then is pumped back to the reactor in a closed loop. The
propellant (or working fluid) can be hydrogen or an argon/cesium mixture.

Specific impulses of twenty-five hundred seconds could be obtained from nuclear-MHD rockets, more than twice the performance of solid-core nuclear rockets and five times better than the
best chemical rockets. Unlike other electrical rockets, the nuclear-
MHD "torch" could produce very high thrust as well.

MHD generators have no moving parts. They are rugged and
comparatively lightweight for their power output. And they have

the peculiar quality of becoming more efficient as they are made larger. Since a nuclear-MHD system could produce about one hundred times more power per pound of equipment than existing electrical rocket systems such as the ion thruster, a nuclear-MHD system could provide high thrust as well as high efficiency. A nuclear-MHD torch that weighs less than two tons could provide thrust in the range of 100 to 300 tons.

Such a torch ship could bring trip times to Mars down to weeks instead of months. If mining expeditions to the Asteroid Belt, which lies beyond the orbit of Mars, are ever to become practical, nuclear-MHD torch ships may well be the propulsion system of choice.

Storm Cellars

No matter what propulsion system is used, interplanetary ships carrying people (*crewed* missions, in NASA's gender-sensitive jargon) will need storm cellars.

Although the structure and equipment of a spacecraft are enough to shield the crew from the normal levels of radiation in interplanetary space, it is foolish to expect space missions lasting many months to avoid solar flares and the lethal doses of radiation that arise in space after a flare erupts. The electronic systems of a spacecraft can be hardened against radiation; human beings cannot be. They need protection.

A storm cellar, then, would be a shielded shelter where the crew could wait out the high radiation levels that can persist for several days after a flare erupts on the Sun. They will have enough warning time to get into the shelter—a matter of hours or even days between the flare's onset and the arrival of the deadly cloud of hard radiation. The shelter must be stocked with enough food to last several days, and of course have adequate water and air systems as well as hardened communications so that the crew can talk with Earth.

The most obvious kind of storm cellar is simply some large mass of material between the crew and the radiation. Solid walls of lead are too massive to be practical on a spacecraft, although the ship's tanks-full of propellants might absorb enough of the incoming radiation to consider putting the storm cellar inside the propellant tankage.

A more elegant solution would be to copy nature and put a strong magnetic field about the storm cellar. After all, it is the Earth's magnetosphere that protects us from deadly solar-flare radiation storms. Superconducting magnets, which retain extremely high field strengths without needing electrical power (once they are charged up), could do the job, as long as they are cooled to a cryogenic temperature.

But a magnetic field powerful enough to deflect the high-energy protons from a solar flare would be so strong that it would warp the magnet out of shape. You would need so much structural mass to hold the magnet together that you might as well build a lead-walled shelter and be done with it.

The truly sophisticated solution is to charge the spacecraft to very high positive electrical potential, so that the high-energy protons are deflected by electrostatic forces: like charges repel one another. To keep the negatively charged electrons in the radiation cloud from reaching the ship and neutralizing its positive charge, a moderate magnetic field is all that is needed; the electrons have comparatively little energy in them, so a weaker field can deflect them well enough.

Whether it's a metal bubble inside a propellant tank or an electrically shielded shelter wrapped by a superconducting magnetic field, the storm cellar can make a good environment for high-tension drama. See my novel *Mars* for an example.

THE WRITER'S PERSPECTIVE

The ongoing effort to produce a viable SSTO, such as the Delta Clipper, offers the writer a rich supply of characters and conflicts. The lone maverick bucking the system. The conflict of bureaucrats who prefer to protect their turf rather than take a chance on something new. The honest (and often heated) disagreements between engineers who believe SSTO can be made to work and those who don't agree. These are raw materials for good fiction, whether it is set in the here-and-now or a thousand years in the future. Human nature won't be that different in a mere millennium.

Draw your characters from life. Do not be afraid to use actual people as models for your fictional characters. You will find that you blend together several different people as your characters grow and develop, unless you are deliberately trying to draw a portrait of a certain individual.

Most people do not recognize themselves when they are portrayed in fiction. The reason is simple: They do not see themselves as the writer sees them. But if they *do* recognize themselves, and the portrait is not flattering, they might possibly try to sue the writer and publisher.

So use real people as models, but be very wary of unflattering portraits.

Imagination and Knowledge

Einstein said, "Imagination is more important than knowledge."

This book is intended to give you the knowledge you need to write about space travel convincingly. Yet your own imagination is more important than any of the technical details in this or any other book.

How would a 22,300-mile-high Skyhook tower look? What would it be like to ride its elevator? Or to be in a jet plane trying to rendezvous with the swinging cable of the shorter, rotating Skyhook system?

What would a laser booster system look like? Jerry Pournelle described one with detail in his novelette "High Justice." But there are many other possibilities.

The known facts are important. The ideas that you can generate by extrapolating from the known facts are even more important. In science fiction, what we know today is usually the starting point from which exciting stories are begun.

Remember, science fiction writers are free to invent any new ideas they can imagine—as long as no one can prove they are impossible within the context of the story. I can write about a multigigawatt laser boosting a spacecraft into orbit, but if I wrote about using a mass driver in Texas to launch payloads from the ground into LEO most readers would take umbrage—justifiably—unless I did some pretty tall explaining to get around the fact that those payloads would burn like meteors before they got clear of the Earth's atmosphere.

Use the facts to stir your imagination. Use the facts also to keep your imagination from straying too far. It's an exceedingly fine line, the difference between extrapolation and out-and-out fantasy. Don't let the difference worry you too much, as long as you keep your story internally self-consistent. Laser boost and magic carpets don't belong in the same story, although magnificent stories have been written about each of them.

CHAPTER 9

The Solar System

Now is the time to take longer strides—time for a great new American enterprise—time for this nation to take a clearly leading role in space achievement, which in many ways may hold the key to our future on Earth.

John F. Kennedy

TECHNICAL FACTORS

The Moon is a quarter-million miles away. The rest of the Solar System is much farther. The closest planet, Venus, never comes nearer to Earth than 25 million miles; Mars' closest approach is some 35 million miles.

The Sun is at the hub of the Solar System; all the planets, asteroids and comets orbit around it. These orbits are not perfectly circular but ellipses of various degrees of eccentricity.

The Earth's orbit, for example, is very close to being a true circle but not quite. In January, when the Earth is closest to the Sun (perihelion), the distance is slightly less than 91 million miles. In July, at aphelion, we are almost 94 million miles from the Sun. Other planets have much more eccentric orbits. But for the sake of simplicity we will use only their average distances from the Sun in this book.

The Astronomical Unit (AU)

Earth's average distance is just a tad under 93 million miles. Astronomers have turned that average distance into a yardstick that they call the *Astronomical Unit* (AU), a convenient shorthand

Planet	Miles $\times 10^6$	AUs	Light Time
Mercury	35.97	0.39	3.21 mins
Venus	67.23	0.72	6.0 mins
Earth	92.96	1.00	8.3 mins
Mars	141.6	1.52	12.6 mins
Jupiter	483.6	5.20	43.2 mins
Saturn	887.3	9.58	1 hr, 19.3 mins
Uranus	1784.7	19.14	2 hrs, 39.5 mins
Neptune	2795.05	30.20	4 hrs, 9.9 mins
Pluto	3672.47	39.44	5 hrs, 28.3 mins

Note: Pluto's orbit is *very* eccentric; so much so that between 1979 and 1999 Pluto is actually closer to the Sun than Neptune.

TABLE 4 Solar System Distances.

way of talking about distances within the Solar System.

Table 4 gives the distances from the Sun of the nine major planets in three different units: millions of miles, astronomical units, and the time it takes light (travelling at 186,000 miles per second) to go from the Sun to the planet.

Interplanetary Communications

Radio waves are a form of electromagnetic radiation, just as light is, although radio waves are much longer in wavelength than visible light. Radio communications therefore travel at the speed of light. Since light travels from the Earth to the Moon in about 1.3 seconds, round-trip communications between the Earth and the Moon have a nearly three-second lag in them: the time it takes a signal to reach the Moon and return.

Communications to the planets have even greater lag times, of course. When Earth and Mars are closest to each other, for example, it takes more than four minutes for a communications signal to travel from one planet to the other. That means conversations between Earth and Mars will have lags of more than eight minutes at best. When Earth and Mars are their farthest distance apart, communications will take about twenty-one minutes *one way*.

You can see by a glance at table 4 that there will be no real conversations over interplanetary distances. Communications will consist of one party talking and the other listening, then a waiting

Planet	Inclination (deg.)
Mercury	7.004
Venus	3.394
Earth	0.000
Mars	1.850
Ceres (asteroid)	10.600
Jupiter	1.308
Saturn	2.488
Uranus	0.774
Neptune	1.774
Pluto	17.150

TABLE 5 Orbital Inclinations of the Planets.

period, then the second party talks while the first party listens. Can interplanetary business be conducted this way?

Asimov considered the time-lag problem of interplanetary communications between Earth and distant Pluto in a short-short story, "My Son, the Physicist," and came up with the idea that both parties could talk continuously to each other. Questions will be received and answers will be put into the pipeline to be received later. There is no reason to wait—keep talking; eventually, an answer will come back. Asimov described this as "Continuous conversation. Just twelve hours [approximately the round-trip time to Pluto] out of phase, that's all."

Inclinations, Conjunctions and Oppositions

There are three features of planetary orbits that have an important bearing on planning space missions and therefore on plotting science fiction stories.

Inclination refers to the angle between the plane in which a planet orbits and the plane of the *ecliptic*.

Draw a picture of the Sun, and then draw in the Earth orbiting around it. Shade in the area between the Earth's orbit and the Sun. That shaded area is the plane of the ecliptic. The inclination of the Earth's orbit to the ecliptic is therefore, by definition, zero.

The other planets' orbits vary from the plane of the ecliptic by different amounts, as shown in table 5.

Why is inclination important? Because the farther a planet's inclination is from the ecliptic, the more energy it will take to send a spacecraft to that planet. Inclination represents a distance just as real and important as the distance a planet's orbit is from Earth.

As you can see, most of the planets orbit close to the ecliptic, with the exception of Mercury and Pluto—and the asteroid Ceres. Mercury, closest to the Sun, is heavily influenced by the Sun's titanic gravitational pull. Pluto is a maverick world in many ways: Once it was thought to be an escaped moon of Neptune that set up its own rather weird planetary orbit. More on that in a few moments.

Ceres is the largest of the asteroids, not a true planet but a planetoid or minor planet. As we saw in chapter 5, Ceres is only 560 miles wide, more like a very large rock than a real planet. More on the asteroids later, too. For now, suffice to say that its high inclination means that a mission to Ceres will have to spend a considerable amount of rocket propellent on climbing out of the ecliptic plane to get to the asteroid—unless the mission is timed to reach Ceres as it crosses the ecliptic, which every object in the Solar System does twice on each orbit.

Opposition is when a planet is in a position exactly opposite the position of the Sun in Earth's sky. You could draw a straight line from the Sun, through the Earth, to the planet (ignoring differences in inclination, of course). Only planets whose orbits are farther from the Sun than our own can attain opposition. These farther-out planets are called *superior* planets by astronomers. The term has nothing to do with whether or not the planet is better than Earth; superior planets are farther from the Sun that the Earth is, inferior planets are closer.

Conjunction occurs when a planet is exactly on the opposite side of the Sun from Earth's position. We cannot see the planet during conjunction because the Sun hides it. We could not communicate with the planet at that point in its orbit because the Sun would block the transmissions (see figure 8). However, commsats in the L-4 or L-5 positions along the planet's orbit could relay communications. Or a set of satellites could be placed in polar orbits around the Sun at about 1 AU. There's no need to restrict your thinking to the plane of the ecliptic.

In the 1940s and 1950s George O. Smith wrote a series of stories about a manned relay station placed at a Lagrange point on Venus' orbit so that people on Earth and Venus could communicate even when Venus is in conjunction: the *Venus Equilateral* stories. Re-

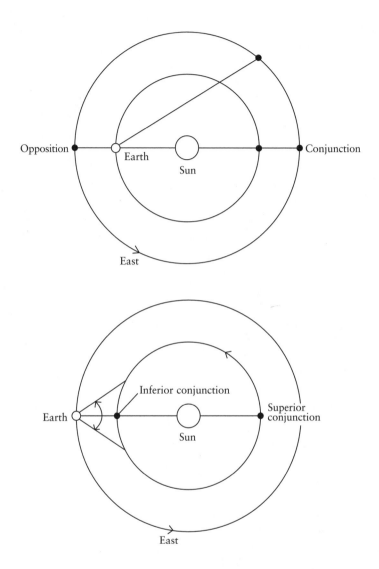

FIGURE 8 Upper drawing shows opposition and conjunction of a superior planet (i.e., one whose orbit is farther from the Sun than Earth's). Lower drawing shows conjunctions for an inferior planet.

membering what we said about the Lagrange points in chapter 6, you can understand what Smith's title refers to.

Both superior and inferior planets can go through conjunctions, although inferior planets, being closer to the Sun than the Earth is, can have *inferior conjunctions*, where the planet is between the Earth and the Sun, as well as *superior conjunctions*, where the planet is on the opposite side of the Sun.

Space missions to a superior planet, such as Mars, are usually planned around the period of opposition, when the Earth-Mars distance is minimal. Missions to Venus and Mercury, the two inferior planets, have the shortest distance to go when those planets are in their inferior conjunction positions.

Transfer Orbits

The first step in heading for the planets is to get into LEO.

Planetary probes such as the Voyager spacecraft that flew past all the outer planets except Pluto are boosted from Earth into LEO, where their systems are checked out. Then they are launched into *transfer orbits* with upper-stage rocket engines such as the Centaur or TOS (Transfer Orbital Stage). Transfer orbits are the trajectories that "transfer" the spacecraft from Earth's position to the position that the target planet will be in when the spacecraft arrives at its vicinity.

Future interplanetary missions will use LEO as an assembly area where spacecraft, their supplies, crews and equipment will be brought together. Then, like the simple unmanned probes of today, they will head out for their destinations on transfer orbits.

The most economical of these interplanetary trajectories are usually called *Hohmann minimum energy orbits*, after the German engineer Walter Hohmann. In 1925 he showed that a trajectory that is tangential to both the Earth's orbit and the orbit of the destination planet requires the least energy and therefore the least rocket propellant.

Minimum energy means longest trip time. The minimum energy orbit to Mars, for example, takes 259 days: eight months, two weeks and five days (see figure 9). The minimum energy trajectory to Jupiter takes two years and nine months.

Faster trip times require more speed. This can be obtained either by a bigger rocket boost when leaving LEO (and coasting the rest of the way) or by using some form of electric propulsion or lightsail that continuously accelerates the spacecraft (at low thrust levels) for long periods of time. A nuclear-MHD torch ship might be able to burn its engine for much longer times than chemical or "straight" nuclear rockets and reduce trip times by accelerating to much higher velocities.

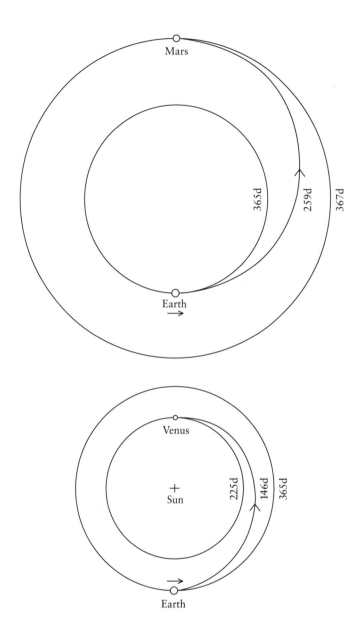

FIGURE 9 Minimum energy transfer orbits to Mars (259 days) and Venus (146 days). Also called Hohmann transfer orbits.

Future missions may start from the Moon or elsewhere, rather than Earth. No matter where your interplanetary missions begin, your explorers will most likely assemble their ships and equipment in low orbit and then head out to their destination on a transfer orbit. If they have a truly advanced propulsion system, such as an MHD torch or a fusion drive, their transfer orbits may be much closer to straight lines than graceful Hohmann curves.

You can get to Mars in hours, if you can just go fast enough.

Gravity Boost

When space engineers began planning in the 1960s for the great interplanetary missions for the *Mariner*, *Pioneer* and *Voyager* spacecraft, they realized that they would not have the propulsion power to fly the spacecraft all the way to the edges of the Solar System. So they utilized the technique of gravity-boosting to help the unmanned spacecraft on their way to the distant planets.

The idea is to use a planet's gravity to add velocity to the coasting spacecraft. You get additional velocity for no cost in propellants—if your aim is good enough.

Assuming that, like the *Voyager* probes, all the rocket thrust for the spacecraft ends within a few minutes of leaving Earth orbit, from there on the spacecraft coasts toward its destination, except for a few tiny squirts of steering jets to fine-tune its trajectory.

As the spacecraft approaches a planet, the planet's gravity attracts it and accelerates it. But the spacecraft's minuscule gravitational field also attracts the planet a teeny bit. If the spacecraft's trajectory is exactly right, the spacecraft can gain some velocity from the encounter. The massive planet actually slows down by an amount so small that it is unmeasurable. But the much-smaller spacecraft gets enough of a boost to speed it on its way farther into space.

Voyager 2, for example, used gravity boosts from Jupiter to go on to Saturn, from Saturn to reach Uranus, and from Uranus to get to Neptune. Both Voyagers have left the Solar System. As of mid-1995, *Voyager 1* was 5.5 billion miles from Earth, travelling at 39,000 mph. *Voyager 2* was 4.3 billion miles away, moving at 36,000 mph. Both spacecraft were still sending back data about the deep-space environment.

In a few million years, these spacecraft may encounter other stars.

The *Galileo* probe was launched from the space shuttle in 1989 without enough velocity to reach its destination, Jupiter, even on a minimum-energy orbit. NASA engineers swung the Galileo spacecraft past Venus and Earth—twice each—to get up enough speed to coast out through the Asteroid Belt and reach Jupiter. In December 1992, *Galileo* zipped a scant 109 miles above the south Atlantic Ocean, on its way to its December 1995 rendezvous with Jupiter.

Earth II

Every now and then some writer gets the idea that there might be another Earth-like planet orbiting the Sun exactly along our own orbit but on the opposite side of the Sun, constantly in superior conjunction so that we never see it.

Nice idea, but it doesn't work. If there were a planet there, we could not see it, but we would detect its gravitational influences on the rest of the Solar System. Its gravitational field would cause wobbles in the orbits of the other planets, as well as perturbing the Apollo asteroids that cross Earth's orbit. It was from such perturbations of the orbit of Uranus that the planets Neptune and Pluto were discovered in 1846 and 1930, respectively, far out in the dark distant reaches of the Solar System.

There is no Earth II, so if you want to write *science* fiction stories, drop that turkey—or invent some reason why our astronomers cannot detect its gravitational influence on the other bodies of the Solar System.

A Middling Star

It's been said that the Solar System consists of the Sun and debris. Ninety-nine percent of the mass of the entire Solar System is in the Sun. The planets, moons, asteroids, comets and loose dust amount to just about one percent of the Sun's mass.

The Sun is a star. An average, middle-class star in many ways. It was born about five billion years ago. It will continue to shine pretty much as it is now for another ten billion years or so. Then it will begin to swell and things will get very interesting—in the jet-jock's use of the word—for anything living on Earth.

We will go into detail about the Sun's origin and lifespan in chapter 10. For the purposes of this chapter all we need to consider is that the Sun will be there for a *long* time to come.

Birth of the Solar System

Although many of the details remain to be settled, astronomers can sketch out with some confidence how the Solar System came into being.

The Sun and planets were born together, some five billion years ago. The material that would become our Solar System originated as a vast cloud of gas and dust—mostly hydrogen—about a light-year in diameter. It was spinning slowly. As it spun, it contracted, and as it contracted it spun faster and faster, just as an ice skater spins faster and faster as she pulls her arms closer to her body.[1]

Most of the original cloud sank into the center and eventually became the Sun. The hydrogen in its core became so dense and hot—more than twenty million degrees—that nuclear fusion reactions began. The cloud lit up. A star was born. Astronomers have seen dark blobs of gas and dust, called *protostars*, turn on their nuclear furnaces and begin to shine.

The early Sun was surrounded by a thin disk of dusty gases spinning out from its middle, left over from the original cloud. This material began to condense into clumps, and the clumps began to aggregate in a process called *accretion*. Early in the Solar System's history the region of the disk was filled with chunks of rock and metal, banging into one another, sometimes sticking together but more often blasting each other into fragments.

Eventually, though, some of the chunks grew big enough to attract other pieces by gravitational pull rather than chance. For eons these protoworlds were bombarded with these smaller pieces of matter—called *planetesimals*. We can see the scars of that bombardment on the face of the Moon.

About 3.5 billion years ago the heavy bombardment ended. Most of the major clumps of matter had either been gathered in by the nine major planets or settled into asteroidal orbits. We still get occasional meteor strikes, of course. A major blow killed the dinosaurs some 65 million years ago. In 1994 Jupiter was struck with the broken-up remains of a comet. But the Solar System has been relatively peaceful for the past 3.5 billion years.

The Water World and Its Moon

To understand the brief sketches of the other planets of the Solar System that are coming up, we should look at a few of the important features of our own planet Earth. There are four factors to consider:

1. *Water*. Earth is the only planet we know of that has *any* liquid water on its surface. In fact, three-fifths of our planet is covered with water. The oceanic basins average about two miles deep. At our distance from the Sun water can remain liquid indefinitely, as long as there is a reasonable atmosphere to protect it from the full fury of the Sun's heat.

2. *Plate tectonics*. Earth's crust is in constant motion. Vast plates of crustal rock, the size of continents, literally float on the denser, hotter mantle rocks beneath them. These movements cause earthquakes, build mountain chains, and rearrange the land masses of Earth with slow, ponderous inexorability.

Plate tectonics are driven by the heat from the Earth's interior; our planet has a molten core of iron-nickel. The heat is partly from the early times of accretion, when the entire planet was molten from the constant bombardment by infalling meteoroids and planetesimals, and partly from the heat generated by the decay of radioactive elements such as uranium and thorium.

3. *Magnetic field*. As we saw in chapter 4, the geomagnetic field helps to protect Earth's surface from the hard radiation that drenches interplanetary space. Like plate tectonics, the geomagnetic field stems from Earth's molten core. The liquid iron in the core is churning constantly because of our planet's daily rotation. This makes the electric currents that run through the iron core generate the geomagnetic field. In effect, the Earth is a huge dynamo, very much like an electric generator, in which moving electrical currents create a magnetic field.

4. *Large moon*. Our moon, the Moon, is about one-quarter the size of the Earth. That's big, as moon-planet relationships go.

The gravitational influence of the Moon not only pulls oceanic tides, it has also stabilized Earth's *precession rate*. Our planet spins like a top, and like a top it tends to wobble around on its axis. The Moon prevents that wobble from becoming so great that it would cause major climate shifts. Mars, for example, with only two tiny moons, has a much greater precession rate and most likely climate shifts—over eons of time—of enormous dimensions.

Put these four characteristics together and you have a world with plenty of liquid water, plate tectonics that pull heavy metals out of the mantle and distribute them (unevenly) along the crust, a protective geomagnetic field, and a Moon that helps stabilize the global climate. What does this add up to?

Life. Not only life, but life-forms that can utilize the metals so nicely lifted up by plate tectonics.

No other planet in the Solar System has all of these same characteristics. No other planet that we know of bears life.

Not only does Earth bear life, life changes the Earth. Our atmosphere is nearly 20 percent oxygen, a corrosive highly reactive gas that would quickly combine chemically with rocks if living plants were not constantly pumping more of it into the air. British chemist James Lovelock and American microbiologist Lynn Margulis have championed the concept of *Gaia*, the proposition that Earth's entire biosphere represents a single interdependent organism that actively regulates the planet's environment to promote the continued existence of life.

Plenty of material for science fiction stories there! See, for example, Ursula LeGuin's "The Word for the World Is Forest."

Nine Different Worlds

Now that we know what makes Earth unique, we can examine the other worlds of our Solar System.

If there is one thing that our space probes have taught us, it is that each of the Solar System's nine major planets is different from all the others. Each planet is a unique world. The nine planets can be roughly grouped, however, into two types—plus a question mark.

The four innermost planets (Mercury, Venus, Earth and Mars) are comparatively small, rocky worlds. They have been called the *terrestrial* planets because they resemble Earth in a superficial way. The next four (Jupiter, Saturn, Uranus and Neptune) are called *gas giants* because they are much larger than the terrestrial planets and they are composed primarily of gases such as hydrogen, helium, methane and ammonia, although there may be rocky cores imbedded within their deep atmospheres. The question mark is the farthermost planet, Pluto, which is too small to be a gas giant; in fact, it is the smallest planet of them all.

Space probes have visited every planet of the Solar System except distant Pluto. Much of what we know about the planets has come from their close-up inspections.

Detailed discussions of the Solar System's planets are beyond the scope of this book. But we do want to get a feeling for what makes each planet unique. So, for each planet we will give nine key characteristics and a brief description—just a glance to whet your curiosity. For more details, see the books listed in the bibliography, and keep up-to-date by reading magazines such as *Science News, Sky & Telescope, Mercury, Ad Astra* and *The Planetary Report*. Information on how to obtain these magazines is given in the bibliography.

The nine key planetary characteristics are these:

1. Length of year: that is, the time it takes the planet to complete one orbit around the Sun, expressed in Earth days or Earth years.
2. Length of day, expressed in hours or Earth days.
3. Diameter of the planet, given in two ways: miles, and in relationship to Earth (Earth = 1).
4. Mass of the planet, expressed in terms of Earth's mass (Earth = 1).[2]
5. Density of the planet, in relationship to water (Water = 1).
6. Surface gravity (Earth = 1).
7. Escape velocity, in miles per second.
8. Temperature; for the rocky inner planets, this will be the average surface temperature. For the gas giant outer planets, the average temperature at the tops of their cloud decks. In degrees Fahrenheit.
9. Atmospheric constituents. As we will see, some planets have no atmosphere, although most have a lot.

Mercury

The closest planet to the Sun, Mercury is a rocky, dense, sun-scorched world.

Earth-based astronomers have a hard time seeing Mercury, because it is always so close to the Sun's glare. This led to one of the great mistakes of astronomical history.

Since Mercury is so difficult to see, for centuries astronomers made their observations when the planet was at its farthest point from the Sun (which astronomers call its greatest *elongation*). What they saw in their telescopes was a small, fuzzy image that seemed always to present the same markings. They concluded that Mercury turned on its axis once in the same period as its orbit around the Sun, just under 88 days. Thus, they reasoned, Mercury's

MERCURY

Year	= 87.97 Earth days
Day	= 58.6 Earth days
Diameter	= 3031 miles, or 0.38 of Earth
Mass	= 0.055 of Earth
Density	= 5.43 × water
Surface gravity	= 0.38 of Earth
Escape velocity	= 2.67 mps
Surface temperature	= 800°F in daylight; -300°F at night
Atmosphere	= None

rotation is locked, just as the Moon's is, and—like our Moon—it keeps one side always facing the Sun and one side constantly in darkness.

For more than a century astronomers (and science fiction writers) accepted the "locked" Mercury, where one half of the planet was always broiling beneath a mammoth blazing Sun while the other side was always in cryogenic sunless darkness.

Alan E. Nourse wrote of the heroic first crossing of the subsolar hemisphere during perihelion (to make sure the party really had the record for hottest walk) in "Brightside Crossing."

But it wasn't so. In 1965, radar observations of Mercury showed that the planet's rotation is not locked. Mercury spins slowly on its axis, taking 58.6 days to make one revolution.

This leads to a strange situation. Mercury's rotation rate of nearly fifty-nine days is exactly two-thirds of the planet's year. Because Mercury's orbit is so eccentric, if you were standing on the surface of Mercury (well protected inside a space suit, of course), you would see the Sun moving from east to west across the dark airless sky, but it would slow down noticeably as you watched, then reverse its direction and head back east for a while, before resuming its westerly motion. At some locations on Mercury the Sun would rise briefly, dip below the horizon, and then rise again for the rest of the "day." After sunset the Sun would peek back up above the horizon before setting for the "night."

If you measured a Mercurian "day" from the time the Sun appeared directly overhead (local noon) to the next time it reached that point, it would take 176 Earth days. From the standpoint of noon-to-noon, the Mercurian "day" is longer than its year!

The Sun looms large in the Mercurian sky: It appears twice as big as we see it from Earth when Mercury is at aphelion (about 43.5 million miles from the Sun) and three times larger at perihelion (28.6 million miles).

And it is *hot*. Daytime temperatures soar to more than 800°F, hot enough to melt zinc. Your space suit had better have plenty of thermal insulation and active cooling systems. At night, temperatures drop to -300°F because there is no atmosphere to retain the day's heat; it radiates away into space.

The blazing Mercurian heat that endangered both humans and positronic robots was the basis for one of Isaac Asimov's Laws of Robotics puzzle stories, "Runaround."

An Iron World

Mercury is a dense planet, with a large iron core and a relatively thin overlying layer of silicon-based rock. This may be because the planet formed so close to the Sun that most of the silicate material in the solar disk was too hot to condense and solidify; it remained gaseous and was eventually blown away on the solar wind, leaving little material for the planet to build on except iron and other metals.

Another possibility, though, was revealed by the *Mariner 10* spacecraft when it flew by Mercury three times in 1974 and 1975. Mercury's battered, airless surface looks very much like the Moon's. The spacecraft cameras photographed a huge bull's-eye of circular mountain ridges some twenty-three hundred miles wide. Named Caloris Basin, this impact crater is the center of faults that run hundreds of miles across the rocky surface.

A sixty-some-mile-wide meteoroid smashed into Mercury nearly four billion years ago, gouging out the Caloris Basin and perhaps blowing away most of the planet's original rocky crust.

Yet there may be ice on Mercury! Radar studies of the planet show unexpectedly bright returns from Mercury's north and south polar areas, the kind of radar "signature" that ice would give. The rest of the planet looks bare and rocky in the microwave frequencies used by the radar probes.

Can there be water ice cached in deep craters near Mercury's poles? If sunlight never touches the interiors of those craters, the answer might be—surprisingly—yes.

VENUS

Year	= 224.7 Earth days
Day	= 243 Earth days (r)*
Diameter	= 7521 miles, or 0.95 of Earth
Mass	= 0.82 of Earth
Density	= 5.25 × water
Surface gravity	= 0.91 of Earth
Escape velocity	= 6.46 mps
Surface temperature	= 900°F (average)
Atmosphere	= 96.5% CO_2, 3% N_2

* Venus' rotation is *retrograde*, opposite of the rotation of the other planets. Seen from their north poles, all the other planets rotate counterclockwise. Venus rotates clockwise.

Venus

In Earth's night sky there is no more beautiful sight than Venus, shining gloriously. Every culture that has looked at the planet has named it after their goddess of love and beauty.

Venus is our nearest planetary neighbor; it is the second planet from the Sun while Earth is third. It sometimes gets as close to Earth as twenty-five million miles.

In bygone years astronomers often referred to Venus as Earth's twin, since the planet is almost the same size as Earth. They theorized that Venus would be hotter than Earth, since it is closer to the Sun. They found that "Earth's sister world" is completely covered by clouds, so that they could not see its surface.

Science fiction writers such as Edgar Rice Burroughs, Stanley G. Weinbaum and Otis Adelbert Klein often depicted Venus as a jungle world, a land of dinosaurs and dripping swamps. Even as astronomers began to learn that this was unlikely, science fiction writers found a "Mesozoic" Venus too good to ignore.

Unfortunately, modern astronomical observations—including several space probes and the first spacecraft to land on another planet, the U.S.S.R.'s Venera 7—have shown that Venus is nothing like the dinosaur jungles of Earth's Mesozoic Era.

Our "sister planet" is as close to hell as anywhere that can be imagined. Its surface temperature is hot enough to melt aluminum. Its atmosphere consists mainly of unbreathable carbon dioxide, at a pressure of some 1300 pounds per square inch, or nearly 90 times Earth's normal sea-level atmospheric pressure: equivalent to the pressure some 3000 feet below the surface of the ocean on Earth, deeper than most submarines can go.

Sister planet? Venus rotates on its axis once in 243 Earth days—backwards. In astronomical parlance, the planet's rotation is *retrograde*. If you could see the Sun through the perpetual cloud cover it would rise—very slowly—in the west. And those clouds are laced with sulfuric acid, which apparently comes from volcanic eruptions that constantly spew sulfur dioxide into the atmosphere.

Spacecraft Observations

Most of what we know about the Venerian surface has come from spacecraft. The Soviet Venera 7 was the first spacecraft to land successfully on another planet, on December 15, 1970. Several more Veneras have touched down on Venus and photographed a bleak landscape of flat volcanic rocks. Enough sunlight comes through the perpetual clouds for cameras to work normally. Russian spacecraft have also released instrument-laden balloons to ride through Venus' dense, still atmosphere, making measurements and radioing them back to Earth.

Orbiting spacecraft such as the American Pioneer Venus and Magellan have mapped the planet with cloud-piercing radar. Their images show that Venus has been hit by massive meteoroids from time to time and that its mountains seem to be volcanic in origin. There is also evidence that plate tectonics, which is the driving force shaping the continents and seas of Earth, were active on Venus up until about 500 million years ago but are no longer operative.

There is no water on Venus' surface, of course, not with an average temperature four times higher than water's boiling point. But there is a "rainfall"—of sulfuric acid.

Water vapor makes up about 0.5 percent of the atmosphere. Apparently it rises to the upper atmosphere, where ultraviolet light from the Sun dissociates the water molecules into hydrogen and oxygen. Sulfur dioxide from volcanic eruptions also rises and is similarly dissociated by solar ultraviolet. The elements recombine to form concentrated sulfuric acid, which gives Venus' clouds their characteristic yellowish tinge. The sulfuric acid condenses into droplets and falls, but long before it reaches the ground the intense heat breaks it down into sulfur dioxide and water vapor again, and the cycle continues.

Perhaps the best description of Venus' surface conditions is in Larry Niven's short story "Becalmed in Hell." While the turgid Venerian atmosphere at ground level displays hardly any movement at all, because it is so dense, at higher altitudes there are winds of more than 200 miles per hour. These Force 5 hurricane winds are driven by solar heating; Venus rotates so slowly that the upper atmosphere overheats at the subsolar region and gives rise to powerful, perpetual wavelike winds that cross the planet's sunlit hemisphere.

Such a thick atmosphere must erode surface features very rapidly. Venus is not heavily cratered, most likely because craters are "weathered" even more quickly than on Earth. Yet Venus is mountainous, which indicates that mountain-building is alive and well on our "sister planet." Radar maps show many volcanolike features, and there is enough sulfur dioxide in the atmosphere to convince most planetologists that volcanism is quite active on Venus.

Runaway Greenhouse

Venus' extremely high surface temperature came as a surprise to astronomers. Even though the planet receives twice as much solar energy as Earth does, its cloud deck reflects about 76 percent of that energy away. How did the surface get hot enough to melt aluminum?

Venus is apparently the victim of a runaway greenhouse effect. That thick atmosphere of carbon dioxide traps incoming heat and holds it. The higher the temperature goes, the more heat the atmosphere can store. Earth escaped such a fate when the earliest plant species began to take carbon dioxide out of our atmosphere and replace it with oxygen. Today Earth's atmosphere contains less than 1 percent CO_2, constantly replenished by animal respiration. Venus' atmosphere is 96.5 percent CO_2.

This is why environmentalists worry about our civilization's outpouring of CO_2 and other greenhouse gases, such as methane. Venus is a powerful example of what happens when a greenhouse effect takes over.

Mars

In the night sky of Earth, Mars is a glowering red star. It was named after the Roman god of war because it reminded the ancient peoples of blood.[3]

MARS

Year	= 686.98 Earth days
Day	= 24 hrs 37 mins
Diameter	= 4222 miles, or 0.53 of Earth
Mass	= 0.107 of Earth
Density	= 3.9 × water
Surface gravity	= 0.38 of Earth
Escape velocity	= 3.11 mps
Surface temperature	= -81°F (average)
Atmosphere	= 95.3% CO_2, 2.7% N_2, 1.6% argon, 0.2% O_2

Going outward from the Sun, Mars is the fourth planet. No planet except Venus comes closer to Earth; at its nearest approaches, which come every two years or so, Mars is within 35 million miles of Earth.

Mars is the most Earth-like of all the planets of the Solar System. Its atmosphere is thin enough so that ground-based astronomers can see its surface. The planet has polar caps, its day is only slightly longer than twenty-four hours, and its axis is tilted so that it even has seasons like Earth, although its year (and each season) is about twice as long as ours—a fact that Edgar Rice Burroughs used for dramatic effect in his novel *The Warlord of Mars*.

Canals? Canal Builders?

Once it was thought Mars was the abode not merely of life but of intelligent life. In 1877 the Italian astronomer Giovanni Schiaparelli observed what he thought were straight lines crisscrossing the planet's face. He called them *canali*, the Italian word for "channels." This was mistaken for "canals," and the idea blossomed that Mars might be populated by intelligent creatures capable of planetary-wide engineering feats.

Astronomers knew that Mars was cold and dry. No liquid water had been observed on its surface. And its atmosphere was much thinner than Earth's. A dying planet, it appeared to be, slowly losing its water and air. Could it be that Martian engineers were tapping water from the polar caps (presumed to be water ice) to irrigate farms and provide drinking water for cities, desperately struggling to keep their civilization alive even as the planet's natural resources were dwindling away?

The American astronomer Percival Lowell spent his life observing Martian canals. He drew ever more intricate maps of the canal systems. Science fiction writers such as Edgar Rice Burroughs set wildly romantic adventures on the Mars that Lowell was describing. H.G. Wells, in *The War of the Worlds*, imagined resource-hungry Martians invading Earth. Even as late as the 1950s, Ray Bradbury wrote of intelligent Martians and their canals in *The Martian Chronicles*.

But it just was not so. The "canals" were optical illusions. What the astronomers were seeing were dark markings on the faint, fuzzy image in their telescopes. They were unconsciously linking these markings into straight lines. Photographs of Mars never showed canals, and spacecraft—starting with the Mariner 4 flyby in 1964— detected no canals at all.

A Spectacular World

Yet Mars is a spectacular world in its own right. The highest mountain in the Solar System is there, Olympus Mons, three times taller than Everest. It is a huge volcano that seems to be silent now, although its mighty lava flows have covered an area the size of Washington state. Olympus Mons is part of a group of volcanoes that have risen on an uplifted section of Mars called the Tharsis Bulge. What caused the bulge and gave rise to the massive volcanoes is problematical, since Mars seems too small and its core too cold to have active plate tectonics.

Mars has only a weak magnetic field, further evidence that its metallic core is either very small or too cold to remain liquid—or both.

Mars has been battered by meteoroids, which is hardly surprising, since it orbits much closer to the Asteroid Belt than Earth does. Its atmosphere is too thin to erase meteor craters through weathering, although there are planet-wide sandstorms occasionally that could erode landscape features over *long* periods of time. Interestingly, one hemisphere of Mars is much more heavily cratered than the other.

There must have been running water on Mars in the past. Spacecraft photos show sinuous trails that look very much like dried out river beds (*not* like the straight-line "canals" that Lowell thought he was seeing). And the most spectacular Grand Canyon in the Solar System is Valles Marineris (the valley discovered by the

Mariner 9 spacecraft), a split in the Martian crust deep enough to swallow the Alps and longer than the distance between New York and San Francisco.

Mars' atmosphere is only about ¹⁄₁₀₀ the density of Earth's, equivalent to the air pressure at about 100,000 feet of altitude on Earth. Even if it were pure oxygen it would be too thin for a human to breathe. It is mostly carbon dioxide, with just 0.2 percent oxygen. Yet that oxygen content in the atmosphere means that human explorers could extract oxygen from the Martian atmosphere, condense it, and use it for life support.

Thin though the Martian atmosphere is, it still blows dust storms that sometimes cover the entire face of the planet. Wind velocities of more than 100 miles per hour have been seen, although since the atmosphere is so thin, there is very little force in the wind. A 100-mph wind would have the impact of a gentle breeze on an astronaut standing on the surface of Mars.

Life Needs an Atmosphere
Mars' thin atmosphere has determined its fate. The Martian atmosphere, thinner than Earth's high stratosphere, cannot hold much heat. At noon in summer along the Martian equator, the ground temperature might rise to 75°F. But the air temperature a few feet above the ground would be about zero, and on that same night the temperature would plummet to -100°F or lower. Whatever solar heat the ground absorbs during the day radiates away into space; the atmosphere stores almost none of it.

If Venus is suffering from a runaway greenhouse effect, Mars is suffering from the lack of any greenhouse at all.

Liquid water would immediately boil away in the near-vacuum of Mars' surface. There is water on the planet, however, frozen into ice at the poles. The polar caps also contain dry ice: frozen carbon dioxide. During springtime, the icecap shrinks, and the Viking landers photographed frost on the ground—evidence that the ice at the poles *sublimes* (goes directly from solid to gaseous state) and is then carried toward the equator by the seasonal winds. Although the north polar cap is larger than the south, it sometimes disappears completely during the northern hemisphere summer.

There is some reason to believe that ice exists below the ground, too, as permafrost. If true, there should be ample water available for human explorers. And perhaps for local life forms.

The Martian atmosphere contains about 0.03 percent water vapor, just about the limit it can hold, considering how cold it is. Frost occasionally mantles the ubiquitous rocks, and clouds, fogs and hazes have been observed on Mars, although the thin atmosphere is usually so clear that Mars receives about the same amount of solar energy on the ground that Earth does, despite its being farther from the Sun.

The two *Viking* spacecraft that landed on Mars in 1976 conducted a rudimentary set of experiments to see if life could be detected in the Martian soil. They found no life but a soil (or, more properly, regolith) loaded with oxides—somewhat like laundry bleach, only stronger. Not a good prospect for life. Moreover, *Viking*'s sensors found no trace of long-chain carbon molecules in the Martian regolith. No organic material at all.

Mars is a cold, dry desert. Its red color comes from iron; the Martian sands are oxides of iron. Rust.

Once and Future Life?

But Mars was probably not always the way it is now. In earlier times, eons ago, Mars might have been considerably warmer, with a thicker blanket of atmosphere than it now holds. We know there have been Ice Ages on Earth, when glaciers covered much of Europe and North America. Perhaps Mars is now undergoing its version of an ice age. Perhaps there is life buried deep underground, or nestled in some sheltered valley.

Late in 1995, scientists discovered colonies of bacteria living deep underground near the Columbia River in Washington. They do not need sunlight; they obtain their nutrients from underground water and the basalt rocks in which they live. Could similar organisms live deep below the harsh surface of Mars, without needing photosynthesis to generate their energy?

In August 1996 a team of NASA scientists announced they had discovered what may be the fossilized remains of Martian bacteria, in a meteorite that was blasted off the surface of Mars millions of years ago and, after wandering through space, fell into the perpetual ice of Antarctica.

As of this writing (September 1996) no one is absolutely certain that the microscopic structures seen inside the meteorite are actually the fossils of Martian bacteria, yet the evidence seems to point that way. More studies of the meteorite's material are underway, and plans for searching for life—or fossils—beneath the surface of Mars are being discussed.

If the meteorite evidence turns out to be true, life did begin on Mars some 3.5 billion years ago, close to the time when life began on Earth. While the surface of Mars seems inhospitable to life today, Martian life forms may still exist deep underground.

Or perhaps life on Mars was wiped out, completely eradicated from the entire planet by a cataclysm similar to the meteoroid strike that extinguished Earth's dinosaurs some sixty-five million years ago.

We have seen that Mars has been more heavily bombarded by meteoroids than Earth. The impact basin called Hellas Planitia (the Plain of Hellas) is a gigantic crater, roughly 1200 miles wide and several miles deep. On the opposite side of the planet lies the Tharsis Bulge, where the great volcanoes have arisen.

Did a massive meteoroid smash into Mars hard enough to gouge out Hellas Planitia, send a shock wave through the solid body of the planet and raise the Tharsis Bulge and its volcanoes? If so, the shock of that impact might have been so severe that it blasted most of Mars' atmosphere out into space. Or caused a planet-wide "nuclear winter" type of dust cloud that blotted out the Sun for months or years.

Either way, such a meteor impact could have wiped out whatever life might have existed on Mars.

Perhaps the first human expeditions to Mars should include paleontologists.

The Moons of Mars

Mars has two moons, Phobos and Deimos, named after the horses that pulled the war-god's chariot in Greek mythology: fear and panic. Both appear to be asteroids that have been captured by Mars' gravitational field into satellite orbits around the red planet.

Don't make the mistake, as many authors have, of describing the disks or crescents of these moons. Neither of the Martian moons is round. And they are so small that, from the surface of Mars, they would appear to the unassisted eye as nothing more than rapidly moving specks of light.

Deimos is only about nine by seven miles across. Its orbit, about 14,600 miles high, is almost geosynchronous (or *areo*synchronous, since we are talking about Mars, not Earth).[4] Deimos revolves around Mars in one Martian day plus a bit more than six hours.

Astronautical engineers have suggested that Deimos could serve as a refueling base, where explorers could mine its rocks for rocket propellants and life support supplies, much as the lunar regolith would be mined for oxygen, hydrogen, aluminum, etc.

Phobos is nearly 17 miles long and 12 miles across. It orbits a scant 5800 miles above the Martian surface. Like an artificial satellite of Earth, it rises in the west and hurtles eastward, completing its orbit in slightly more than 7½ hours.

In the 1960s, the Russian astronomer I.S. Shklovskii suggested that Phobos' orbit is decaying so rapidly that it could not be a solid body of rock; perhaps it is hollow. Perhaps it is a space station, built either by intelligent Martians or by visitors to the planet from somewhere else!

Phobos actually is rock and it is not hollow, later calculations—and spacecraft photos—have shown. But it could be used as a "ready-made" space station by human explorers and its rocks mined for supplies, as was suggested for Deimos.

The Asteroid Belt

As we saw in chapter 5, more than five thousand asteroids have been discovered so far; there are probably millions of them too small to be seen from Earth. Two of them have been photographed close-up by the spacecraft *Galileo* as it coasted out toward its 1995 rendezvous with Jupiter.

Gaspra was the first asteroid to have its picture taken, in 1991. Gaspra looks like a lumpy potato, about 12.5 miles long and 8 miles wide; roughly the same size as Mars' moon Deimos—or Manhattan Island. Almost two years later *Galileo* photos of Ida showed that the asteroid had a small "moon" tagging along with it.

The asteroids fall into two major classes: stony and metallic.

Stony asteroids of the carbonaceous chondritic type contain organic matter (long-chain carbon molecules) as well as hydrates: water molecules chemically linked to the rock. They will be treasured resources for future space operations, "oases" floating through interplanetary space, where spacefarers can find water and equally valuable organic material to replenish their life-support supplies.

The metallic asteroids are mainly iron-nickel of very high quality. MIT astronomer Tom McCord estimated that there are hundreds of millions of *billions* of tons of high-grade iron ore in the asteroids.

A Thin Belt

Although it's called the Asteroid *Belt*, don't think that the asteroids are strewn so thickly that they present a hazard to navigation. There is plenty of empty space between them. Robot spacecraft have flown through the Belt with no difficulties whatsoever.

In fact, when the *Galileo* spacecraft was sent to photograph asteroids Gaspra and Ida, the craft had to be carefully maneuvered to make rendezvous with these tiny chunks of rock orbiting in the vast emptiness of the "Belt."

Leftovers or Remnants?

The asteroids are not an unmixed blessing, however. Most of the meteoroids that still impact Earth and the other planets are probably fugitives from the Asteroid Belt, kicked out of their Sun-circling orbits by the gravitational influences of the planets.

From meteorites recovered on Earth we know that the asteroids are very old, probably dating back to the very beginnings of the Solar System, when the planets were accreting. The asteroids in the Belt probably were prevented from gathering together to form a planet by the constant gravitational interference of the giant planet Jupiter. Thus the asteroids offer scientists an invaluable sampling of what the very early Solar System must have been like.

Of course, there is the faint possibility that the asteroids are actually the remains of a fully formed planet that somehow broke apart. This is exciting fare for science fiction writers, and indeed gave a kick-start to the famed comic strip *Superman*. The first edition of the comic book showed the planet Krypton exploding and a sleek, art-deco rocket ship carrying the infant Superman to Earth.

But astronomers—and their mathematics—do not support the busted-planet idea. While Jupiter's gravitational pull could prevent a planet from forming, it is difficult to see how it could disrupt a planet already formed. Besides, if you put all the material in the Asteroid Belt together, there would not be enough to make a planet even the size of Mercury.

If you are going to blast a planet apart, you will need more than a Jovian planet's gravitational influence to do it.

Jupiter

Jupiter is the giant of the Solar System, eleven times wider and nearly 318 times more massive than Earth. Yet this enormous

JUPITER

Year	= 11.86 Earth years
Day	= 9 hrs 55 mins
Diameter	= 88,733 miles, or $11.2 \times$ Earth
Mass	= $317.9 \times$ Earth
Density	= $1.3 \times$ water
Surface gravity	= $2.54 \times$ Earth
Escape velocity	= 37.28 mps
Surface temperature	= -243°F (cloud tops)
Atmosphere	= H_2, He, CH_4, NH_3, H_2O

world spins so fast that its "day" is only nine hours and fifty-five minutes long.

Jupiter is spinning so rapidly that even a glance at the planet shows a noticeable flattening at the poles, like a squashed beach ball. And like a beach ball, Jupiter is colored with gaudy stripes of red, white and brownish hues.

The atmosphere is mostly hydrogen, with about 10 percent helium. There are three layers of clouds: the highest is composed of ammonia ice crystals, the middle is of ammonium hydrosulfide (a mixture of ammonia and hydrogen sulfide), and the lowest may contain water ice or even drops of liquid water. The clouds cover the planet completely; it is impossible to see below them.

The clouds zip along, strung out in bands parallel to the equator, one band heading east and the adjacent band west. Driven by the planet's rapid rotation and by heat welling up from the interior, hurricane-strength wind speeds are common. The cloud bands rub against one another and stir up eddies the size of Earthly continents.

And, of course, there is the Great Red Spot, an enormous oval system three times the size of Earth. It is obviously some form of atmospheric disturbance, but that is like calling a killer hurricane a low-pressure weather system. It rotates counterclockwise, completing one rotation in about six Earth days. The Great Red Spot has been observed for more than three hundred years. Is it a perpetual storm? How far down into Jupiter's interior does it reach? What gives it its red coloration? Unknown, until spacecraft delve beneath those cloud tops to investigate the hidden world of Jupiter.

Heated From Within

Even though the temperature at the cloud tops averages -238°F, Jupiter is hotter than it should be if its only source of heat were sunlight. Something deep inside the planet is generating heat. Perhaps Jupiter is still contracting, its massive gravitational field pulling the planet in on itself, and this contraction generates the heat flow. The temperature at Jupiter's core has been estimated at 36,000°F.

Astronomers believe Jupiter may be a "failed star," that is, a body that might have become a star if it had collected more mass during its accretion phase. Could our Solar System have been a double-star system? Jupiter's mass is 0.001 the mass of the Sun, much more than all the other planets combined but still much too low to trigger hydrogen fusion reactions and become a true star.

Astronomers believe there may be objects in the sky that are "almost" stars, that is, bodies that are far more massive even than Jupiter yet not quite massive enough to generate the fusion reactions in their interiors that would make them true stars. They call such bodies *brown dwarfs* (dwarf stars, that is). Brown dwarfs should radiate in the infrared, sullenly giving off heat generated by their contraction.

Jupiter is not big enough to be a brown dwarf, even though it is generating heat internally. As we shall see in chapter 12, astronomers have found a brown dwarf orbiting one of our stellar neighbors.

Jupiter's density, only 1.3 times that of water, shows that it is composed mainly of hydrogen and helium, just as the Sun is. While the inner planets were too close to the Sun to retain light gases, which quickly boiled away, at its distance from the Sun (5.2 AU) Jupiter was able to hold onto a good deal of the hydrogen and helium it collected from the solar disk. And the more it pulled in, the more massive the protoplanet became, the stronger its gravitational field, the more additional material it could gather.

Jupiter's Interior

Spectroscopic studies of Jupiter's clouds confirm that they are mainly hydrogen and helium, with ammonia and methane (both hydrogen compounds) as minor constituents, plus traces of ammonium hydrosulfide and water.

What lies beneath the clouds? The fact that Jupiter's rapid rotation has noticeably flattened the planet's sphere shows that much of Jupiter must be either gaseous or liquid. However, calculations show that the planet should have a dense core that is some 10 to 20 times the mass of Earth.

Thousands of miles beneath the clouds, pressure squeezes Jupiter's hydrogen into the form of a liquid metal (somewhat like mercury). Metallic hydrogen conducts electricity, and it is believed that electrical currents in the metallic hydrogen, abetted by the planet's rapid spin rate, generate Jupiter's intense magnetic field.

There may be a solid rocky core beneath the metallic hydrogen, but there is no way of knowing if this is so, as yet.

An Ocean World?
If Jupiter has a solid rocky core, like the terrestrial planets, it is buried beneath thousands of miles of atmospheric gases that condense with depth and pressure into metallic hydrogen.

Yet at some depth below the clouds the gases of the atmosphere must condense into liquids, squeezed by the weight of the gases above. At some level beneath those clouds there must be a planet-wide ocean. Of water? Traces of water vapor have been detected in the cloud tops. More likely any ocean in Jupiter will be liquid hydrogen. Yet, because of the heat welling up from the planet's core, there might be layers of liquid ammonia, liquid methane, even liquid water.

Ammonia and methane seem noxious to us, yet they were very common ingredients in Earth's early oceans and atmosphere, nearly four billion years ago, when life began on our planet.

Life in Jupiter?
An ocean more than ten times bigger than Earth, warmed from beneath by whatever is driving Jupiter's interior heat flow. Might there be life beneath the Jovian clouds?

As of this writing, we simply do not know. The *Galileo* spacecraft dropped its probe into Jupiter's swirling clouds, to give us our first observation of what's going on in the planet's interior. Although it detected the presence of organic molecules—carbon-chain molecules that are essential to life—it did not detect living organisms, because it could not get deep enough into Jupiter's atmosphere before being destroyed. But, as Carl Sagan has often said, absence of proof is not proof of absence.

If you want to write stories about alien life in our Solar System,

Jupiter seems like the best bet, at present. Aquatic life, swimming in an ocean ten times larger than Earth, unable to see through Jupiter's swirling clouds, chained to their planet by its heavy gravity. Yet—perhaps—not merely alive but intelligent.

Clarke wrote of huge life forms floating in the Jovian clouds, creatures that might have some form of intelligence, in his story "A Meeting With Medusa." In "Call Me Joe," Poul Anderson had humanity colonizing Jupiter by proxy, using artificial life-forms controlled electronically by human minds from the Galilean moons of Jupiter. He postulated using metallic hydrogen and water as building materials for the man-made creatures.

Magnetosphere and Radio Emissions

Jupiter possesses the most powerful magnetic field in the Solar System, some twenty thousand times stronger than Earth's.

The Jovian magnetosphere is so wide that it encompasses Jupiter's seven innermost moons; it actually is wider than the Sun's 850,000-mile diameter. If our eyes could see magnetic fields, Jupiter's magnetosphere would look as big as the full Moon in our night sky.

That huge magnetosphere traps charged particles from the solar wind, just as the Earth's geomagnetosphere does. Jupiter has its own set of Van Allen belts, where the levels of radiation are much higher and more dangerous than Earth's. The Jovian radiation belts are so broad that they encompass the orbits of Jupiter's four major moons—the Galilean satellites (more on them shortly). Thus, human explorers will need heavy radiation shielding if they hope to stand on the surfaces of Jupiter's major moons.

Jupiter is also the noisiest planet of the Solar System in radio frequencies. Powerful bursts of radio energy flicker all around the planet, most likely caused by massive lightning bolts deep within the clouded atmosphere. There is also a form of radio emission caused by Jupiter's moon Io as it orbits through the intense Jovian radiation belts.

Jupiter's Galilean Moons

When Galileo first turned a telescope to the heavens, in 1610, he saw four "stars" orbiting around Jupiter. These four moons are called Jupiter's Galilean satellites. In order of their distance from Jupiter, they are named Io, Europa, Ganymede and Callisto.

Name	Distance*	Diameter**	Year Discovered
Metis	79,510	25	1979 (Voyager)
Adrastea	80,140	16 × 10	1979 (Voyager)
Amalthea	112,660	106 × 93	1892
Thebe	137,880	42	1979 (Voyager)
Io	261,970	2256	1610
Europa	416,880	1951	1610
Ganymede	664,870	3268	1610
Callisto	1,170,000	2983	1610
Leda	6,893,500	9	1974 (Pioneer 11)
Himalia	7,133,300	115	1904
Lysithea	7,282,500	22	1938
Elara	7,293,000	47	1905
Ananke	13,173,100	19	1951
Carme	14,043,000	30	1938
Pasiphe	14,602,000	31	1908
Sinope	14,726,500	22	1914

* In miles from Jupiter
** In miles: for comparison, Earth's Moon is 2160 miles in diameter

TABLE 6 The Moons of Jupiter.

The largest moon in the Solar System, Ganymede is 8 percent larger than the planet Mercury, and three-quarters the size of Mars. Callisto is 2 percent larger than Mercury. Yet these moons look minuscule next to giant Jupiter.

Io is the closest of the Galilean satellites. With a diameter of 2,255 miles it is about 2 percent larger than Earth's Moon. Called "the pizza world," Io's surface is a mottled red, yellow, orange, white and black. The colors come from sulfur compounds spewed out by volcanoes that are apparently powered by the enormous tidal pull that Jupiter exerts on Io's crust and interior. The constant flexing of the moon's entire body keeps Io's interior molten.

Nine active volcanoes have been seen on Io, plus some 200 volcanic craters larger than 12 miles across. These volcanoes spew up about 11 billion tons of sulfur-bearing material each year, which erases any evidence of impact cratering on Io. Sulfur compounds are hurled to escape velocity (Io's escape velocity, not Jupiter's) so that there is a ring of thin sulfurous gas girdling Jupiter along Io's orbital path. This doughnut of sulfur compounds interacts with Jupiter's powerful magnetosphere, causing intense electrical currents that generate powerful radio emissions.

The other Galilean satellites are ice worlds, with densities not much above that of water. Craters pockmark their surfaces, and long cracks scratch their icy surfaces. However, the ice is often covered with darker material, perhaps carbon-based dust or soot.

Clarke suggested that life may bloom beneath the ice mantle of Europa in his novel *2010: Odyssey Two*. Europa is not as heavily cratered as the other Galilean moons, suggesting that its ice surface has melted and then refrozen, erasing the oldest craters.

In 1995 the Hubble Space Telescope detected a very tenuous atmosphere of molecular oxygen on Europa, barely one hundred billionth of Earth's atmospheric pressure. On Earth, molecular oxygen is pumped into the atmosphere by photosynthetic plants. Considering Europa's -229°F surface temperature, astronomers don't believe the oxygen on Europa stems from life. Rather, they think that the intense radiation of Jupiter's magnetosphere "sputters" water molecules off the moon's icy surface and then dissociates the water into hydrogen and oxygen. The hydrogen quickly escapes; the heavier oxygen remains.

Still . . . perhaps Clarke is onto something.

More Moons, and a Ring

Jupiter has a total of sixteen moons that we know of; there may be a few that have so far escaped even the sharp camera eyes of the Voyager spacecraft and the Hubble Space Telescope. While the Galilean satellites are planetary-sized bodies, the other moons seem to be captured asteroids. *Voyager 1* discovered in 1979 that Jupiter also is orbited by at least three faint rings of fine rocky particles, apparently the remains of one or more moons that got too close and were broken up by tidal forces.

Cataclysmic Comet Crash

In 1994, Jupiter was struck by twenty-one fragments of Comet Shoemaker-Levy 9, which had been broken up during a close encounter with the planet on an earlier swing through the Solar System. Blasting into Jupiter's atmosphere at an estimated 130,000 mph, the cometary fragments hit Jupiter with the energy of a million hydrogen bombs.

Every major telescope on Earth, as well as the Hubble Space Telescope and cameras aboard the Galileo spacecraft, watched the cataclysmic event. Each fragment of the comet exploded shortly after it penetrated the Jovian cloud tops, throwing up huge plumes of hot gaseous debris, almost as wide as North America, which rose nearly two thousand miles above the clouds. The plumes were composed of methane, ammonia, oxygen, carbon monoxide, sulfur, water and even metals—although which constituents came from the comet and which from Jupiter itself is still uncertain.

Nine months after the impacts, several of the sites were still visible to Earth-based telescopes, bright patches against the cloud deck. The largest impact scar is almost the diameter of Earth.

If there is life beneath Jupiter's clouds, could it have survived such a disaster? Rick Cook and Peter L. Manly considered that question in their story "Symphony for Skyfall." I did, too, in my short story "Life As We Know It."

Mining Jupiter's Clouds

We saw in chapter 7 that helium-3 from the Moon can be a vital fuel for fusion power generators, although how much helium-3 can be recovered from the lunar regolith is unknown at this time.

Jupiter's bright, swirling clouds are composed mainly of hydrogen and helium, undoubtedly including isotopes such as deuterium and helium-3. Isotopes that are rare or even nonexistent on Earth may be plentiful in Jupiter's atmosphere.

Future expeditions to Jupiter may scoop up tons of atmospheric gases and carry them back Earthward to power fusion generators and provide hydrogen to be combined with lunar oxygen for water.

Galileo

Launched in 1989, the *Galileo* spacecraft spent six years in space before it reached Jupiter in December 1995. The spacecraft orbiter will make eleven orbits of the giant planet over twenty-three months, making close flybys of each of the four Galilean moons. Sensors will also study Jupiter's tenuous rings and its massive magnetosphere.

An atmospheric entry probe separated from the main spacecraft and entered the Jovian clouds on December 7, 1995. Slowed by a heat-shield aeroshell and then by parachute, the *Galileo* probe carried the first instruments to enter Jupiter's tremendously deep atmosphere. The probe transmitted data for 58.5 minutes as it sank into Jupiter's deep, turbulent atmosphere, about twenty minutes longer than required for the mission's primary scientific objectives.

About half an hour after the last data transmission, the temperature of Jupiter's atmosphere was more than 1200°F, hot enough to melt the probe's Dacron parachute. Within six hours the probe plunged to a depth of more than six hundred miles below the cloud tops, where the 3000°F temperature melted its titanium structure.

Data transmission from Jupiter was slowed by the fact that *Galileo*'s main antenna never opened fully, but preliminary analysis showed that the Jovian atmosphere contains neon, argon, hydrogen sulfide, ammonia, methane and organic compounds, including hydrocarbons. This is the first time organic compounds have been found on any of the planets of our Solar System.

Water vapor was unexpectedly low and two heavy inert gases—krypton and xenon—unexpectedly high. Astronomers believed that the probe would find considerable water vapor, since Jupiter is rich in hydrogen and oxygen should be as plentiful as it is in the Sun, since it is the most abundant element after hydrogen and helium. Also, many of Jupiter's moons are covered with water ice.

However, only about one-tenth of the expected amount of water vapor was detected by the *Galileo* probe's mass spectrometer, a finding that puzzled planetary astronomers. Yet the discovery of organic chemicals in the Jovian atmosphere gives hope that life may exist deeper beneath Jupiter's cloud decks.

Helium was found to be only half as abundant as in the Sun, however. Astronomers suggest that helium condenses into droplets and rains down into the deeper levels of the Jovian atmosphere, below the altitudes the *Galileo* probe sampled.

Wind speeds at the cloud tops were more than 220 mph and increased to more than 335 mph before the probe's signals ended. This indicates that Jupiter's winds are driven by the planet's internal heating rather than by solar energy, as the winds of Earth are powered.

On its way toward Jupiter, the spacecraft encountered several dust storms. Dust motes about the size of smoke particles—a tenth of a micrometer—hit the spacecraft's detectors at a rate of up to twenty thousand particles per day. The usual rate of dust particles, between the storms, was one particle every three days. The storm particles were moving at nearly twenty-five miles per second, but

---

SATURN

Year	= 29.46 Earth years
Day	= 10 hrs 39 mins
Diameter	= 74,568 miles, or 9.45 × Earth
Mass	= 94.2 × Earth
Density	= 0.7 × water (!)
Surface gravity	= 1.08 × Earth
Escape velocity	= 22.37 mps
Surface temperature	= -301°F (cloud tops)
Atmosphere	= H_2, He, CH_4, NH_3

---

they were so small that they did not damage the spacecraft or its sensors. *Galileo* was well past the Asteroid Belt when the dust storms occurred; the dust apparently emanates from Jupiter itself, since the detectors picked up the particles only when they pointed at the planet.

As we saw in chapter 5, *Galileo* also photographed two asteroids—Gaspra and Ida—as it cruised through the Asteroid Belt.

Saturn

With its intricate system of broad circling rings, Saturn is the loveliest sight in the sky. Like Jupiter, Saturn is a gas giant, slightly smaller, slightly colder, not quite as colorful as its bigger neighbor. But breathtakingly beautiful.

The speculations we made about what's going on beneath Jupiter's clouds apply to Saturn, but less so. There might be a planet-girdling ocean beneath Saturn's yellow and tan clouds, but it seems less likely than on Jupiter. Deeper down there is likely to be metallic hydrogen and then, perhaps, a rocky core of about 10 to 15 Earth masses. Perhaps the *Cassini* spacecraft, now scheduled to be launched in 1997, may tell us something about Saturn's interior.

Saturn's density is so low that the planet would actually float on water if you could build a pool ten times the size of Earth. This means that it is composed more of the lightest elements, hydrogen and helium, than any of the other planets.

Saturn's Rings

Saturn's beautiful rings are composed of particles of ice or ice-covered dust, although some of the "particles" are as big as houses. The rings are about 250,000 miles in diameter but not much thicker than a hundred yards. Their total mass amounts to that of an icy satellite about sixty miles in diameter. They are undoubtedly the remains of one or more moons that got too close to the planet and were broken up by gravitational (tidal) forces.

The dynamics of the rings are fascinating. The *Voyager* spacecraft detected "shepherd" satellites, small moons that circle just outside or just inside the rings and apparently keep them in place with their tiny gravitational influence. The main rings are actually composed of hundreds of thinner "ringlets" that appear to be braided together.

Spacecraft time-lapse photos also showed mysterious spokes weaving through the largest of the rings, patterns of light and dark that remain unexplained and fascinating. Perhaps Saturn's extensive magnetosphere electrically charges the dust particles in the ring, and this gives rise to the spokes.

Saturn's Moons

The *Voyager* spacecraft showed eighteen moons orbiting Saturn, most of them apparently captured asteroids, although Tethys, Dione, Rhea and Iapetus range in diameter from 650 to nearly 900 miles, bigger than the largest asteroid in the Belt.

Mimas is only 242 miles across, but it is scarred by a crater almost one-third its diameter. The crater, named Herschel after the astronomer who discovered Mimas in 1789, makes the moon look eerily like the "Death Star" from the movie *Star Wars*.

Satellites have also been found at the Lagrangian points on the orbits of two of Saturn's moons. Helene (19 miles across) rides along in the same orbit as 696-mile Dione, 234,500 miles from Saturn. Telesto and Calypso (both about 16 miles across) were found in the orbit of 659-mile-wide Tethys, about 183,000 miles from the planet.

In 1995 four additional satellites of Saturn were found by the Hubble Space Telescope, bringing Saturn's total retinue of moons to twenty-two.

Its moons and rings make Saturn one of the most fascinating neighborhoods in the Solar System.

Titan and Los Angeles

Titan, though, is the aptly named giant of Saturn's brood, with a diameter of 3,190 miles. The only larger satellite in the Solar System is Jupiter's Ganymede.

Titan has something not even Ganymede has: a substantial atmosphere. Titan is the only moon in the Solar System to possess a thick mantle of gases. Io has a thin haze of sulfur dioxide, from its volcanoes; Europa an even thinner whiff of oxygen; and—as we shall soon see—Neptune's moon Triton has a thin atmosphere, as well. But Titan's atmosphere is actually about 50 percent thicker than Earth's.

It is composed mainly of nitrogen, laced with methane and perhaps traces of other hydrocarbon compounds such as ethane (an ingredient in gasoline).

Shine sunlight on that atmosphere and you get the same result that you do in Los Angeles: photochemical smog. When the *Voyager 2* spacecraft photographed Titan in 1981 it found a world shrouded in orange smog. However, the Hubble Space Telescope was able to peer through Titan's cloudy atmosphere in 1995 and produce photographs of its surface.

Titan's surface may be "a bizarre, murky swamp" of "hydrocarbon muck," in the words of a *Voyager* scientist. The methane and other hydrocarbons in the atmosphere could produce hydrocarbon rain or snow. There could be lakes of methane-ethane on the surface. Imagine the titanic tides, though, pulled by massive Saturn—thousands of times stronger than the pull of the Moon on Earth's tides. On Titan, a lake or larger sea might literally crawl all the way around the world, pulled by Saturn's immense gravity.

Nitrogen, hydrocarbon compounds, liquid methane: could life exist on Titan? With a surface temperature averaging about -300°F, it is hard to think of the chemical processes we call life being possible. But we simply don't know what chemistry—or biology—is capable of producing under alien conditions.

Enough is *not* known for you to write stories about alien life on Titan. But your aliens had better be able to digest gasolinelike liquids at cryogenic temperatures.

Uranus

Although Uranus is less than half the size of Saturn, it is still more than four times larger than Earth and certainly qualifies to be called a gas giant.

URANUS

Year	= 84.01 Earth years
Day	= 17 hrs 14 mins (r)
Diameter	= 32,560 miles, or 4.11 × Earth
Mass	= 14.5 × Earth
Density	= 1.3 × water
Surface gravity	= 0.91 of Earth
Escape velocity	= 13.04 mps
Surface temperature	= -323°F (cloud tops)
Atmosphere	= H_2, He

Uranus is weird. The other planets of the Solar System (excepting Pluto) have axial tilts ranging from Jupiter's 3.1° to 26.7° for Saturn. Earth's axis is tipped 23.4°, a tilt that gives us our seasons. Mars has a similar tilt, 25.2°.

Uranus, though, is tilted 97.9° from the vertical. Its north pole points toward the Sun for part of its year, while half a Uranian year later the south pole points sunward. What kind of climate does that produce?

The planet's "day" is 17 hours, 14 minutes long, but it spins from east to west: *retrograde*, in astronomical parlance.

If the planets all formed together, at the same time, why is Uranus tipped over so far and spinning backward, relative to most of the other planets? We might explain Venus' slow and retrograde rotation by theorizing that it was hit by a very large meteoroid. But Uranus is about fifteen times more massive than Venus; it would have had to be struck by a meteoroid the size of a planet to tilt it like that.

Even to the Voyager cameras Uranus seems a bland, quiet world, with none of the swirling bands of clouds that mark Jupiter and Saturn. Uranus is smaller than they, of course, and considerably colder. If there is a heat source deep within the planet, it does not seem to roil the clouds noticeably. Uranus looks like a greenish-blue world of hydrogen and helium clouds, tinted by frigid methane.

Magnetosphere

Like Jupiter and Saturn, Uranus has a powerful magnetosphere: some forty-eight times stronger than Earth's. But where all the other planetary magnetospheres are roughly aligned with the planet's axis of rotation, Uranus' magnetosphere is tilted almost 59° away from the planet's rotational axis. And the center of the magnetic field does not coincide with the planet's center but is offset by nearly 4800 miles, almost one-third of Uranus' radius. Weird indeed. What's going on inside Uranus that generates such a lopsided magnetic field?

Discovery and Naming

While all the planets out to Saturn were known from primeval ages, Uranus was the first planet to be discovered in historic times. Although the planet can be seen by the unaided eye—just barely, under ideal conditions—it was not known to be a planet until 1781, when the German-born astronomer William Herschel detected its motion against the background of true stars and plotted its orbit.

Herschel named his discovery Georgium Sidus (the Georgian Star) after his patron and fellow Hanovarian, King George III of England. But the German astronomer Johann Bode pointed out that since all the other planets were named after classical gods, this new one should be similarly named. Starting with Mars, each planet outward from the Sun was named after the previous one's father; Jupiter was the father of Mars, Saturn the father of Jupiter. Uranus, the oldest of the Greek gods and their god of the heavens, was the father of Saturn. Thus the "new" planet was named.[5]

Rings and Moons—and Carbon

Uranus is orbited by a system of dark, narrow rings, so faint that they were only discovered in 1977 and then photographed by *Voyager 2* in 1986.

Uranus has at least fifteen moons, ten of them apparently captured asteroids. The five major satellites—Miranda, Ariel, Umbriel, Titania and Oberon—show fascinating and puzzling surfaces pitted by craters and wrinkled by grooves and cliffs. Each of these moons is different from the others; like the planets themselves, each moon is unique. Carbon-based dust seems to cover much of Uranus' moons; we have already seen that carbon dust and carbon compounds are plentiful among the moons of Jupiter and Saturn.

Apparently the outer Solar System is rich in carbonaceous dust, which may have been driven away from the inner worlds by the Sun's heat and solar wind. The terrestrial planets may have ab-

---

NEPTUNE

Year	= 164.79 Earth years
Day	= 16 hrs 7 mins
Diameter	= 31,350 miles, or 3.88 × Earth
Mass	= 17.14 × Earth
Density	= 1.64 × water
Surface gravity	= 1.19 × Earth
Escape velocity	= 14.91 mps
Surface temperature	= -373°F (cloud tops)
Atmosphere	= H_2, He

---

sorbed a good deal of this carbon as they accreted from the original solar disk.

Carbon is the building block of life, of course. But at the frigid temperatures of the outer Solar System, carbon chemistry seems unlikely—unless there are special conditions on Uranus or its moons that have not yet been discovered.

Neptune

Although Neptune is slightly smaller than Uranus, and certainly colder, it seems to be a more active world than Uranus.

Neptune is a blue world, much like Uranus, and most likely due to the same reason: the presence of methane in its cloud tops. But Neptune's atmosphere is more active than Uranus'. In its 1989 flyby, *Voyager 2*'s cameras showed belts of clouds and a large, dark oval storm system that immediately reminded observers of Jupiter's Red Spot. When the Hubble Space Telescope was trained on Neptune in the mid-1990s, however, the dark spot had disappeared, although a different one showed up in 1994, near the planet's north pole.

Both dark spots were edged with white clouds, presumably of methane ice crystals that form at higher altitudes than the spots themselves.

In late 1994 the Hubble Space Telescope observed bright areas in the planet's blue disc: weather patterns—giant storms, actually— that change over periods as short as a few days.

Neptune also has rings, but the surprising thing about them is that they don't seem to be complete. Rather, they are arcs of fine particles that go only partway around the planet. Or, if they are complete rings, they are far thinner in some places than in others. How? Why? Perhaps we are seeing rings that have just formed out of a crumbling moon; or maybe ancient rings that are breaking up and dropping their particles into Neptune's thick atmosphere.

Neptune's Interior

Neptune is denser than the other gas giants; its interior most likely contains less hydrogen and helium and more methane, ammonia and water. The pressure at its core is so great, because of the weight of thousands of miles of material pressing on it, that core temperatures must be high enough to melt rock. A mantle of liquid hydrogen probably surrounds the core, with an ocean of water—mixed with ammonia and methane and heated from below—above that.

Discovery of Neptune

Within a few years of Herschel's discovery of Uranus, astronomers began to find that the new planet was not following the orbit they had predicted mathematically. Something was perturbing Uranus, tugging gravitationally at it. The mass and probable position of the disturbing object were calculated, and in 1846 Neptune was discovered.

This was the first time that the presence of an unseen heavenly body had been predicted by using Newton's Law of Universal Gravitation and its accompanying mathematics. (See the discussion of Earth II earlier in this chapter.)

Triton

Neptune has seven small moons, ranging in size from about 30 to nearly 250 miles in diameter. It also has Triton, which at 1,675 miles is roughly three-quarters the size of our own Moon. Triton orbits Neptune in retrograde fashion, backwards, compared to most of the other bodies of the Solar System. It may be a captured body that once orbited the Sun but strayed close enough to Neptune to be caught by the planet's gravitational pull.

Triton is itself surprising. It has a thin atmosphere of molecular nitrogen (N_2) and methane, with a high haze layer floating above it. We know that our Moon is too small to hold an atmosphere; how can Triton hang onto one? The answer is that at Triton's distance from the Sun, temperatures are so low that even a smallish body can hold an atmosphere. The gas molecules are moving so sluggishly at

PLUTO

Year	= 248.6 Earth years
Day	= 6.39 Earth days
Diameter	= 1430 miles, or 0.17 of Earth
Mass	= 0.0025 of Earth
Density	= 2.03 × water
Surface gravity	= 0.05 of Earth
Escape velocity	= 0.62 mps
Surface temperature	= -419°F
Atmosphere	= N_2, CH_4

temperatures of -373°F that they cannot achieve escape velocity.

Triton has a geologically "young" surface; that is, there are relatively few craters in its methane and nitrogen-ice covered exterior. This is also surprising; what geological forces can be at work in this frozen ice ball to erase old craters? Or has Triton somehow escaped the meteoric bombardment that has peppered the other moons and planets?

Triton also has a polar cap, probably of nitrogen frost. Most surprising of all, Triton has volcanoes. Well, perhaps geysers would be a more accurate term. *Voyager 2*'s cameras spotted dark plumes of gases erupting, indicating that there must be some internal heating within Triton. Perhaps geysers resurface Triton by spewing out gases that settle on the ground and refreeze there.

Pluto—and Charon

With a diameter of 1430 miles, Pluto is slightly smaller than Neptune's moon, Triton. Yet it is accompanied by a moon of its own, Charon, that is slightly more than half its size: 789 miles across. Thus the Pluto-Charon system is more like a double planet even than the Earth and its Moon.

Charon is only 12,000 miles from Pluto, so close that the two are gravitationally locked together; Charon orbits Pluto in the same 6.39 days that Pluto turns on its axis. There is some indication that Pluto's tenuous atmosphere of nitrogen and methane extends far enough to envelop Charon, too. The two bodies share the same atmosphere.

Pluto's rotational axis is tipped 122.5° from the plane of its orbit, even farther than Uranus'. This means that Charon's orbit around Pluto passes in front of and then behind the planet, as seen from Earth. These *transits* (when Charon moves in front of Pluto) and *occultations* (when it moves behind) have allowed astronomers to measure the diameters of the two bodies accurately and even to map out bright and dark spots on them. The poles on both Pluto and Charon are brighter than the equatorial regions, indicating the presence of polar caps, probably ices of methane and nitrogen.

No spacecraft has yet visited Pluto, so all we know of the planet and its satellite comes from Earth-based observations and the Hubble Space Telescope in LEO.

Astronomers once thought that Pluto might be a former satellite of Neptune that somehow escaped the planet. After all, Pluto's highly eccentric orbit actually crosses Neptune's orbit. Since 1979, Pluto has been closer to Earth than Neptune is. Its orbit will recross Neptune's in 1999, when Pluto once again becomes the outermost planet of the Solar System for another 220-some years.

Yet it is difficult to imagine how Pluto could have begun as a satellite of Neptune, then escaped and captured Charon. More likely, Triton was once in an independent orbit and was captured by Neptune, while Pluto and Charon were always "on their own."

Pluto's nitrogen/methane atmosphere is thinner than Mars', and at its gelid surface temperature of -419°F even methane will freeze. Indeed, Pluto's surface seems to be covered with methane ice, while Charon apparently is mantled with water ice.

In his story "Construction Shack," Clifford Simak posed the idea that Pluto was an artificial world, used by the alien beings who built the Solar System. Charon was unknown at the time the story was written; Simak might have written it into the story as the portable lavatory that is found at any construction site.

It is summertime on Pluto now. The planet passed its perihelion point—the closest it ever gets to the Sun—in 1989. As it moves in its orbit away from perihelion, its thin nitrogen/methane atmosphere will condense into snow and freeze onto the ground, waiting another two centuries before "springtime" arrives again.

Pluto's Discovery

Irregularities in the orbits of Uranus and Neptune led astronomers to believe that another planet, even farther out, must be perturbing them gravitationally. For a quarter-century astronomers searched in vain; not until 1930 was Pluto found by American astronomer Clyde Tombaugh and named after classical mythology's god of the dark and cold underworld.[6]

However, Pluto is too small and too distant to affect Uranus and Neptune. Either the perturbations were not real (they may have been mathematical errors in those pre-computer days) or something else was creating the disturbances. Astronomers have searched for a planet even beyond Pluto, but "Planet X" has yet to be found.

Beyond Pluto

Pluto is called the outermost planet of the Solar System, but there are objects even farther out from the Sun that raise the question of whether Pluto should really be regarded as a planet at all.

After all, Pluto is smaller than our own Moon. And in 1977 a body was discovered orbiting between Saturn and Uranus. With a diameter of about 215 miles, *Chiron* (pronounced KY-ron, and not to be confused with Pluto's moon Charon) seems to be a large asteroid. But it is a long way from the Belt.

Planets or Asteroids or Comets?

Is Chiron a small planet, a large asteroid, or perhaps the nucleus of a comet that is too far from the Sun to show a tail? Are there more such bodies out there beyond the orbit of Saturn, perhaps another Asteroid Belt? Is Pluto really a planet or merely the closest member of another belt of asteroids?

And what about comets? Where do they come from, and how do they fit into the rest of the Solar System?

In ancient times comets were regarded with superstitious dread. Hanging in the sky night after night like a pointing, accusing finger, they were associated with death and catastrophe.

Icebergs in Space

Comets are actually miles-wide icebergs sprinkled with carbonaceous dust. As they come closer to the Sun they begin to heat up; their ices start to boil away and they develop the long tails of gases and dust that in Latin were called *coma*, meaning "hair."

No matter which direction the "hairy star" is moving, a comet's tail always points away from the Sun, its gases and dust driven by the solar wind.

Comet orbits are elongated ellipses that apparently start in the farthest reaches of the Solar System, out beyond Pluto, and swing through the inner regions, where the comets brighten and sprout the tails that give them their name.

Some comets swing through the inner Solar System and are never seen again. Either they gained enough velocity to break free of the Sun forever, or their orbits are so elongated that it will be millennia before they return to our neighborhood. At least one comet has been observed to crash into the Sun, drawn to a fiery death by the Sun's powerful gravitational field like a moth that fluttered too close to a candle flame.

Halley's Comet
Many comets are regular visitors. They are called the *short-period* comets. The most famous of these is Halley's Comet, the first whose return was predicted.

In 1705 Edmund Halley used Newton's spanking new theories of motion and gravity to predict that a comet that had been observed in 1531, 1607 and 1682 would return in 1758. It did indeed, and even though Halley had died seventeen years earlier, the comet has been called by his name ever since.[7] A search of ancient records has shown observations of Halley's Comet dating back to 240 B.C.

When Halley's Comet returned to Earth's vicinity in 1986, spacecraft from Europe, Japan and the Soviet Union went out to study it. Halley's nucleus proved to be a 10×5 mile oblong of ice, covered with extremely dark dust, darker than coal. Bright jets of gas spurted from its body when sunlight struck it, blowing off millions of tons of water vapor, carbon monoxide, carbon dioxide and complex organic (carbon) compounds. The particles in the tail included mixtures of hydrogen, carbon, nitrogen, oxygen and silicates.

The Oort Cloud and the Kuiper Belt
Where do comets come from?

In 1950 the Dutch astronomer Jan Oort postulated that there must be a vast reservoir of trillions of comets orbiting far beyond the orbit of Pluto, the icy remains of the original building blocks of the Solar System. Oort envisioned a spherical cloud of cometary bodies—mainly big chunks of ice—drifting out at the fringes of the Sun's gravitational influence, far beyond Pluto's orbit, between 20,000 and 100,000 AUs from the Sun. Perhaps the Oort Cloud even extends halfway to the next nearest star, the Alpha Centauri system, which is about 275,000 AUs from the Sun.

Every so often, the gravitational interactions among the comets in the Cloud, or the particular lineup of the planets, or even the faint gravitational influence of a distant star will nudge a comet into a trajectory that sends it plummeting toward the inner regions of the Solar System.

Oort's original idea of a spherical cloud of comets orbiting beyond Pluto was refined by the Dutch-American astronomer Gerard Kuiper, who pointed out that many short-period comets—those that return to the inner Solar System in periods of less than two hundred years (like Halley's Comet)—must originate in the inner fringes of the Oort Cloud. That region, now called the Kuiper Belt, is thought to contain millions of comets that orbit around the Sun in the same direction as the planets, within 30° of the ecliptic.

Mining Comets

We know now that comets are invaluable sources of water and other life-support chemicals for space inhabitants. Halley's Comet, for example, boiled away more than thirty million tons of water vapor into space during the six months of its approach to the Sun in 1985-86. Halley's ten-mile-long nucleus of dust-covered ice shrank by some twenty to thirty feet during its last visit to the Solar System. At that rate of loss, it still contains enough ice for thousands more orbits.

Spacefarers will want to capture the water and organic chemicals boiled away by comets. They will develop scooper ships to take advantage of this natural bonanza.

The first step in this direction will be NASA's *Stardust* spacecraft, scheduled for launch in 1999 on a five-year mission to sample dust and gases spewed by Comet Wild-2, which travels between the orbits of Earth and Jupiter. In 2004 *Stardust* will fly to within sixty-some miles of the comet's icy nucleus, taking the most detailed pictures ever of a comet nucleus and sweeping up microscopic dust particles spewed by the nucleus using a collector made of aerogel, the lowest density solid material known. The aerogel will gently slow the particles from impact speeds of nearly 12,500 miles per hour so that researchers back on Earth can get their first close-up look at cometary matter. *Stardust* will return its comet samples to Earth in 2006.

Mining the comets beyond Pluto for water or hydrocarbons to manufacture food is a recurring theme in many of Frederik Pohl's novels, such as *Gateway* and its sequels. It will be far easier, though, to scoop the gases and dust from comets' tails as they swing through the closer inner regions of the Solar System.

If the Oort Cloud does reach out halfway to Alpha Centauri, maybe that system has an Oort Cloud of its own that comes close to ours, or even intermingles with it. Perhaps cometary bodies, coasting through the cold darkness at the edges of planetary systems, form a sort of link between the stars: stepping stones across the vast gulfs of the interstellar distances.

Incidentally, Oort's hypothesis has been borne out by observation. Since 1992 ground-based telescopes have detected twenty-three objects at the distance that the Oort Cloud should be. All of them are more than sixty miles across—huge, for comets.

In 1995 the Hubble Space Telescope picked out thirty more members of the Cloud, ranging in size from four to six miles across, more like a typical comet.

THE WRITER'S PERSPECTIVE

As we discussed when considering space habitats in chapter 6, the question of human motivation is central to stories involving journeys to other worlds. Who would go? And why? Those questions can be the starting point for powerful, exciting stories.

Of course, you can place stories on the other worlds of our Solar System in the far future, when humans have been living on those worlds for generations. In that case, the physical nature of the world can be a major driving force in the story's plot. Venus' searing heat, the deadly cold of Titan, the crushing pressures of Jupiter's ocean, the boiling surface of a comet—they can be much more than mere background for a story.

My personal favorite is the idea of a tidal sea on Titan that is pulled all the way around the moon by the immense gravitational attraction of Saturn. I touched on this, very softly, in my novel *As On a Darkling Plain* and again in *Sam Gunn, Unlimited*.

Terraforming

Here I should interject a personal prejudice against the concept of *terraforming*, the idea of transforming a planet's natural environment into a world as completely Earth-like as possible. Walking around in your shirtsleeves on the surface of Mars may sound very nice, but it is an idea—I think—whose time has gone.

Terraforming would be a long and difficult and incredibly expensive task. Turning Venus' hellhole conditions into an Earthly paradise would take centuries by any method currently conceivable—unless you pull a rabbit out of your hat as the makers of the Arnold Schwarzenegger film *Total Recall* did. They transformed Mars' atmosphere into an Earthly one within a minute or so, using "alien technology." That's fantasy, not science fiction. There is no explanation, no possible rationale within the context of the story, for such a miraculous event. The shock wave of such a sudden jump in air pressure would have flattened any structure on the planet and killed the inhabitants.

On the other hand, science fiction writers have produced scientifically plausible ways of converting alien planets into more Earth-like environments. In "The Martian Way," Asimov had his protagonists mine the rings of Saturn for ice chunks. They transported these huge cubic-mile-sized icebergs to Mars where they were crash-landed to melt and provide moisture for the terraforming.

Carl Sagan's ideas for seeding the clouds of Venus with blue-green algae that would, over time, bring down the planet's temperature to more Earth-like levels, are discussed in the seminal book he co-authored with I.S. Shklovskii, *Intelligent Life in the Universe*.

More recently, Kim Stanley Robinson "terraformed" the planet Mars in his novels *Red Mars*, *Green Mars* and *Blue Mars*.

It seems like a terribly expensive way to create Earth-like real estate.

If you really need to create a terrestrial environment, Gerard O'Neill and his Princeton students showed it can be done within the limits of known technology. Build L-5 type habitats. Much cheaper, and you get Earth-like gravity inside to boot.

Besides, why transform Mars or any other planet into another version of Earth? Why not use the alien conditions as elements of your story? If you want Earth-like conditions, keep your characters on Earth. Or in a space habitat.

In my novel *The Winds of Altair*, a team of religiously motivated young men and women are sent to a planet orbiting the star Altair. Their mission is to terraform the planet, prepare it for colonization by emigrants from Earth. They find native animals on the planet that are on their way to becoming as intelligent as humans.

Terraforming the planet will wipe out all its native life-forms.

It was during the writing of that novel that I came to the conclusion that terraforming is a poor idea, both technically and as a subject for science fiction—unless you write about the problems the terraformers must face.

◆ ◆ ◆

[1] This is due to the *conservation of momentum*, one of the consequences of Newton's Laws of Motion. The amount of angular momentum involved in a body's spin remains constant (barring outside forces), so if the body becomes smaller, the rate of spin increases. If the body gets larger, the spin rate decreases, which is why a spinning ice skater slows down when she spreads her arms.

[2] For what it's worth, Earth's mass is just about 6×10^{21} tons. That's 6 billion trillion tons.

[3] Interestingly, the bright red star in the constellation Scorpio (the Scorpion) is named *Antares*, from the Greek meaning "the rival of Ares," Ares being the ancient Greek name for their god of war and for the planet we call Mars.

[4] The prefix *areo* (from *Ares*, the Greek equivalent of the Roman Mars) is used in reference to Mars the way *geo* is used in reference to Earth.

[5] The German chemist Martin Klaproth was so excited by the discovery of Uranus that he changed the name of a new element he had just discovered from *klaprothium* to *uranium*.

[6] The first two letters of Pluto are also the initials of Percival Lowell, the American astronomer who believed so fervently in Martian canals and who urged with equal fervor that his fellow astronomers search for the ninth planet.

[7] Newton died even earlier, in 1727.

CHAPTER 10

The Stars

. . . to explore strange new worlds, to seek out new life and new civilizations, to boldly go where no one has gone before.

Gene Roddenberry

TECHNICAL FACTORS

Distances again.

When we move from the outer fringes of the Solar System to the stars we are taking such a big jump in distances that a whole new scale must be used.

You recall from the previous chapter that astronomers use the Astronomical Unit as a convenient yardstick for measuring distances within the Solar System. Now imagine a map in which the AU—the 93-million-mile average distance between the Sun and Earth—is shrunk down to one inch. How far away, on that scale of one inch equaling one AU, would the nearest star to our Solar System be?

Four and a third miles.

The difference between the distances inside the Solar System and the distances to the stars is the same as the difference between inches and miles.

Lightyears

Astronomers use a different yardstick when they deal with interstellar distances: the lightyear.

Light travels at about 186,000 miles per second. There are 31,536,000 seconds in a 365-day year. Therefore, light travels some 5,865,696,000,000 miles in a year—just a tad less than six trillion miles. That distance is called a lightyear. Note that this is a measure of *distance*, not of time.

It is one of those odd coincidences that there are just about the same number of AUs in a lightyear (63,072) as there are inches in a mile (63,360).

The nearest star to our Solar System is Alpha Centauri, at 4.3 lightyears. Most of the stars that you can see in the night sky are within a few hundred lightyears, although Polaris, the North Star, is one thousand lightyears away.

Multiple Stars

Alpha Centauri is actually a triple star system. Alpha Centauri A is a yellowish star very much like our Sun, only slightly brighter. The B component is an orange star, a bit cooler than the Sun although about the same luminosity. Alpha Centauri C, often called *Proxima* Centauri, is actually the closest star to our Solar System, at 4.3 lightyears. The A and B components are about a tenth of a lightyear farther away.

Proxima is a dwarf red star that orbits roughly 10,000 AUs from A and B, which are some 40 AUs from one another, about the same distance apart as the Sun and the planet Pluto. While A and B orbit around a common center of gravity in about 80 years, Proxima's orbit around A and B takes thousands of years.

If there were an Earth-like planet orbiting Alpha Centauri A at the same distance that Earth orbits the Sun, its inhabitants would see A very much as we see the Sun. B would be a very bright star, perhaps brighter than the full Moon. C would be a dim star, barely recognizable against the background stars of the night sky.

Many, perhaps most, stars exist in multiples. Single stars like the Sun might be in the minority. Could planetary systems form around multiple stars? Would stable planetary orbits be possible? Yes, given the right distances and sizes. The Alpha Centauri system, for example, could harbor a set of planets close to A, with B holding its own clutch of planets around it as the two stars orbit around a common center of gravity.

See Stephen Gillett's *World-Building* for the fascinating details.

Colors and Lifespans

Stars come in many colors and sizes. And ages. The bigger and hotter a star is, the shorter its lifespan and the more violent its death.

Color is the clue to a star's temperature. Like the gas flame of a

Spectral Class	Surface Temperature	Color	Examples
O	above 25,000	blue-violet	rare
B	11,000–25,000	blue	Rigel, Spica
A	7500–11,000	blue-white	Sirius, Vega
F	6000–7500	white	Canopus, Procyon
G	5000–6000	yellow	Sun, Capella
K	3500–5000	orange	Arcturus, Aldebaran
M	less than 3500	red	Betelgeuse, Antares

Note: Temperatures are given in Kelvin scale; Sun's surface temperature is 11,300°F.

TABLE 7 Stellar Spectral Classes.

kitchen stove, colors toward the blue end of the spectrum indicate higher temperatures than reddish colors. Astronomers classify the stars in seven major groups, which they call *spectral classes.*[1]

The spectral classes are based on stellar temperatures; originally they were arranged in strict alphabetical order. But continuing measurements of the stars showed that B-class stars were actually hotter than A, O-class stars were hotter still, and some other categories could be dispensed with. So the spectral order now reads, starting with hottest stars, O, B, A, F, G, K, M—plus a few other letters reserved for uncommon stellar types, such as R, N and S.

To remember the order of the major spectral classes, from hottest to coolest, use the mnemonic "Oh, be a fine girl/guy, kiss me."

Hot blue giant stars such as Rigel are burning up their nuclear fuels at rates thousands of times faster than the Sun. Rigel must be so young that it was not shining when the earliest humans roamed the savannas of eastern Africa. And Rigel will not last much longer. At the rate it is consuming its nuclear energy sources, Rigel will explode within a few million years.

Conversely, the small red dwarf stars are burning their resources so slowly that they can chug along for trillions of years.

Stars of All Descriptions

The stars we can see in Earth's night sky have been studied since prehistoric times, when primitive observers created the *constellations*, fanciful imaginary pictures that linked the stars into groups. Modern astronomers identify stars as belonging to constellations, which is an easy way to tell in which part of the sky the star is located. Alpha (α) Canis Majoris, for example, is the brightest star in the Big Dog constellation, the star named Sirius. Beta (β) Canis Majoris is the second-brightest star in that constellation; and so forth.

The brightness of the stars as we see them depends on their intrinsic luminosity—how much light they are actually emitting—and their distance. Our Sun, for example, is really a fairly dim star. But it is only one Astronomical Unit away, rather than lightyears, so it appears overpoweringly bright to us.

Apparent magnitude is how bright a star looks to us. *Absolute magnitude* is how bright the star would look if it were 10 parsecs (32.6 lightyears) away. *Luminosity* is the star's intrinsic output of visible light.

Table 8 shows the fifteen stars that are nearest to our Solar System.

Notice that of the fifteen nearest stars, at least five are multiple systems: four binary stars and one triple. Also, most of these stars are small, reddish, M- and K-class stars, much dimmer than the Sun.

Now take a look at the brightest stars seen from Earth, as shown in table 9. Here the B- and A-class stars predominate, even though they are hundreds of times farther from the Sun than the nearest stars: hot, blue and blue-white stars with thousands of times the luminosity of the Sun. It is clear that these stars look bright because they *are* extremely luminous.

Parsecs

Even using lightyears, the numbers are getting unwieldy. For the larger distances in the universe, astronomers use the *parsec*, which is equal to 3.26 lightyears. If you think of the lightyear as a "foot," the parsec is a "yard." As we will see, cosmic distances are so huge that astronomers frequently speak in terms of kiloparsecs and megaparsecs, thousands and millions of parsecs, respectively.

Star	Distance	Spectrum	Luminosity	Comment
Sun	1 AU	G2	1	
α Centauri A	4.4 LY	G2	1.4	LY = lightyears
" B	"	K0	0.44	
" C	4.3 LY	M5	5.8×10^5	Proxima
Barnard's Star	5.9 LY	M5	4.4×10^4	
Wolf 359	7.7 LY	M8	1.7×10^5	
Lalande 21185	8.2 LY	M2	5.2×10^3	
Luyten 726-8A	8.5 LY	M5	6.3×10^5	
" B	"	M5	4.0×10^5	
Sirius A	8.6 LY	A1	23	
" B	"	wd	1.9×10^3	white dwarf
Ross 154	9.5 LY	M4.5	4.0×10^4	
Ross 248	10.2 LY	M6	10^4	
ε Eridani	10.7 LY	K2	0.30	
Ross 128	10.8 LY	M5	3.3×10^4	
Luyten 789-6	10.8 LY	M6	1.20×10^4	
61 Cygni A	11.1 LY	K5	0.076	
" B	"	K7	0.036	
ε Indi	11.2 LY	K5	0.13	
τ Ceti	11.3 LY	G8	0.44	
Procyon A	11.4 LY	F5	7.6	
" B	"	wd	5.2×10^4	white dwarf

Note: Spectral classes are divided into ten grades, with 0 the hottest. The Sun and Alpha Centauri are both G2 stars (hotter than G3 stars, but not as hot as G1 stars).

TABLE 8 The Nearest Stars.

The Lifespans of Stars
The Sun as a Star

Stars are born, live out their lifespans, and then die—sometimes very violently. The Sun is a moderate star, weighing in at about 2×10^{27} metric tons, or roughly 333,000 times more massive than the Earth. Its diameter is slightly more than 850,000 miles, more than one hundred times bigger than Earth.

We saw in chapter 9 that the Sun condensed out of a lightyear-sized cloud of gas and dust between 4.5 and 5 billion years ago. All the stars were born that way. Astronomers have photographed dark

The twenty brightest stars visible from Earth, ranked in order of their true luminosity.

Name	Distance (LYs)	Spectral Class	Luminosity (Sun = 1)
1. Deneb	1400	A2	48,000
2. Rigel A	815	B8	43,500
" B	—	B9	120
3. Betelgeuse	489	M2	13,000
4. β Crucis	489	B0	5700
5. Antares A	391	M1	5200
" B	—	B4	110
6. β Centauri A	293	B1	3600
" B	—	?	174
7. α Crucis A	391	B1	3300
" B	—	B3	2000
8. Spica	260	B1	2300
9. Canopus	98	F0	1450
10. Achernar	65	B5	200
11. Capella A	46	G0	150
" B	—	M0	0.013
" C	—	M5	0.0005
12. Arcturus	36	K2	110
13. Aldebaran A	52	K5	100
" B (wd)	—	B3	0.0013
14. Vega	26	A0	52
15. Pollux	39	K0	40
16. Sirius A	8.6	A1	23
" B	—	wd	0.0019
17. Fomalhaut A	23	A3	13
" B	—	K4	0.1
18. Altair	17	A7	10
19. Procyon A	11.4	F5	7.6
" B	—	wd	0.0005
20. α Centauri A	4.4	G2	1.45
" B	—	K0	0.44
" C*	4.3	M5	0.000058

Note: wd = white dwarf

* α Centauri C is also known as Proxima.

TABLE 9 The Brightest Stars.

clumps of gas and dust that they call *protostars* and then returned their telescopes to the same region of the sky a few years later and seen some of those clumps transformed into glowing stars.

Nuclear fusion is the energy source that powers the stars. At the core of the Sun, where the temperature exceeds 20 million degrees, the Sun is transforming the nuclei of hydrogen atoms into the nuclei of helium atoms. When four protons (hydrogen nuclei) fuse into a helium nucleus, the helium is 0.7 percent lighter than the four original protons. That 0.7 percent of the original mass is converted into the energy we see as sunlight, following Einstein's famous equation, $E = mc^2$, where E stands for energy, m for mass, and c the speed of light.

The Sun loses four million tons of mass every second; four million tons of the Sun's matter are converted into the energy equivalent of 10^{10} megatons of TNT each second. Ten billion megatons of TNT each second! For more than four billion years! Yet this outpouring of energy represents only 0.7 percent of the mass involved in the fusion process. If the Sun converted all its hydrogen into helium it would be only 0.7 percent smaller than it is now.

During this long summer of its life, the Sun is said to be a *main sequence* star (see figure 10). It will shine steadily for some ten billion years more, converting four million tons of matter into energy every second through the hydrogen fusion process.

Could life exist inside our sun? It would be very different from anything we know—some form of organized plasma. Hal Clement described such a life-form in "Proof."

> They had evolved far down near the solar core, where pressures and temperatures were such that matter existed in the "collapsed" state characteristic of the entire mass of white dwarf stars. Their bodies were simply constructed: a matrix of close-packed electrons—really an unimaginably dense electrostatic field, possessing quasi-solid properties—surrounded a core of neutrons, compacted to the ultimate degree. Radiation of sufficient energy, falling on the "skin," was stabilized, altered to the pattern and structure of neutrons; the tiny particles of neutronium which resulted were borne along a circulatory system—of magnetic fields, instead of blood—in the nucleus where it was stored.

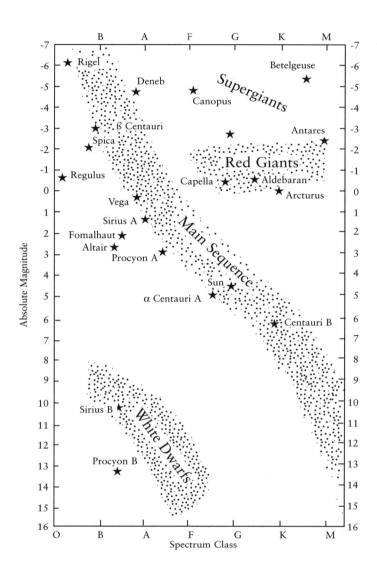

FIGURE 10 A Hertzsprung-Russell Diagram.

The H-R diagram has nothing to do with a star's position in space. In the early twentieth century astronomers found that when they plotted the brightness (absolute magnitude) against the color (spectrum class) of large numbers of stars, they got a characteristic distribution. Stable stars such as the Sun fell into the broad region labelled Main Sequence, while giant stars and dwarf stars occupied their own groupings. In time, the Sun will move toward the red giant section of the diagram and eventually evolve into a white dwarf star.

It takes a powerful imagination and a solid understanding of plasma physics to create plausible life-forms that live inside a star. Such creatures may not exist in the real world, but Clement was able to make a convincing case for them, so that the reader was not only willing to suspend disbelief but anxious to see what these fascinating creatures could do.

Red Giant Phase

Long before the Sun consumes all its hydrogen, it will begin to change. In ten billion years or so, the Sun will have converted so much of the hydrogen in its core into helium that the core will be much denser and hotter than it is now. This increase in core temperature will force the Sun's outer envelope of plasma to expand. It will swell to a huge size, swallowing the orbit of Mercury, then Venus, and even the Earth.

The distended Sun's surface will be cooler and redder than it is now, but it will be so huge that the total amount of energy it radiates will be far higher than today's energy output. Long before the Earth is swallowed by the expanding Sun, its increased heat will have burned off Earth's atmosphere and boiled away the oceans.

The Sun will become a red giant star. For a while.

What is happening inside the Sun is that, in its predominantly helium core, the temperature has soared to 100 million degrees. At that point, the helium nuclei begin to fuse together, and helium fusion begins to create new elements: carbon, oxygen and neon.

Helium fusion reactions go much faster than the earlier hydrogen fusion. Soon (in the cosmic time scale) the helium supply at the core runs low. But the core temperature and density are now so high that the carbon, oxygen and neon begin to fuse into still-heavier elements.

The cycle keeps repeating in ever-tightening coils: Fusion reactions produce heavier elements that increase the core's density and temperature, which leads to new fusion reactions that produce even heavier elements. Each new cycle goes faster than the previous one.

The Sun is behaving like the Hemingway character who, when asked how he went bankrupt, replied, "Two ways . . . Gradually and then suddenly."

White Dwarf Phase

The Sun is heading for disaster. New energy sources will not be forthcoming forever. Outwardly, the Sun will continue to swell in its red giant phase, possibly engulfing even the orbit of Mars.

But eventually it will run out of energy sources and collapse. Its huge distended layers will fall in on themselves, and the Sun will shrink to about the size of the Earth. All those 10^{27} metric tons of matter will condense into a sphere the Earth's size. A teaspoonful of the Sun's matter will weigh tons.

The Sun will become a white dwarf star, all of its inner energy sources gone, a slim rim of nuclear reactions still simmering near its surface, perhaps. Gradually it will cool off and become dark, a burned-out cinder surrounded by the charred hulks of its inner planets and the much-reduced remnants of the outer planets, whose thick mantles of gases were boiled away into space when the Sun glowered fiercely as a red giant.

Not all stars are so lucky, though.

Violent Deaths

A star's mass determines how violently it will die.

The stars are cosmic cookers. They start with little more than hydrogen and helium—the two lightest elements—and through nuclear fusion they create heavier elements: carbon, oxygen, neon and more, all the way up to iron.

Through all these fusion processes, the star has been a battle-field between two opposing forces: gravity, which is constantly trying to pull the star in on itself; and gas and radiation pressures, which are trying to push the star's matter outward. The Sun is a very neat balance between these two forces, stable and bright for billions of years.

As a star's core creates constantly heavier elements, the core becomes constantly denser and hotter. Gas and radiation pressures increase and the star swells into a red giant.

A star can continue to make constantly heavier elements in its core, fusing heavier and heavier nuclei to make still-heavier new elements, until it reaches the point where it is producing iron nuclei in its fusion cooker. When it tries to fuse iron nuclei, the game is over.

All the earlier nuclear fusion processes, starting with hydrogen-to-helium, yield net energy gains. Iron fusion, however, *consumes* energy. Once iron fusion begins, there is no new energy coming out of the star's core. The outward-pushing gas and radiation pressures drop off drastically.

Gravity is always there, though, and at this point gravity wins the ancient battle. The star collapses.

A star of the Sun's mass will collapse down to a white dwarf. For a star whose core is between 1.4 and 3 times the mass of the Sun's core, something stranger happens.

Neutron Stars

A white dwarf star stops collapsing when the atomic particles forced together by the star's gravity get so close to one another that they resist further squeezing. It's like a room full of people, where the walls are pushing in. When the people are packed so tightly that they are all shoulder-to-shoulder, they are strong enough to keep the walls from squeezing them further.

But for a star with a core 1.4 times more massive than the Sun's core, the gravitational field is more powerful, powerful enough to keep on squeezing until the atomic particles themselves crush together and turn into neutrons—nuclear particles slightly more massive than protons but electrically neutral. In our analogy of the roomful of people, the walls squeeze so hard that the people are mashed together. Ugh!

A star composed entirely of neutrons can shrink down to a few miles' diameter. An entire star that was originally more massive than the Sun, squeezed down to a solid ball of *neutronium* no more than a few miles wide. A teaspoonful would weigh thousands of tons.

The core collapse happens suddenly, and the outer envelope of the star's plasma just as suddenly falls inward, then explodes in a shattering *supernova* blast, brighter than thousands of Suns for a few weeks to a few months, before it gradually fades. The outer envelope is blown away into space, leaving the core of neutronium.

The remaining core—a neutron star now—still has the same angular momentum (spin) as it had originally, but since it has become so much smaller, it spins blindingly fast. Where the Sun turns once on its axis in roughly a month, a neutron star's spin rate is measured in fractions of a second.

Pulsars and LGM

In 1967 British radio astronomers detected a strange, pulsating radio signal. The bursts were 0.001 to 0.002 second long, and they came every 1.33730113 seconds. The precise timing was as accurate as an atomic clock's.

Intelligent signals from an extraterrestrial civilization? For a few weeks the astronomers considered the "LGM theory": the possibility that "little green men" were sending deliberate signals across interstellar space.

It turned out, however, that the *pulsars*, as they were soon dubbed, were fast-spinning neutron stars that are beaming out natural radio signals the way a lighthouse swings its beam across the sea.

Pulsars are neutron stars, although presumably not all neutron stars are pulsars. There is a pulsar, however, in the heart of the Crab Nebula, a star that exploded centuries ago. The light of that supernova blast was bright enough to see in midday, and Chinese astronomers recorded the arrival of the "guest star's" light in the year 1054. On July 4, no less.

Supernovas

Stars sometimes explode. In ancient times, before telescopes were invented, naked-eye astronomers would occasionally see a "new" star appear in the heavens. What they were seeing, of course, was a star that had been too dim for naked-eye observation, which had suddenly flared in brightness.

Such *novas* (from the Latin meaning "new") are usually stars that are part of a double-star system, orbiting so close to one another that one star sucks up the outer layers of its companion star, becomes unstable, and blows away its outer envelope in an explosion that can increase the star's brightness—briefly—to 100,000 times the Sun's luminosity.

Nova stars are often repeaters, although there may be centuries or millennia between outbursts. Under certain conditions a white dwarf may accumulate so much of its companion's mass that it explodes in a much more spectacular supernova cataclysm. The star completely destroys itself. Astronomers call this type of stellar catastrophe a Type I supernova.

The Crab Nebula pulsar is the remains of a Type II supernova explosion, the kind that happens when a very massive star, such as Rigel or Spica, blows itself apart in a spectacular eruption when it collapses at the end of its red giant phase.

"Spectacular" hardly gives a hint of a supernova's brilliant violence. A typical Type II supernova can release as much energy in its first twenty-four hours as the Sun emits in a million years.

But the star's death leads to new life. For when a supernova blasts most of the star's material into interstellar space, it is seeding the galaxy with the material for new stars. Not only does the star's plasma contain all the elements up to iron, but the titanic energy of the supernova explosion produces additional nuclear reactions that create even heavier elements, up to uranium and beyond. Elements that do not exist naturally on Earth, and have been produced only in nuclear laboratories, have been detected in the glaring light of supernova explosions.

And, as we saw in chapter 4, supernovas apparently also generate the ultra-energetic subatomic particles mistakenly called cosmic "rays."

Signposts in Space

Supernova explosions are *bright*. Supernovas can be seen in galaxies millions of lightyears from us. They are used as a rough gauge to help estimate intergalactic distances. Assuming that supernovas are roughly the same brightness wherever they occur, astronomers can estimate the distance to a remote galaxy by measuring the apparent brightness of supernovas in that galaxy. The difference between the supernova's apparent brightness and the assumed true brightness is caused by the distance.

Astronomers estimate that there is at least one supernova in the Milky Way galaxy per century, although very few of them are in regions where we can see them from Earth, since the Milky Way's thickest, most star-rich regions are hidden from us by deep clouds of interstellar dust. It seemed ironic that the last great supernova clearly visible from Earth happened in 1604, just before the invention of the telescope.

Then, in 1987, astronomers' dreams came true: a supernova flared in the Large Magellanic Cloud, a satellite of our Milky Way, visible to all the sensors that modern technology could aim at it.

Arthur C. Clarke made a supernova the center of his famous short story "The Star." Its brightness and distance from Earth were an integral part of the story. He wrote:

> When a star becomes a *supernova*, it may for a little while outshine all the massed suns of the galaxy. The Chinese astronomers watched this happen in A.D. 1054, not knowing what

it was they saw. Five centuries later, in 1572, a supernova blazed in Cassiopeia so brilliantly that it was visible in the daylight sky. There have been three more in the thousand years that have passed since then.

Writing in 1955, Clarke of course could not know that another supernova would occur in 1987.

Building New Stars

For reasons we will discuss in chapter 12, cosmologists assume that the earliest stars were built from clouds that contained only hydrogen and helium (with perhaps a trace of lithium). These stars created heavier elements in their cores through fusion processes, and then even heavier elements in supernova explosions. Thus the interstellar medium—the clouds of gas and dust floating through the galaxy—have been enriched in heavy elements by the earliest stars. Some of these heavy elements are wafted into space by the stars' "solar" winds; some are blown into the interstellar medium by nova and supernova explosions.

Astronomers call any element heavier than helium a "metal." Our Sun is composed of about 99 percent hydrogen and helium and 1 percent "metals": heavier elements that were cooked inside elder stars and then spewed out into the interstellar medium. Our Sun, then, is not among the first stars of the Milky Way. In fact, most cosmologists believe our Sun is a "third generation" star. Younger stars have even more "metals" available to them.

In actual fact, then, you and I are composed of stardust. The atoms in our bodies of the elements heavier than helium were created in stars that exploded and spewed their materials into interstellar space. Our Sun and Solar System are built of their scattered atoms. Stardust.

This has an important effect on the possibilities of locating intelligent extraterrestrial civilizations, as we will see in chapter 12.

Planets?

We know that the Solar System was created as a family group, Sun and planets together. Do planets exist around other stars?

Science fiction writers have always tacitly assumed they do, and astronomical theory predicts that other stars would form planetary systems just as our Sun did. In recent years, space-borne sensors have detected dust clouds surrounding several nearby stars, flattened whirls of debris that are assumed to be accretion disks: the building material for planets.

But planets are small and dim, and so close to their parent stars that their reflected light is drowned out in the glare of the stars themselves. It should have been no surprise, then, that the first planets to be found orbiting another star were discovered by radio astronomers.

No surprise. But a heartbreak to those seeking living alien civilizations.

Pulsar Planets!

The first extrasolar planets to be discovered were found orbiting around a pulsar in the constellation Virgo: PSR B1257+12. (Not a romantic name; it refers to the pulsar's position in the sky.) PSR B1257+12 is a neutron star that rotates hundreds of times per second. Astronomers studying the pulsar with the thousand-foot Arecibo radio telescope in Puerto Rico detected tiny fluctuations in the arrival time of the star's radio signals, which suggested that the pulsar wobbles as it moves through space. They concluded that the best explanation for the wobbling would be the gravitational tug supplied by two or possibly three unseen planets orbiting the pulsar.

This is indeed strange. One would assume that the star-wrecking supernova explosion that created the pulsar would have destroyed any planets orbiting the star. But there they are. Perhaps they were originally *very* massive planets, much bigger even than Jupiter, and all that remains of them are their rocky cores. Or were these planets formed out of the roiling plasma of the supernova explosion itself? Can planets accrete out of the debris from a supernova blast?

Either way, those planets do not seem to be attractive sites for life. But remember Einstein's dictum, "Imagination is more important than knowledge." A science fiction writer can use imagination *and* knowledge to create stories that challenge all our assumptions.

Robert Forward used his knowledge as a physicist and his imagination as a science fiction writer to produce *Dragon's Egg*, where his characters are microscopic creatures living on the surface of a neutron star.

Planets of Sunlike Stars

For decades astronomers have tried to ferret out the presence of planets around our stellar neighbors by looking with optical telescopes for slight wobbles caused in a star's motion by the gravitational tug of unseen planets.

Peter van de Kamp, at Swarthmore College outside Philadelphia, Pennsylvania, pioneered this astrometric technique. In the 1950s he announced that he had measured slight wobbles in the paths of several of the nearest stars, including Barnard's Star (6.1 lightyears away) and Lalande 21185 (7.9 lightyears), caused by "unseen companions": i.e., planets.

Yet other astronomers were unable to duplicate van de Kamp's findings. Some even claimed that the telescope and measuring equipment van de Kamp used were incapable of making such precise measurements.

More recently, instead of trying to measure slight changes in a star's position in space, astronomers have developed a more sensitive technique, based on spectrographic analysis. By taking spectra of a star and looking for the Doppler shifts[2] in the starlight caused by the star's movement, astronomers can measure extremely small motions.

In mid-1995 this technique paid off—twice. Planets were discovered orbiting two stars: 51 Pegasi, a Sun-like star forty-two lightyears away from us, and GL229, thirty lightyears away. The discoveries have been confirmed by other observatories and accepted by the astronomical community.

A yellowish star of G4 spectral class, 51 Pegasi is a little cooler than the Sun, yet slightly brighter. This implies that it is somewhat larger than the Sun.

The planet orbiting 51 Pegasi is almost as massive as Jupiter, yet its orbit is only one-sixth that of Mercury, the closest planet to our Sun. It orbits around 51 Pegasi in just 4.2 days. How can such a massive planet exist so close to its star? If you towed Jupiter that close to the Sun most of its gaseous material would be quickly boiled away into space.

Perhaps the planet is not a gas giant, as Jupiter and the other large planets of our solar system are. Perhaps there are more ways to form planets than we have seen in our own Solar System.

A Brown Dwarf?

GL229 is a dim red dwarf star, about four-tenths the mass of the Sun. Its companion, dubbed GL229B, orbits about forty-four astronomical units away, slightly farther than Pluto orbits from the Sun.

GL229B is a supergiant, twenty times the mass of Jupiter. Astronomers quickly deduced that it is not a planet in the usual sense, but a *brown dwarf* star, a body almost massive enough to trigger thermonuclear reactions in its core and thus become a true, shining star. Almost massive enough, but not quite.

Calculations have shown that a body must be at least 0.08 percent of the Sun's mass in order to sustain nuclear fusion reactions in its core. GL229B is not that massive. Brown dwarf stars would radiate in the infrared, giving off heat from their slow contraction. GL229B was detected by infrared sensors and photographed both in the infrared and in visible light by the Hubble Space Telescope. Methane and water vapor have been detected in its spectrum, which implies a surface temperature below 2400°F.

Astronomers believe they have found two other brown dwarfs in the Pleiades star cluster, a loose batch of stars in the constellation Taurus, the Bull.

Brown dwarfs offer an interesting setting for science fiction stories: much more massive than ordinary planets, almost big enough to support fusion reactions at their cores, simmering with the heat of their gradual contraction. How about a brown dwarf with a few more ordinary planets orbiting around it?

Goldilocks and Liquid Water
Within a few months of the 51 Pegasi discovery, astronomers found two more planets around the Sunlike stars 70 Virginis (in the constellation Virgo) and 47 Ursae Majoris (in Ursa Major, also known as the Big Dipper).

The planet orbiting 47 Ursae Majoris is about 3.5 times more massive than Jupiter. Orbiting the star at about twice the distance of the Earth from the Sun, the planet takes roughly three years to complete one revolution. Although its surface temperature is a chill -130°F, its atmosphere could contain liquid water, the astronomers calculate.

The planet orbiting 70 Virginis has a mass about eight times that of Jupiter and orbits less than half Earth's distance from the sun, although its orbit is highly elliptical. Its discoverers call it Goldilocks because it's not too far from its sun and not too close; with an average surface temperature of about 180°F Goldilocks could conceivably have abundant liquid water, oceans and rain—and perhaps life.

Other Planetary Systems

Now we know that other stars have planets. And we can see that our Solar System is probably not the "standard model" for other planetary systems!

In 1997 NASA plans to install the Near Infrared Camera and Multi-Object Spectrometer (NICMOS) on the Hubble Space Telescope. NICMOS should be able to detect a planet orbiting a star as distant as four hundred lightyears away, if the planet is at least six times more massive than Jupiter and its orbit is farther from the star than Jupiter's is from the Sun.

Future improvements in telescopes and their electro-optical systems might bring planets as small as Earth into view.

Black Holes and Spacetime

Neutron stars and brown dwarfs seem pretty weird. But it gets weirder still.

When a truly massive star collapses, its gravitational field is so powerful that not even neutronium can withstand the crushing force. If the star's core is more than three times the mass of the Sun, the star's collapsing matter continues to shrink and as it does, the gravitational field grows ever more powerful, until not even light can escape from the collapsing star. It disappears from our universe. It has become a black hole.

It's like the old joke about the man who dug a hole, jumped in, and pulled the hole in after him.

Our understanding of physics breaks down here. The perimeter around the collapsing star at which light can no longer get away is called the *event horizon*. What happens inside the event horizon is unknown. Perhaps the star shrinks down to a *singularity*, a point of zero dimension but infinite density. Perhaps the star digs a *wormhole* through spacetime and emerges somewhere—and some when—else in the universe. Or perhaps it emerges into another universe.

Since Einstein first enunciated his relativity theories, physicists have thought of time as a dimension of our universe. Spacetime consists of the three spatial dimensions—length, width and height—plus time. H.G. Wells popularized this concept in *The Time Machine* when Einstein was still a teenager (a fact I used as the basis for my short story "Inspiration").

The only thing that seems clear is that a black hole warps spacetime. For more than sixty years science fiction writers have played with the idea of "space warps" as a means of moving across interstellar distances faster than the speed of light. Black holes appear to be natural spacetime warps; one day humans may learn how to use them as portals to other parts of the universe(s) and then to build such warp devices to suit ourselves.

But be careful. Some very heavyweight physicists have declared that they do not believe black holes can actually exist. Certainly none has been unequivocally discovered as yet. How do you discover something that, by definition, cannot be seen? From the hard radiation generated as cosmic dust and star debris are sucked into the black hole's insatiable maw, according to the orthodox view. There are a number of X-ray sources in the sky that might be the stormy sites of black holes. Might be. The evidence is not yet conclusive.

The Milky Way Galaxy

Our Sun and all the stars around us are part of the Milky Way galaxy, a vast pinwheel of more than 100 billion stars, with enough loose gas and dust in it to make perhaps another 100 billion more. When you look at the sky on a clear, dark night you can see the shimmering band of the Milky Way arching across the heavens. You are looking at billions upon billions of stars so far away that their light blends together into a whitish haze.

The Milky Way is a spiral galaxy, roughly 100,000 lightyears across and about 30,000 lightyears thick in its central bulge. Our Solar System is imbedded in one of its spiral arms, some 30,000 lightyears from the galactic center.

Something violent seems to be going on at the core of the Milky Way. Perhaps a very massive black hole is gobbling up stars by the thousands, generating enormously energetic radiation in the process. We do not know for certain, because we cannot see the Milky Way's core; it is hidden by thick veils of interstellar dust, the building material for new stars. Radio and, to some extent, infrared wavelengths penetrate the dust, however, and observations at those frequencies indicate that our galaxy's core is a violent, dangerous place.

Galaxies by the Billion

The Milky Way is merely one galaxy among billions that have been seen by our largest telescopes. Many of these galaxies are

FIGURE 11 The beautiful spiral galaxy in the constellation Andromeda, some two million lightyears from Earth. Also known as M31 and NGC224 in the Messier and New Galactic Catalogues, respectively. (Courtesy National Optical Astronomy Observatories)

spirals, such as the famous M31 in Andromeda, assumed by astronomers to be a near-twin of the Milky Way (see figure 11). The largest galaxies are called *ellipticals*; instead of a spiral structure they appear to be huge oval collections of thousands of billions of stars. There are smaller, irregularly shaped galaxies, as well. The two Magellanic Clouds that are satellites of our Milky Way are irregulars.

Use the term galaxy correctly. In Hollywood the word has been misused time and again to mean a solar system: a star and its accompanying planets. That is wrong. A galaxy is a collection of billions of stars, nothing less.

There is no reason why science fiction stories should be restricted to the Milky Way galaxy. It's a big universe out there, and there are many, many galaxies to choose from. Some galaxies have very violent things happening inside them. One of the most massive, M87, has a jet of intensely hot plasma spurting from its core. The jet is some three kiloparsecs long and is a powerful source of radio emission.

Other galaxies, such as the irregular M82, seem to be in the process of exploding. As we have seen, there are strong indications of violence in the core of our own Milky Way. In Stanley Schmidt's novel *The Sins of the Fathers*, a highly advanced alien species caused the explosion at the Milky Way's core; it was, in Schmidt's phrase, "an industrial accident" that will make the entire galaxy uninhabitable because of the lethal levels of hard radiation generated by the explosion. In his Known Space series, Larry Niven postulates the explosion of the galactic core as the major motivation of the actions of one of his alien races.

In the next chapters we will look at the problems and possibilities of building starships and then at the nature of the universe itself, to see how it might be possible to roam the starry heavens even out to the edges of infinity.

And we will take a special look at the enigmatic quasars.

THE WRITER'S PERSPECTIVE

It's an enormous universe out there, with plenty of story material. And it may not be the only universe we have to play with. More on that in chapter 12.

One thing to keep in mind is that it's all in motion. The Earth orbits around the Sun at a speed of some 18.6 miles per second. The Sun orbits around the center of the Milky Way galaxy at a speed of about 12.4 miles per second, dragging the rest of the Solar System along with it. Every year the Sun covers a distance of 4.2 AUs.[3] Even so, it takes 200 million years for the Sun to complete one swing around the Milky Way's center. That 200-million-year orbit is sometimes referred to as a "galactic year."

There is nothing more ludicrous than the idea of having a starship hover in space. When an actor playing the captain of a starship cries out, "Full stop!" you know that neither the writer, director nor producer knows or cares much about the real world.

We will discuss how starships might actually look in the next chapter. For now, let's consider some of the dramatic potential in the interstellar environment.

Sight-Seeing

In our position in the galaxy, some 30,000 lightyears away from the Milky Way's core, the neighborhood is rather bland.

Of the forty stars within sixteen lightyears of the Sun, most are quiet little red dwarfs, the kind that will continue to slowly burn their hydrogen fuel for hundreds or even thousands of billions of years (if the universe lasts that long). Some of them may have planets orbiting around them, but red dwarfs are so dim and cool that a planet would have to be very close to the star—say, at Mercury's distance from the Sun—to be able to have liquid water and support life. Stephen Gillett's *World-Building* shows what kinds of stars might harbor Earth-like planets.

Sirius, at 8.6 lightyears, is more interesting. It's a blue-white A-type star, the brightest true star in Earth's night sky. Its actual luminosity is 23 times the Sun's; there are many more luminous stars out there: Deneb, for example, is some 48,000 times more luminous than the Sun, but at 1400 lightyears' distance, its true luminosity is greatly diminished. Sirius outshines every other star mainly because it's so close to us.

Sirius has a white dwarf companion, and since Sirius has since ancient times been called the Dog Star (it is in the constellation of Canis Major, the Big Dog), its dwarf companion—discovered telescopically in 1862—has been dubbed the Pup. Astronomers are not known for stand-up comedy.

The fact that the Pup has evolved into a white dwarf stage means that interesting things have happened on Sirius. Did the Pup flare up in a nova explosion when it collapsed? Could it have been seen on Earth? Was it the Star of Bethlehem?

Have there been supernovas close enough to Earth to shower our planet with hard radiation? Did a supernova trigger the extinction of the dinosaurs sixty-five million years ago? Will a future supernova threaten us?

Poul Anderson considered the effects of a nearby supernova on an alien race that had to decide who could be evacuated and who must stay and die in "Supernova" (later retitled "The Day of Burning").

Deeper in Space

Even more spectacular vistas await us deeper in interstellar space. Leaf through any astronomy book and you will see photographs of stunning beauty:

• Planetary nebulas, smoke rings blown out by stars

• Turbulent clouds of gas and dust such as the Horsehead Nebula in the constellation of Orion, where new stars are being born

• Shattered remnants of supernova explosions; the Crab Nebula

The sight-seeing is breathtaking and offers the backgrounds for hundreds of stories.

Think of a close binary pair of stars, spinning around one another in days or hours, a crackling, blazing bridge of white-hot plasma pouring from one star to its companion. Think of the energy there and how future generations of scientists might harness that energy. Or perhaps alien scientists have already learned how to.

Immortality Through Star Flight

You recall in chapter 6 that the overriding reason for expanding into space, beyond the limits of Earth, is to ensure that the human race can survive even if some cataclysm makes our home world uninhabitable. Spaceflight separates the fate of humankind from the fate of planet Earth.

Star flight—the ability to travel to other stars—can separate the fate of humankind from the fate of the Sun. Stars die. Perhaps it is foolish to think in terms of billions of years, but science fiction writers can and should look far ahead.

However, the problem may not be so far in the future, after all. The Sun may not be the well-behaved main sequence star astronomers believe it to be.

The Neutrino Problem

For more than a quarter of a century, astrophysicists have been trying to detect neutrinos generated by the fusion processes taking place in the Sun's core. Neutrinos are very elusive particles that have no electrical charge and very little mass, if any. A typical neutrino could slip through several *lightyears* of lead without being stopped.

Still, physicists' calculations show that neutrinos could be detected by suitable equipment deep underground, where the detectors are shielded from spurious signals triggered by cosmic rays and other false alarms. In more than twenty-five years of trying, the physicists have detected only about one-third of the neutrinos they predicted they would find.

This means either their equipment is not working the way they thought it would, or the Sun is not producing the number (or kind) of neutrinos they believe it should be. If the Sun is not producing neutrinos as expected, perhaps the fusion reactions in the Sun's core are not working the way the astrophysicists think they are.

Is the Sun on the brink of a catastrophe? No reputable scientist believes it to be. Yet . . . where are the neutrinos?

Flee or Fix?

Astronomer Michael Hart has said, "If you're planning to destroy life with a nuclear war you better do it soon, because once life spreads to the stars it will become impossible to destroy."

A species that has star flight has racial immortality in its grasp. Even if its original star dies, or merely begins to expand into a red giant, star flight guarantees that it will be possible to move to other stars. Or to live in artificial habitats between the far-flung stars. And if the core of our galaxy is actually in violent eruption, we may need to flee the Milky Way itself, eventually.

On the other hand, if we master the energies involved in propelling ships to the stars, perhaps we can learn how to control the evolution of our home star and prevent it from swelling into a red giant, making Earth uninhabitable. A.J. Austin and I built two novels around that concept: *To Save the Sun* and *To Fear the Light*.

◆ ◆ ◆

[1] *Spectral*, as used here, has nothing to do with ghosts. It refers to the rainbow of colors, ranging from red to violet, that make up the *spectrum* of visible light. Visible light is itself only a small slice of the full spectrum of electromagnetic energy, which also includes radio waves, microwaves, infrared, ultraviolet, X-rays and gamma rays.

[2] Any wave motion—light, sound, etc.—can exhibit a Doppler shift: When the source of the waves is approaching, the waves pile up and the observer senses the wavelengths shortening; when the source is moving away, the waves stretch out and the observer senses them lengthening. When a source of light is moving away, the observer sees the light shifted toward the longer-wavelength red end of the visible spectrum. An approaching source is blue-shifted. This phenomenon is named after Christian Doppler, the Austrian physicist who studied it in connection with sound waves. French physicist Armand Fizeau applied Doppler's work to light waves. Purists call it the Doppler-Fizeau Effect when dealing with light.

[3] Which brings up a problem about time travel. Even if a time machine could be built, if you go back in time one year you will arrive in cold interplanetary vacuum, 4.2 astronomical units away from Earth—unless your time machine somehow moves you through space, as well.

CHAPTER 11

Starships

There can be no thought of finishing, for "aiming at the stars," both literally and figuratively, is a problem to occupy generations, so that no matter how much progress one makes, there is always the thrill of just beginning.

Robert Goddard

TECHNICAL FACTORS

The first starships from Earth are already plying their way through the vacuum of interstellar space. Having completed their planetary flyby missions, *Voyagers 1* and *2* and the earlier *Pioneers 10* and *11* are coasting out beyond the Solar System on journeys that will take millions of years before they arrive in the vicinity of another star.

We have seen that the distances to the stars are vast. This means that star flight will require enormous amounts of energy—and enormous amounts of time.

To escape the Sun's gravitational pull, a spacecraft must achieve a velocity of 10 miles per second: Solar System escape velocity. If a spacecraft could maintain that 10 mps speed indefinitely, instead of slowing down as it coasts, it would take 80,000 years to reach Alpha Centauri.

Even if you could travel at the speed of light it would take 4.3 years to get to Proxima Centauri. And that's the closest star to us.

Project Orion

We could probably build a starship today, except that it's illegal.

In the 1960s, a group of scientists that included Freeman Dyson, of the Institute for Advanced Study at Princeton, suggested using nuclear bombs to propel a spacecraft to interstellar velocity.

The bombs would be exploded at the rear of the ship, and a portion of their energy would be exerted against a heavily shielded plate that would literally push the spacecraft forward. By exploding bombs every few seconds, the ship could be accelerated to interstellar velocity, perhaps as much as a third of the speed of light, which would get an Orion-type ship to Alpha Centauri in slightly less than three years.

The idea was dubbed Project Orion, and it seemed technically feasible, although the engineering problems were considerable. Dyson and his cohorts were enthusiastic. The nearer stars, at least, seemed within reach.

But the scheme fell apart when the United States ratified the Outer Space Treaty of 1967. Among the treaty's provisions was a ban on putting nuclear weapons in space. Despite the efforts of Dyson and others to show that the nuclear bombs were to be used for propulsion and not as weapons, Project Orion was stopped before it really got started.

(We will discuss the legal aspects of spaceflight in chapter 13 and the military aspects in chapter 14.)

The Generations Ship

Still, we could begin building a different type of starship today. A space habitat, such as those discussed in chapter 6, could be turned into a starship if you could provide it with a propulsion system that will accelerate it to 10 mps. And if its life support systems were truly closed-cycle.

Once it achieves Solar System escape velocity, the habitat could coast outward to the stars—for thousands or even millions of years. Children would be born, live out their lives in the habitat, and die, generation after generation. An interstellar Noah's ark.

Science fiction stories about such *generations ships* have been written since Tsiolkovskii's time. Heinlein wrote one of the most memorable, "Universe," in 1941. In many such stories, the distant descendants of the original star-travellers have forgotten the mission's original purpose; they believe that their vast ship is the entire universe and know nothing of the cosmic immensity beyond their ship's hull. As electronic information systems become smarter and easier to use, however, this notion becomes more difficult to carry off successfully. Today's readers find it harder to believe that the ship's inhabitants would forget everything that their ancestors knew, unless some sort of cataclysmic accident befell the ship.

A generations ship would have to be big, large enough to house enough people to provide an adequate gene pool, so that genetic defects would not creep into the ship's population and gradually destroy it. That means a breeding population of thousands, at least.

And the ship would have to be completely self-sufficient, all its life-support systems completely closed-cycle. Farmers will be just as important to the generations ship as electronics technicians, and the problems of maintaining the ship so that it functions properly over many millennia will keep everyone busy.

Our growing knowledge of biology and genetics should help immensely if and when we decide to build a generations ship. Some have suggested sending an automated *seed ship* to the stars, carrying a cargo of human embryos that will be kept frozen until the ship arrives at its destination. Then the fetuses will be brought to term by automated equipment, and the human babies will eventually become settlers on the new world.

An automated ark would have either to be preprogrammed toward a definite star, which presupposes that an adequately Earth-like planet has already been detected there, or it will need sensors and navigation systems that can search out an Earth-like world and guide the ship to it.

Another alternative is to have a "live" crew running the seed ship and directing the birth and education of the babies once they arrive at their new home world. But the crew would have to spend many generations in transit, and the problems of defects in the gene pool arise once again. A variation of this idea is to bring several crews, but keep only one of them awake and active at a time. A crew would remain on duty for a certain number of years, then revive its replacement crew and go into cryonic suspended animation for the rest of the voyage. More on cryonics shortly.

Lightsails and Magsails

We saw in chapter 2 that solar sails may be used to propel spacecraft within the Solar System and, boosted by powerful laser beams, might even be used for interstellar missions. As long as the laser beam can reach the sail, the spacecraft will be continuously accelerated, even reaching speeds close to the velocity of light, over years of travel. Robert Forward and others have worked out designs in which the sails can also be used to decelerate the starship when it is time to slow down at the ship's destination.

It might also be possible—and even preferable—to use particle beams instead of light. Like the accelerators used in "atom-smashing" physics labs, particle-beam accelerators produce focused beams of subatomic particles, such as protons. While the particles travel somewhat slower than photons of light, they have mass (which photons do not) and thus impart more momentum to the sail when they strike it. A particle-beam sail could thus be smaller than a true lightsail and accelerate faster. The ship's crew would have to be shielded against the energetic particles constantly bombarding it, however.

Another possibility is to use a form of magnetic sail for interstellar propulsion. Deep space is pervaded by magnetic fields: While the field strength of the galactic field is low, the field is so vast that it represents a titanic amount of energy. By using a "sail" made of a non-material magnetic field generated by superconducting magnets, a starship might be able to use the galactic magnetic field to accelerate itself close to lightspeed, somewhat in the way that subatomic particles are accelerated by magnetic fields in "atom smasher" facilities in physics labs.

The Lightspeed Limit and Tachyons

Lightsail and magsail ships will take many, many years to travel between the stars. And although generations ships have made excellent subjects for science fiction, most writers want to get their characters to their destinations faster.

Since Einstein published his Special Theory of Relativity in 1905, physicists have understood that nothing in the universe travels faster than light: 186,000 miles per second seems to be the universal speed limit.[1] Every test of Special Relativity, every measurement made since 1905, confirms that limitation.

Some physicists, though, have postulated the concept of *tachyons*—particles that always travel faster than light and cannot move slower than 186,000 mps.

Tachyons are just the reverse of ordinary particles, which are whimsically referred to as *tardyons*. The faster a tachyon goes, the less energy it needs. Thus tachyons make the ideal propellant for faster-than-light (FTL) craft. The mathematics is all there for writers to use.

Although no one has captured a tachyon yet, and they might not exist at all, you can use the idea of a tachyon drive for your starship, following the Second Law of Science Fiction: Science fiction writers are free to extrapolate from today's knowledge and to invent anything they can imagine—so long as no one can prove that what they have "invented" is wrong.

The Energy Requirements

In the world that physicists can measure, nothing moves faster than light. In fact, Einstein's $E = mc^2$ shows that the closer you get to lightspeed, the more massive your starship becomes.

Energy changes into mass when you approach the speed of light. Particle accelerators such as synchrotrons have pushed electrons to velocities in excess of 90 percent of lightspeed. At such speeds, the electron's mass increases. When more energy is pumped into the electron, most of it is converted into mass, not speed. The electron grows heavier.

Notwithstanding this very real problem, let us now picture a starship heading into the cosmos. Let's say we want it to accelerate to at least 95 percent of the speed of light. How do we do it?

Fusion Rockets

Plasma physicists have been laboring to produce a controlled fusion reactor for half a century. Let us assume that they will eventually be successful and will learn how to convert hydrogen into helium to release energy.

Even converting a mere 0.7 percent of the hydrogen fuel's mass into energy will allow a fusion-propelled ship to make a round-trip mission to Alpha Centauri in twenty-nine years. The ship would accelerate at one Earthly *g*—32 feet per second, each second—for several months. It would then be travelling at better than 95 percent of lightspeed and could coast the rest of the way. The same procedure would be used on the return journey.

While the total elapsed time for the round-trip would be twenty-nine years, to the crew of the ship the trip time would seem slightly shorter. This is because time itself begins to change when you move at velocities near lightspeed. We will go into *time dilation effects* more deeply in a few moments.

The bad news: Such a fusion ship would need something like 1.6 billion tons of hydrogen propellant for every ton of payload. The mass ratio is 1.6 billion to one. Hardly economical.

The good news: You may not need to carry all that hydrogen with you.

Interstellar Ramjets. Back in the 1960s, physicist Robert W. Bussard of the Los Alamos Scientific Laboratory in New Mexico invented the concept of the interstellar ramjet.

A rocket must carry all its propellant. But suppose you could pick up your propellant along the way? Your ship could carry much more payload, and its range would be unlimited—it could go anywhere, at close to lightspeed, as long as it could find propellant to feed its fusion engines.

Interstellar space is filled with hydrogen gas. "Filled" is perhaps too optimistic a word, though. While there is enough hydrogen gas floating in the Milky Way galaxy to build 100 billion stars or more, it is spread *very* thinly—no more than a few atoms per cubic inch.

Bussard calculated that a starship of a thousand tons' payload could scoop up enough hydrogen to run its fusion engines if it had a funnel some twenty-five hundred *miles* wide in front of it.

Although there is certainly plenty of space out among the stars, Bussard was not envisioning a solid structure twenty-five hundred miles across. His scoop would be a powerful magnetic field instead. Using a laser beam to ionize the interstellar hydrogen atoms and make them electrically conducting, the ionized atoms could then be scooped up by a magnetic field and fed into the starship's fusion drive.

Larry Niven popularized Bussard's idea in science fiction stories where he used "ramscoop" starships.

Bussard's magnetic scoop has another advantage to it. Interstellar space is drenched with hard radiation, including primary cosmic "rays." A starship would be constantly bombarded by this radiation, endangering both the crew and the ship's electronic systems. That huge magnetic scoop, however, can act as a shield—very much the way the geomagnetosphere shields Earth from cosmic radiation. The scoop can also be an umbrella!

Antimatter
Star Trek's good ship *Enterprise* uses antimatter fuel. And an excellent choice it is. For while hydrogen fusion converts 0.7 percent of mass into energy, in matter-antimatter interactions, 100 percent of the mass is converted to energy. It's hard to do better than 100 percent.

Antimatter is the mirror image of normal matter. Where a normal electron carries a negative electrical charge, an antielectron has a positive charge, and is thus called a *positron*. Antiprotons have negative charge. For every particle that physicists have discovered, they have found an antiparticle that mirrors it.

When a particle and antiparticle meet they destroy each other in a reaction that converts *all* of their mass into energy. That energy can be used either to heat or otherwise accelerate a working fluid (as in a nuclear or electrical rocket) or directly to propel the ship through some yet-to-be-invented means.

The universe we live in seems to consist entirely of normal matter. Antimatter has been produced only in physics facilities. This puzzles the physicists, because there doesn't seem to be any good reason for the universe to be all one kind of matter.

Are there antimatter stars out there, somewhere? Antimatter galaxies? Whole universes of antimatter?

The universe that we can observe is apparently entirely normal matter. If you want antimatter for your starship, you're going to have to produce it in a particle accelerator or some other kind of nuclear facility.

And shield it carefully! Since antimatter reacts explosively with normal matter, you must "contain" your antimatter fuel—most likely in a *magnetic bottle* that will suspend the antimatter within its powerful magnetic field and not allow the stuff to touch the solid walls of its container.

Whereas a fusion rocket would need 1.6 billion tons of hydrogen propellant per ton of payload, an antimatter ship would need "only" 40,000 tons of propellant, half of it antimatter—still a payload ratio of 40,000 to 1, but perhaps within the realm of practicality for rocket engineers.

You could do even better: carry only the 20,000 tons of antimatter you need and scoop the normal matter from the interstellar hydrogen you're flying through. Or even better: produce the antimatter out of the normal matter being scooped in, using a shipboard particle accelerator.

Jack Williamson (under the penname of Will Stewart) wrote a series of stories based upon a human civilization in the Asteroid Belt trying to make use of antimatter (he called it Seetee—CT—contraterrene matter). The Seetee turns out to be alien artifacts.[2]

Time Dilation

Einstein showed that when an object—whether an atomic particle or a starship—travels at a velocity close to the speed of light, time begins to move at a different rate for that object. When you get close enough to lightspeed for time dilation effects to come into play, it's said you are moving at a *relativistic velocity.*

When a starship begins moving at better than 90 percent of lightspeed, time aboard the ship begins to slow down noticeably. Clocks aboard the ship will tick slower and slower as the ship's speed gets closer and closer to the speed of light. Everything aboard the ship, equipment and humans alike, will slow down with respect to the passage of time on Earth.

Yet aboard the ship itself everything will seem quite normal. And everything on the ship will be normal, even though years of time might pass on Earth before a second elapses on the ship. The only difference is that time itself is moving at a different rate aboard the speeding starship than it does for objects that are not travelling at relativistic velocity—such as the Earth and everyone on it.

This is the basis of the *twin paradox* of relativity. If one twin stayed on Earth while her sister flew to a star at relativistic velocity, when the flying twin returned to Earth she would be younger than the sister she left behind.

Suppose a ship flew at better than 90 percent lightspeed to Polaris, the North Star, which is one thousand lightyears away. Ignoring details such as the time spent in accelerating to top speed and decelerating to landing speed again, the ship could make the round-trip flight in a *subjective* time of 20 years. That is, to the ship's crew only 20 years will have passed. But when they return home they will find that 2000 years have elapsed on Earth.

In *Time for the Stars*, Robert Heinlein made use of actual sets of twins, selected and trained to be in telepathic contact, so that faster-than-light communications are possible. What happens when one twin is still a teenager and the other has become a grandfather?

With time dilation, perhaps the stars are within our reach, after all. The German mathematician Eugen Sänger calculated that a ship flying at 99 percent of lightspeed could cross the entire observable universe in a subjective time of only forty years.

Not only does this put the farthest galaxies in reach, it means that the maintenance problems of starships can be brought down to easily manageable levels. Instead of trying to keep a generations ship working for millennium after millennium, we can put into port for repairs and maintenance (and R&R) after only a few decades.

A few decades of ship time, that is. Thousands or millions of years will have elapsed for the rest of the universe. Will there still be a port to receive the starship?

Sleeping to the Stars

The crew need not stay awake through the entire flight. It should be possible to freeze the crew in liquid nitrogen, which would suspend their life functions so that they can sleep away the decades in flight without consuming air, food or water. This technique is known as *cryonics*, a word that combines cryogenics with bionics.

Cryonics was first suggested in the 1960s as a way of evading death. The idea was that if you are dying of some disease, you have yourself frozen immediately upon being declared clinically dead, before your body and brain begin to decay. You are betting that: (a) medical science will learn how to cure the disease sometime in the future; and (b) you can be thawed successfully. Once returned to consciousness and cured of the disease that "killed" you, you return to life—decades, perhaps centuries, in the future.

Dozens of people in the United States have had their bodies frozen after being declared clinically dead. No one has yet been brought back from freezing, although apparently mice have been successfully thawed in laboratory experiments.

In my novel *Voyagers*, the astronaut protagonist is frozen in the depths of interplanetary space as he makes rendezvous with an alien spacecraft that has entered our Solar System. Eighteen years later, he is retrieved, brought back to Earth, and revived in the novel's sequel, *Voyagers II: The Alien Within.*

By the time we are ready to build starships, we will probably be able to cryonically freeze the crew and revive them when they reach their destination.

Between time dilation and cryonics, the crew of a starship may feel as if they have spent only a few days in transit to the farthest star.

Here's how Cordwainer Smith described such a trip in "Think Blue, Count Two":

> Before the great ships whispered between the stars by means of planoforming [a faster-than-light drive], people had

to fly from star to star with immense sails—huge films assorted in space on long, rigid, coldproof rigging. A small spaceboat provided room for a sailor to handle the sails, check the course, and watch the passengers who were sealed, like knots, in immense threads, in their little adiabatic pods which trailed behind the ship. The passengers knew nothing, except for going to sleep on Earth and waking up on a strange new world forty, fifty, or two hundred years later.

This was a primitive way to do it. But it worked.

One-Way Trips

Whether we are considering generations ships or antimatter-propelled interstellar ramjets with cryonically frozen crews, all star trips will be one-way journeys.

Generations ships, of course, will be designed for one-way transits. Only the distant descendants of the original passengers will arrive at their ultimate destination.

But the faster ships will be on one-way journeys, too. Even if they zip out to the stars and back again in only a few months, subjective time, millennia will have passed on Earth. Imagine setting out on a journey next week and returning ten thousand years later. It would be like a Neolithic hunter leaving his cave and returning to modern Los Angeles.

You can't go home again. Not when you start flying out to the stars. Not if you are playing fair with the known laws of physics and astronomy.

Unless you can find a way to warp spacetime and produce practically instantaneous travel.

THE WRITER'S PERSPECTIVE

John F. Kennedy, speaking of the problems facing his presidency, said, "I do not fear these challenges. I welcome them."

Writers should welcome the challenges of dealing with the realities of interstellar flight. It's easy to give your characters some sort of wonderful spacetime warp so they can zip about the universe without worrying about time dilation or the vast distances—of both space and time—that separate us from even the nearest stars.

But then why bother to deal with an interstellar setting? It's like writing about a mountain-climbing adventure where your characters ride to the mountaintop in a helicopter.

Engineering Your Star Drive

While magnetic sails, tachyon drives and antimatter propulsion are all valid *concepts* for dealing with interstellar flight, no one has designed or engineered such propulsion systems. It is up to you, the writer, either to think out the details of how such a star drive would work, or to skirt around the details skillfully enough so that the reader will accept the concept without really getting to know how the system works.

Remember what we said earlier about boring your reader with technical details? Unless the minutiae of how your star drive works is vital to the story, do not delve into it. Your "explanation" is apt to be largely arm-waving rather than real engineering, so why bother? Unless it is crucial to the plot, simply show that the propulsion system works. The reader will be quite happy with that.

Faster Than Light

Many writers have refused to let Einstein's speed limit slow them down. They have produced faster-than-light (FTL) propulsion systems for their starships, relying on the Second Law of Science Fiction and the hope that no one can prove them wrong.

E.E. "Doc" Smith was a pioneer in writing stories with interstellar backgrounds. He solved the problem of interstellar flight by "inventing" a propulsion system he called the "inertialess drive," which operated on principles far beyond what was then (or now) known of physics. The basic idea was that this space drive somehow got around Newton's Laws of Motion and allowed starships to fly faster than light. It was unexplained, really, but it worked because Smith was a good-enough writer to make the reader *want* to believe it could work.

Smith's space operas are a good example of the limits of extrapolation, however. The electronics equipment on his starships, for example, was very much like the radios of the 1930s, only bigger. His ships used gigantic vacuum tubes, which were always in danger of overheating. The transistor had not yet been invented when Smith was in his heyday, but he apparently never stopped to think that a civilization that could produce the inertialess drive might develop something better than vacuum tubes to power its communications gear.

Gene Roddenberry, creator of *Star Trek*, was very much aware of Einstein and the lightspeed limit. He also knew about theoretical work on tachyons. Thus he developed the "warp drive" that allowed the *USS Enterprise* to travel faster than light. Roddenberry worked out the major features of the warp drive quite carefully—but ignored the time dilation effects that would mean the *Enterprise* could never return to its own time after flitting out among the stars.

The Real World

Yet the real world is so much more interesting than fictional universes where there are no limits on speed or time.

Some of the most heavily used backgrounds of science fiction are tossed overboard when you write about the universe as it actually exists. Interstellar empires are impossible when it takes thousands of years for messages to travel from the capital to the frontier. Interstellar wars are nonsense when a general orders an invasion knowing that it will be the great-great-grandsons of his troops who make the attack. Why ship minerals across interstellar space when local planets and asteroids contain the same minerals?

There might be interstellar trade in organic materials that are difficult to synthesize, although our rapidly growing understanding of biochemistry makes even that seem doubtful. Interstellar trade would most likely be in intangibles—poetry, literature, art, philosophy. In his Instrumentality stories, Cordwainer Smith made export of religion between planets a capital offense.

A Spacetime Triangle

Think of the story material that the universe is offering you. In my novel *As On a Darkling Plain*, two men love the same woman. One of the men and the woman travel to Sirius to study a primitive band of humanlike inhabitants of a planet there. The other man remains on Earth. When the star-travellers return to Earth, they are still youthful, while the man who remained behind is in his seventies and burning for revenge.

In *The Exiles Trilogy*, a group of scientists exiled from Earth to an orbiting space habitat converts their prison into a starship. Generations go by and the inhabitants change tremendously—and spend almost all their energies just keeping their ship from falling apart. Then they reach a planet that is almost like Earth. Do they genetically alter their unborn children so that they can survive on the new world or limp farther into the starry depths, hoping to find a world exactly like Earth?

The fact that star flights will be one-way journeys offers even more story material. Starship crews will be forced to think ahead in terms of centuries and millennia. They will never know what's coming up next, even if they are visiting a world that they have seen many times before. What a setting for adventure!

Who Will Go? And Why?

Again the question arises: Who would go? One-way journeys, with no possibility of returning to home and family, most likely means that those who travel to the stars will want to bring home and family with them. Unless and until some way of breaking or avoiding the lightspeed barrier is found, starships are going to be family affairs. All starships will be generations ships, no matter how fast they travel. Which also means that starships will have to be big, large enough to serve as permanent habitats not merely for the crew, but for all the crew's families, as well.

Another question: What about aliens who visit Earth from the distant stars? What motivates them? Murray Leinster's classic story "First Contact" clearly showed the dangers involved in meeting extraterrestrials about whom we know nothing except the fact that they exist and have a high order of technology.

Damon Knight's equally famous tale "To Serve Man" strikes directly at the heart of alien motivations. His aliens have come to Earth for food: us.

In Stanley Schmidt's *The Sins of the Fathers* the aliens who arrive at Earth are driven by guilt: They caused the eruption at the core of the Milky Way that is going to make the entire galaxy uninhabitable.

Motivation is the key to character, whether the characters are human or alien.

◆ ◆ ◆

[1] The word "theory," as it is used here, has a special meaning for scientists. It means a model, a systematic ordering of ideas that gives shape and meaning to many observations, and even suggests future observations and experiments. Einstein's *theory* of relativity, then, is not just a hunch or a hypothesis: It is a way of organizing what is known of physics into a system of ideas that makes sense of everything in the field.

[2] The politics of the stories are so relevant to the times in which they were written that they badly date the Seetee tales. This is an important point for writers to keep in mind.

CHAPTER 12

The Universe

The most beautiful thing we can experience is the mysterious. It is the source of all true art and science.

Albert Einstein

TECHNICAL FACTORS

When we look at the stars we are looking backwards in time.

We see the Sun as it existed some eight minutes ago, when the light we observe left its photosphere. We see Sirius blazing in our night sky as it was 8.6 years ago; that's how long it has taken its light to reach us. Sirius might blow up tomorrow night, but we won't know about it for another eight years and seven and a half months.

The Andromeda galaxy is more than two million lightyears away. The farthest galaxies are megaparsecs away. Thus, as we look at very distant objects we are seeing them as they were millions, even billions of years ago. We are looking back into the ancient history of our universe.

It is difficult for astronomers to observe the Milky Way galaxy because we are inside it. They have mapped out its spiral structure and detected evidence of something very violent going on at its core, but they cannot look at the Milky Way in its entirety, the way they can see the great spiral in Andromeda or other galaxies, because great clouds of interstellar dust obstruct our view.

It is even more difficult to make observations of the universe as a whole. We can see parts of it, but to date only two major observations that encompass the entire known universe have been made: the redshifts that indicate the universe is expanding, and the cosmic microwave background radiation that is deduced to be the relic of the universe's violent beginning.

Redshifts and Expansion

The universe seems to be expanding.

Galaxies are grouped in clusters. Our Milky Way is part of a small cluster called, prosaically, the Local Group, which includes us, the M31 spiral in Andromeda, and fifteen smaller galaxies. Other galactic clusters are much larger, with thousands of members.

Outside the Local Group, which is bound together by gravity, all the galaxies and galactic clusters appear to be moving away from us. The farther the galaxy, the faster it is rushing away.

Their motion is deduced from the *redshifts* of their spectra. That is, the light from a distant galaxy will show a shift toward the red end of the spectrum when compared to light from a stationary laboratory source. The light from all the farther galaxies is redshifted; this is assumed to be a Doppler shift (or, more accurately, a Doppler-Fizeau shift). The farther the galaxy, the bigger its redshift. It would seem, therefore, that the universe is expanding.

The Big Bang

It's not that we are in the center of the universe and everything is rushing away from us as if we had a case of cosmic body odor. The entire universe is expanding, like the skin of a balloon that is being puffed up. Picture a balloon covered with dots, where each dot is a cluster of galaxies. As the balloon expands, an observer on any of those dots would see all the others moving away.

Most cosmologists explain the universe's expansion by postulating that the universe began in a primordial blast of incredible energy: the *Big Bang*. All the matter and energy of the universe was once squeezed down to a single point, which somehow exploded. The galaxies, the stars, the planets, you and I are all celestial shrapnel, remnants of that original Big Bang.

Cosmologists and astrophysicists have been able to calculate what must have taken place just after the Big Bang. They have mathematical models for what happened within a few thousandths of a second after it began. They can show that this titanic eruption of energy gave rise to the subatomic particles, which in turn formed the lightest elements: hydrogen, helium, lithium. The heavier elements, up to iron, have been "cooked" inside stars; the still-heavier elements, up to the transuranium kinds, have been created in the fiery blast furnaces of supernovas.

Cosmologists try to trace the expansion of the universe backward in time to determine when the Big Bang happened. To do this they must get an accurate figure for how fast the universe is now expanding. Alas, such a number is not easy to determine. It is called the *Hubble constant*, after the American astronomer Edwin P. Hubble, who first connected the redshifts with universal expansion. The Hubble constant depends on accurate measurements of the distances to the galaxies, and such distance measurements over megaparsecs depend, in turn, on so many variables that there is no firm agreement on the Hubble constant or the age of the universe.

The most likely figure for the universe's age is somewhere between ten and twenty billion years.

The Observable Universe
Can we peer that far into the universe to observe its beginning? Unfortunately, no. The more distant the galaxies are, the faster they are moving away from us. The rate of separation between us grows with distance. For galaxies that are far enough, the rate at which we are moving away from each other approaches the speed of light. For even more-distant galaxies, our separation rate can exceed lightspeed. Neither galaxy is moving at the speed of light, but when you add up the speeds of both galaxies, the rate at which they are moving apart is faster than the speed of light. This is called a *superluminal* velocity.

We could never see such galaxies. Their light would never reach us. (And, when we use the word "light" in this context, we mean all the electromagnetic radiation the galaxy emits: visible light, radio waves, etc.)

Astronomers have seen superluminal objects, that is, objects that are moving away from one another at velocities faster than lightspeed. The speed champion, as of early 1995, is a cloud of radio-emitting gas apparently ejected by a ferociously hot source of gamma radiation called GRS1915+105. The two are separating at an apparent speed of 1.25 times the speed of light. Neither the ejected radio source nor GRS1915+105 is actually moving faster than light, but their separation speed is superluminal.

Cosmologists estimate that we can see galaxies that are within about 300,000 years of the Big Bang. Beyond that, the curtain is closed. Since the actual age of the universe is not known with great certainty, neither is the actual size of the observable universe.

The Cosmic Background Radiation

Is there any evidence remaining of the Big Bang? Yes. Radio astronomers have detected a very faint glow of microwave radiation that is evenly distributed in every direction across the sky. This *cosmic background radiation* is apparently the remains of the primeval fireball of the Big Bang. The microwave radiation has cooled to a very low temperature, barely three degrees above absolute zero. This is precisely the temperature that calculations predicted for the cosmic background, which makes cosmologists confident that they really are seeing the last feeble ember of the original Big Bang.

The discovery of the microwave background radiation in 1967 was the second observation that encompasses the universe as a whole. It greatly strengthened the Big Bang theory, since it was most easily explained as the result of the original cosmic explosion.

Problems With the Big Bang

While most astronomers and cosmologists accept the Big Bang theory as the one that best explains the universe's origin and current condition, the theory is not without its problems.

For one thing, if the universe is "only" about ten billion years old—as some Hubble constant measurements indicate—then there are stars that are older than the universe! Ancient red stars of the Milky Way have been deduced to be older than ten billion years. Most cosmologists believe that the universe is older than that, although some of the most recent Hubble constant measurements lean toward a younger, and more troublesome, age for the universe.

Then there is the problem of the missing matter. By studying the motions of the galaxies, astronomers can estimate the amount of mass they contain. Yet observations of the stars and gas clouds in the galaxies show far less mass than the motion studies require, by a factor of ten or more. There must be a lot of material among the galaxies that we cannot yet see.

Some have suggested that neutrinos—tiny neutral particles that have vanishingly small masses—make up the missing mass. Others suggest perhaps dead, burned out stars are much more abundant than previously believed. But if that is so, the universe must be *much* older than the standard Big Bang model predicts. Other, more exotic ideas have been put forward; none of them has persuasive observational backing.

Another outstanding problem is the lumpiness of the universe.

The original Big Bang resulted in a smooth and very rapid inflationary expansion of the universe. The cosmic background radiation is remarkably smooth: It varies across the sky only a few parts in a hundred thousand. Yet the universe today is decidedly lumpy, with galaxies of hundreds of billions of stars and galactic clusters with thousands of galaxies, and nothing but nearly perfect vacuum in between.

A map of the observable universe, in fact, looks like a froth of soap bubbles: loops of galactic clusters arching through empty cosmic space. How could a smooth beginning produce such lumpy results?

Cosmologists point out that the very tiny ripples in the microwave background radiation must indicate that the universe was not perfectly smooth even at its earliest times. Those ripples are the seeds for future galaxies and clusters. But has the universe existed long enough for such ripples to develop into galaxies? Or will we find that the Big Bang theory needs serious revisions?

Interestingly, recent scans by the Hubble Space Telescope have shown that the universe contains many more faint, young, irregularly shaped galaxies than previously suspected. The deeper into space that the telescope looks—and the farther back in time, therefore—the more of these faint galaxies, rich in young blue stars, can be seen. Galaxy formation started quite early in the universe's history, apparently.

Quasars

Which brings us to the quasars.

Discovered in the 1960s, the quasars are like the Red Queen in *Alice's Adventures in Wonderland,* who made a point of believing six impossible things before breakfast. They seem to be doing impossible things.

Most quasars have enormous redshifts, which means that they are out at the edge of the observable universe—if their redshifts actually are linked to their distances.

The typical quasar emits more energy in radio, infrared, visible light and higher wavelengths than a thousand galaxies such as the Milky Way. More energy than a thousand times 100 billion stars. Yet they seem to be much smaller than ordinary galaxies, possibly no larger than a few times the diameter of the Solar System.

Their size is estimated from the fact that the quasars twinkle;

their brightnesses wax and wane irregularly, often within a few days or less. Since the quasars have been observed to brighten within a few days, they must be small enough for light to cross their entire diameters in a few days. Considering that the Oort Cloud of comets that marks the outer fringes of the Solar System is about a light-day from the Sun, the quasars can't be much bigger than the Solar System.

Redshifts and Black Holes

If the quasars truly are "cosmologically" distant, as their redshifts indicate, then a typical quasar emits more energy than a thousand Milky Way-type galaxies. Astrophysicists have no solid explanation for this prodigious outpouring of energy—especially since it seems to be coming from a region not much larger than the Solar System.

They have suggested that the quasars are powered by supermassive black holes—black holes created not by the collapse of a single star, but thousands or perhaps millions of individual stars. We have seen that something violent seems to be happening at the core of the Milky Way and many other galaxies. Some galaxies appear to have undergone massive explosions in their cores that have hurled enormous filaments of hot plasma over distances of kiloparsecs.

The quasars may be very young galaxies with titanic black holes eating away at their cores, gobbling up stars by the thousands and generating enormous outpourings of electromagnetic energy in the process.

As we saw in chapter 10, however, some physicists doubt that black holes can exist, and none have been definitely observed. This means they are fair game for the science fiction writer, if you are prepared to have your story skewered on the sharp edge of advancing knowledge some day.

"Local" Quasars?

A vocal minority of astronomers has argued, since the first discovery of the quasars, that they are not "cosmologically" distant at all but are "local"—that is, as close as nearby galaxies, not out at the edge of the observable universe.

If the quasars are local objects, it would mean that their energy outputs are much more reasonable. The closer they are, the more their brightnesses are due to nearness rather than intrinsic luminosity. It would also mean that the quasars are not at the cores of young galaxies.

Quasar Redshifts

Then what about their redshifts?

All that a redshift actually means is that the source of light is moving away from the observer. Since Hubble's time, cosmologists have assumed that since all the galactic clusters are redshifted, the universe is expanding. Einstein's General Theory of Relativity predicted such an expansion, although Einstein himself thought the prediction wrong—until the galactic redshifts were observed.

Suppose the quasars are objects from comparatively nearby galaxies that are simply moving very fast, perhaps ejected from the galaxy like a cannonball fired from a gun? Or like the cloud of radio-noise-emitting gas that is rocketing at superluminal velocity away from GRS1915+105. Then their redshifts would have nothing to do with the expansion of the universe.

Two problems with that. One: Where does the energy come from? Even a local quasar must be very massive, perhaps as massive as a million stars or more. How can it be accelerated to the high velocities indicated by their redshifts?

Two: If the quasars' redshifts have nothing to do with the expansion of the universe, what about the redshifts of the galaxies and galactic clusters? Scientists hate to use two explanations for one phenomenon. The principle of *Occam's Razor* says that when you have the choice of two explanations, start by selecting the simpler one. It will usually be correct.

If the quasars' redshifts turn out to be unrelated to the expansion of the universe, the entire structure of the Big Bang theory comes into question.

We simply do not know enough to say conclusively that the quasars are cosmologically distant and associated with the very early stages of galaxy-building. Probably the majority of astronomers and cosmologists are correct, and their model of the Big Bang is on the right track. Only time and more observations will tell.

Where Is Everybody?

Meanwhile, let's turn our attention back to the Milky Way galaxy and a question that Nobel-laureate physicist Enrico Fermi asked half a century ago. If we assume that there are other intelligent species in the galaxy, why haven't they come visiting? As Fermi put it, "Where is everybody?"

Consider: Our Sun is most likely a third-generation star, meaning that it is fairly young, as stars go. After all, the galaxy must be at least ten billion years old; our Sun is only half that age. There are many, many older stars in the Milky Way. If life and intelligence have arisen on some of them, why haven't they made themselves known to us?

Okay, the distances between the stars are vast and forbidding. But radio communications travel at the speed of light. Our radio telescope at Arecibo, Puerto Rico, is powerful enough to beam a signal completely across the Milky Way. Surely older, more advanced alien civilizations could do the same. Or even better.

Moreover, they could have come calling in person. Even using interstellar arks, and star-hopping in generations ships across the galaxy at a rate of one star every thousand years, they could have crossed the entire Milky Way in fifty million years or so—a scant two-hundredths of the galaxy's history. Earth was teeming with life fifty million years ago; the dinosaurs had already gone and it was the heyday of the mammals.

Of course, some people claim that we *have* been visited by aliens, repeatedly. UFO stories are intriguing but lack the firm kind of evidence needed to make them believable. If you were captain of a starship and found a planet with intelligent inhabitants, would you go around kidnapping little old ladies on country roads in the dark of night?

Larry Niven combined alien visitation with time dilation in his ironic "The Green Marauder," introducing a character over two billion (objective) years old. On her last visit to Earth, almost 800 million years ago, she saw great civilizations that were later completely destroyed by planet-wide pollution—free oxygen produced by photosynthetic plants, the oxygen that allowed our kind of life to arise.

So—science fiction and UFO tales aside—where is everybody?

Galactic Geopolitics

To answer that question, consider the "geography" of the Milky Way galaxy.

Our Solar System is in one of the galaxy's spiral arms, some thirty thousand lightyears from the galactic center. The core of our galaxy is much thicker with stars than our "suburban" neighborhood. Although the core is maddeningly hidden from us by interstellar dust clouds, the stars closer to the galaxy's center must be packed so close that there is probably no more than a single lightyear between them.

Stars in the galaxy's core are also much older than the Sun— red giant stars are common there, stars that have used up most of their original hydrogen fuel. The young stars, such as our Sun and hot blue giants such as Rigel, are out in the spiral arms.

It is these younger stars that are rich in metals (remember that to astrophysicists, any element heavier than helium is a "metal"). The older stars in the core regions are metal-poor.

These earliest stars formed out of clouds that had little more than hydrogen and helium in them. The first generation of stars in the Milky Way began with hydrogen and helium, then cooked the heavier elements in their nuclear furnaces. When they eventually collapsed and exploded, these "metals" were blown out into space to form the raw materials for new stars.

First-generation stars, therefore, *could not produce life.* There was no carbon, no oxygen, no nitrogen available when they were shining. If those earliest stars were accompanied by planets, the planets could be nothing but balls of frozen hydrogen and helium. There was no silicon, no aluminum, no iron, none of the elements that form rock and true metals.

Second-generation stars would have a smattering of these heavier elements, although not as much as the Sun. Planets of such stars might be able to support life, perhaps even intelligent life. Could such an intelligent species develop a technological civilization? It all depends on the abundance of the heavier elements, especially the true metals.

Our technology on Earth is built on metals. Our history rings with the echoes of the Bronze Age, the Iron Age, the Steel Age, the Uranium Age. How abundant would these metals be on planets of second-generation stars? We simply do not know.

But we do know this. They are abundant enough on Earth—a planet orbiting a presumably third-generation star—to allow us to develop technology.

Are We the First?

Perhaps the reason that our radio telescopes have heard no intelligent signals and we have not been visited by extraterrestrials (UFO stories aside) is that there are no older, wiser, more technologically advanced species in our region of the Milky Way. Perhaps not anywhere in our entire galaxy.

Maybe we are the first creatures in the Milky Way to have enough metal and enough time to develop a space-faring civilization.

No extraterrestrials? Even though Asimov could write volumes of robot and Foundation stories without alien life forms of any kind mentioned, it seems a cruel blow to remove E.T.s from the ranks of possible story subjects. Fortunately, we simply do not know whether there are aliens out there, intelligent or not. But the universe is large, and we have just started to explore it.

Quasars as Starships

Perhaps we have seen evidence of extraterrestrial intelligence, after all, but simply do not recognize it.

Radio astronomers are searching the heavens for intelligent signals in the program called SETI, the Search for Extraterrestrial Intelligence. But are radio signals the only signs we might expect to find in the heavens?

We saw in chapter 11 that starships would probably be large enough to hold many families, and they would need extremely powerful propulsion systems such as antimatter drives. Assume that we are not the oldest, most advanced critters in the Milky Way. Assume that intelligent aliens have achieved star flight. What would their starships look like, from Earth?

Even extremely large starships would be too small for our telescopes to image over interstellar distances. But what about the plumes of hot plasma from the exhausts of their rocket engines? Big clouds of very hot plasma that show strong redshifts, if they are moving away from Earth, and strong blueshifts if they are heading our way. Clouds that might well get brighter or dimmer as the ship changes its power settings.

Quasars?

Perhaps the quasars are not merely "local," in the sense that they are associated with nearby galaxies. Perhaps they are well within the Milky Way itself, starships plying the interstellar trade routes. If they are within our own galaxy, they would be much smaller and their energy output consequently also smaller than even "local" quasars would be.

Why are they all redshifted, moving away from us? Because (perhaps) those are the only ones we have noticed. After all, astronomers have been on the lookout for objects showing significant redshifts since the 1920s. Blueshifted objects would be much harder to detect, because a blueshifted cloud of hot rocket exhaust would most likely be shifted up into the X-ray or gamma-ray regions of the electromagnetic spectrum.

The only way to detect such objects would be with satellite sensors; the Earth's atmosphere absorbs most ultraviolet, X-ray and gamma-ray wavelengths.

Interestingly, since the 1960s satellites have detected bursts of gamma radiation that seem to be coming from all around us. Some astronomers believe there are powerful gamma-ray sources far out in intergalactic space, "cosmologically" distant. Others argue that the gamma-ray "bursters," as they are called, come from a halo of neutron stars on the fringes of the Milky Way.

Could they be blueshifted starships? Probably not. If they were, they should show some motion across our field of view, as well as blueshifts indicating that they are approaching us. (Or, in the case of the quasars, redshifts indicating that they are moving away from us.) Astronomers call such crosswise movement "proper motion"; no proper motion has yet been detected in the gamma-ray bursters or the quasars.

Still, the speculation that these astronomical objects might be starships could be the fuel for interesting science fiction.

Or consider this: Perhaps the quasars are "local" objects with the mass of a million Suns or so, ejected from nearby galaxies— deliberately. Now ask yourself the questions: Who? Why? When? How?

Space Warps

Although we don't know of any way to propel ourselves through space except some form of rocketry or sailing, there might be other ways of travelling across the stars that we simply have not yet discovered.

Einstein's general relativity shows that spacetime is curved by the presence of massive stars and galaxies. You can picture spacetime as a sort of thin rubber sheet, and the mass of a star as a metal ball bearing that dimples the sheet. In fact, Einstein saw gravity in terms of geometry: masses of matter warp the fabric of spacetime.

The universe's curvature might be saddle shaped or spherical. It might even be corrugated like corduroy; we simply do not know. Not yet.

But it might be possible to use the warping effect caused by very massive objects such as black holes to burrow through spacetime, dig a *wormhole* that connects here and now with someplace and sometime else. A few astronomers even suggested that the quasars are explosive "white holes" of energy erupting into our universe at the other end of wormholes generated by black holes of collapsing galaxies.

If you need instantaneous interstellar travel, or at least you want to get around the problems of time dilation and relativistic veloci-ties, you can use black holes and wormholes—either natural or man-made. Or made by aliens, as Frederik Pohl has done in his series of novels about the long-extinct alien race called the Heechee.

Other Universes

A space warp might even land you in a different universe, where the laws of physics are not the same as those in our universe. Andrei Linde, a Russian astrophysicist now at Stanford University, has suggested that once a Big Bang generates a universe, that universe generates other universes, rather like a crystal replicates itself in a nutrient medium.

New Big Bangs may be happening all the time in this view, and the universe—or *multiverse*, really—is much larger and more var-ied than anyone had thought.

Lasers in Space

The one universe we can see is various enough, though. Would you believe natural lasers can exist?

The laser was invented in 1960. It is a device that greatly ampli-fies the emission of light from suitably excited atoms. In fact, the word "laser" is an acronym for "light amplification by stimulated emission of radiation."

Astronomers were surprised to find in the 1970s that natural conditions in the atmospheres of Mars and Venus sometimes give rise to laser action. The carbon dioxide in those planetary atmo-spheres occasionally emits pulses of laser light.

In 1995, sensors aboard NASA's Kuiper Airborne Observatory,

a high-altitude plane used for astronomical observations, detected laser action from the hydrogen gas cloud surrounding a faint star in the constellation Cygnus: MWC 349. Under highly excited conditions, the hydrogen emits red laser light. When less excited, it emits yellow beams.

While astronomers assume these cosmic lasers are natural, might not a science fiction writer consider that they could be artifacts created by alien technology? Perhaps they are the signals that SETI is mistakenly seeking with radio telescopes. I wrote of such a possibility in a short story, "Answer, Please Answer."

Who knows what else is out there, waiting to be discovered?

Dyson Spheres

Our exploration of the universe may reveal to us engineering feats of truly staggering proportions.

Tsiolkovskii suggested in 1895 that humans might eventually begin to rebuild the Solar System. Pointing out that the Earth receives only 5×10^{10} of the energy the Sun puts out, Tsiolkovskii speculated that we might turn the Asteroid Belt into a chain of space cities so that we can intercept and use more solar energy.

In 1960, Freeman Dyson went a giant step farther. He postulated that a truly advanced civilization could build a sphere around its parent star, so that it could capture and use *all* the energy the star emitted. A "Dyson sphere" in our Solar System would be built out of the material of the planet Jupiter, at a radius of one AU from the Sun—so that its interior surface would be at the same temperature regime as the Earth is now.

Larry Niven dealt with such gigantic engineering works in his novel *Ringworld*.

Might we find Dyson spheres out among the stars, built by alien races far advanced beyond our own technological capabilities? A Dyson sphere would have a diameter the size of a planetary orbit, and it would most likely be radiating in the infrared, to get rid of the excess heat from its central star. Might brown dwarf stars actually be Dyson spheres?

More than half a century ago, English geneticist J.B.S. Haldane said, "The universe is not only queerer than we imagine—it is queerer than we *can* imagine."

There is a challenge for science fiction writers!

THE WRITER'S PERSPECTIVE

Lee DuBridge, who served as President Nixon's science advisor, summed up the question of extraterrestrial life in one beautiful sentence: "Either we are alone or we are not; either way is mind-boggling."

Mind-boggling indeed. To think that we are the only form of intelligent life in a universe of billions upon billions of stars and galaxies is beyond belief. Yet we have found absolutely no evidence of any trace of intelligence elsewhere in the Solar System or among the stars.

Very likely this is because we have barely begun to look. The universe is large, and we simply have no inkling of how common life and intelligence may be.

Alien Visitors

Suppose, for example, Earth was visited by intelligent aliens a thousand years ago. They noted a promising little civilization cooking, not yet capable of crossing the planet's oceans, but apparently fairly bright. They make a note of returning for another look in ten thousand years. After all, there are a lot of worlds to investigate.

Clarke used a variant of this idea in *2001: A Space Odyssey*. His aliens left an artifact on the Moon for us to discover when we had risen to the level of space flight. Once uncovered, the artifact sent a message to the aliens that we were ready to be contacted.

Or perhaps they are watching us now and all the UFO stories are true. They don't want to make their presence known, though, because they realize that would warp our development. Like *Star Trek*'s explorers, they have a Prime Directive against interfering with a local species' development.

Our chances of finding intelligent aliens—or being found by them—depend critically on how abundant life is in the universe. Even if there are plenty of intelligent species among the stars, however, how likely is it that we will find one that is enough like ourselves to make meaningful contact?

The Postage Stamp Analogy

The problem is this:

Consider the history of the planet Earth. Let the height of the Empire State Building represent the planet's 4.5 billion years of existence. We can then represent humankind's measly million years or so by a one-foot ruler stuck at the top of the building. The thickness of a dime placed atop the ruler stands for the length of time since humans developed agriculture and civilization: roughly ten thousand years. A postage stamp glued onto the dime represents the length of time since we have developed modern science, about three hundred years.

If other intelligent species are out there among the stars, what are the chances of our meeting one at our own level of development—that is, within the thickness of that postage stamp? The overwhelming chances are that any alien species we encounter will be far below or far above us.

For example, we may find intelligent species that are younger than ourselves, with a correspondingly simpler technology and social development. Aside from letting them worship us as gods, there is probably very little we could do for them—or they could do for us.

Certainly we would want to study them and learn more about how intelligence and societies develop. We would most likely observe them from orbit and try to remain invisible to them, so that we do not disturb them in any way. The Prime Directive. We have seen how the European intrusion into the Americas and the islands of the Pacific destroyed those societies and nearly extinguished their whole populations. We would want to avoid that.

What happens if we make contact with a species much more advanced than we? The same thing, only in reverse. We would have precious little to offer them, except perhaps curiosity value. And they would be wise enough not to tamper with us. We hope. A really advanced race would most likely go its own way, aloof and serene, no matter how hard we tried to be friendly. The picture that comes to mind is a puppy chasing a monorail train. I used that concept in my novel *Orion Among the Stars*.

The species that are more or less at our own stage of development—somewhere in the thickness of that postage stamp—those are the species that we will interact with. That is where the fun will be. And the danger.

We will interact with species that have something to gain from us. And vice versa. Cavemen and angels have so little in common with us that they won't affect us very much, nor we them. But species at a similar intellectual, technological and moral level will provide the interstellar action. And the stuff of science fiction stories.

CHAPTER 13

Legal Aspects

The first thing we'll do, let's kill all the lawyers.

William Shakespeare, *Henry VI*, Part II, act 4, scene 2

Distressing though it may be, there will be laws—and lawyers, eventually—in space. A good deal of law regulating activities in space has already been enacted.

In fact, when the Soviet Union placed the first artificial satellite in orbit, Sputnik I, on October 4, 1957, it caused an international legal flap.

Territorial Rights

Since Roman times, territorial rights had been assumed to extend from the borders of your property up into the air and out to infinity. When aircraft first began flying across national boundaries, international agreements had to be worked out to permit such overflights of "sovereign" territory. Every nation had, and still has, the legal right to deny access to its airspace to another nation's aircraft. In the extreme, that right can be backed by force—a nation can shoot down an "intruding" plane.

But when Sputnik I went beeping away in orbit in 1957, it crossed the borders of virtually every nation on Earth without permission from any government. The Soviets had not bothered to ask for permission to overfly other nations' territories.

No one could do anything about it, because there was no way to destroy the satellite, even if any nation had wanted to take that extreme step. The Soviets had established the de facto principle that air rights end at the upper fringes of the atmosphere— therefore, satellites, in space, could cross national boundaries without hinderance.

Several years later, when the first American reconnaissance satellites went into orbit, the Soviets protested vehemently at the "spy satellites" peeking down at them. But they themselves had established the principle that nations did not need anyone's permission to orbit a satellite. The best they could do was to put up their own surveillance satellites as quickly as possible.

And they started to develop antisatellite weapons. More on that in the next chapter.

COPUOS and the 1967 Outer Space Treaty

Almost immediately after Sputnik, the United Nations General Assembly created the Committee on the Peaceful Uses of Outer Space (COPUOS), which attempted to come up with rational principles to guide space exploration and utilization. These principles were incorporated in 1967 into "The Treaty on Principles Governing the Activities of States in the Exploration and Use of Outer Space, Including the Moon and Other Celestial Bodies."

The 1967 Outer Space Treaty, as it soon became known, was eventually signed and ratified by the U.S., U.S.S.R., and virtually every other nation in the world, except for a few countries in Latin America, Africa and the Middle East.

The first article of the 1967 Outer Space Treaty deals with the freedom to explore and use space. It declares that "outer space, which includes the Moon and other celestial bodies, can be freely explored and used by all countries." The treaty further states that no nation may claim any part of the Moon or any other body in space as its national territory. That is why, when Armstrong and Aldrin landed at Tranquility Base in 1969 they announced that they "came in peace, for all mankind." Since the U.S. had agreed to the 1967 treaty, they were not allowed to claim the Moon or any part of it for the United States.

Further articles in the treaty call on nations to provide assistance to astronauts who need help, regardless of their nationality; thus, if American astronauts crash-land a shuttle in another nation's territory, that nation stands pledged to help the astronauts and return them to the United States. G. Harry Stine dealt with this situation in his novel *Shuttle Down*, in which the shuttle's crew makes an emergency landing on Easter Island.

The 1967 treaty also establishes that any damages caused by a space mission are the responsibility of the nation from which the mission was launched. For example, when radioactive nuclear power generators in Soviet satellites fell onto Canadian soil, the U.S.S.R. paid for the cleanup and removal of the debris. Even private ventures, such as the commercial launches now taking place in the U.S., are the responsibility of the federal government if they cause any property damage or injury to people anywhere in the world.

One of the legal problems the U.N. lawyers tried to grapple with was the definition of just where space begins. This is not as simple a question as a physicist or a pilot would see it. Legally, is the space shuttle orbiter "in space" when it reenters the atmosphere for its return to Earth? If not, does the U.S. have to obtain permission from the nations the shuttle overflies when it is coming back from orbit for its landing?

To date, the U.N. has tried to work with the concept of "space activities" and leave moot the definition of where space begins and air rights end.

Weapons in Orbit

The 1967 Outer Space Treaty bans "weapons of mass destruction" in space and outlaws any kind of military bases on the Moon.

Weapons of mass destruction are understood to mean nuclear, chemical and biological weaponry. Thus Project Orion, which was to use nuclear bombs to propel a starship, was scrapped before it truly started, because it would have required placing "weapons of mass destruction" in space. To the Project Orion enthusiasts the nuclear "devices" were part of a propulsion system. But to the lawyers and politicians they were bombs that could have been used to rain destruction on targets on the ground.

With the Cold War ended and nuclear weaponry being scrapped by the United States and Russia, perhaps we can look forward to a renewal of Project Orion and a trip to Alpha Centauri early in the twenty-first century.

Incidentally, although nuclear weapons in space are banned, the Soviet Union did develop a "Fractional Orbit Bombardment System" (FOBS) in an attempt to get around that restriction. More on that in the next chapter.

The Geostationary Orbit

As we have already seen, in the 1970s a clique of Third World countries that called themselves the Group of 77 claimed that the geostationary orbit, where commsats are placed, legally belongs to the nations that lie along the equator. This conflicted with the 1967 treaty's principle of the freedom of space, however, and the claim was ignored. Since the Group of 77 had no power—legal or military—to enforce its claim, it was quietly dropped. But as more nations acquire the technology to build antisatellite weapons, GEO may become a battleground, at least legally.

Which nations are entitled to place commsats along the geostationary orbit, and which positions along that orbit are they entitled to? If these decisions were left to a "first come, first served" basis, a few nations would dominate global satellite communications, to the detriment of the smaller nations.

These decisions are made by the International Telecommunications Union, an organization based in Geneva that dates back to 1906 and the very early days of radio broadcasting. The ITU has divided the geostationary orbit into three major segments: Region 1 is the section of the orbit that covers Africa, Europe, and the Confederation of Independent States (formerly the U.S.S.R.); Region 2 covers the Americas; and Region 3 covers Asia and the island nations of the Pacific Ocean.

Within each region, nations are granted "slots" (locations along GEO) in which they can place commsats. The ITU also allocates the frequencies that commsats and other satellite radio equipment may use.

"Spy" Satellites

The U.N.'s COPUOS also tries to deal with the problems raised by observation satellites. Some nations do not want reconnaissance satellites taking pictures of their territory, even if the imagery is only for the purpose of locating natural resources. These nations worry that those wealthy enough to buy satellite data will exploit their natural resources before their own governments have a chance to protect those resources or develop them on their own.

In addition, many nations do not want "outsiders" looking at them from orbit. Observation satellites make totalitarian governments uncomfortable, especially when the world's news media have access to the satellite imagery. COPUOS tries to protect various nations' claims to privacy, but space technology moves much faster than international law, and the American tradition of "freedom of information" appears to be winning out over other nations' desires to keep themselves—and their people—in the dark.

The Moon Treaty

When the U.S. signs a treaty, and the Senate ratifies it (a two-thirds majority is needed for ratification), the provisions of that treaty acquire the same legal standing as federal laws. Thus, even if a private company wants to build—let's say—an Orion-type starship in orbit, it would be a violation of federal law. The FBI would shut them down.

In 1979 the U.N. drafted a new treaty titled "Agreement Governing the Activities of States on the Moon and other Celestial Bodies." The Moon Treaty was an attempt to govern *all* space activities. It was based on the idea that space—and all the planets, moons, etc. in space—belong to the "common heritage of mankind," and therefore no nation may exploit them without the agreement of all the other nations, such agreement to be worked out, presumably, through the U.N.

Although the U.S. government was ready to sign the Moon Treaty, American space activists quickly became aroused by fears that the treaty would prevent private enterprise from operating in space. The major aim of the treaty was to create a system for sharing the wealth that is found and developed in space. But American opponents to the treaty felt that the system the U.N. was fostering was designed to freeze private enterprise out of space and leave space development to some vague U.N. bureaucracy. They claimed that the treaty called for an "OPEC-like monopoly" that would "control, regulate, and probably itself exploit outer space resources."

As a result of that opposition, the United States did not sign that treaty. Neither did the Soviet Union, the other major space power at that time, although the Soviets' reason was based on their refusal to allow *anyone* any measure of control over their space activities. Even though many nations did sign, including France and Canada, the treaty is now regarded as a dead issue.

Use But Don't Claim Ownership

Thus the legal standing of any nation or private venture that wants to develop facilities in space is rather tricky. If a private company (or a government) wants to establish a base on the Moon and begin mining lunar resources, the 1967 Outer Space Treaty says they are perfectly free to do so—as long as they don't claim that they own the ground on which the base stands.

This is a different kind of situation from the one we are accustomed to on Earth. You can *use* lunar resources—scoop up the regolith and process its oxygen for sale, for example—but you cannot claim ownership either of the ground on which your equipment stands or the regolith materials you are processing! Interesting material for science fiction stories.

What happens, for example, if your characters latch onto a metallic asteroid and begin mining it for gold, and a rival group lands on the other end of the same asteroid and begins mining there?

What happens if one company processes lunar regolith for its oxygen, but another company hijacks an oxygen shipment, claiming that since no one can claim ownership of it, anyone can take it for free? This was an element in my novel *Privateers*.

Clearly these are points that need to be worked out, not only by lawyers but by science fiction writers as well. In fact, by presenting possible scenarios in their stories, science fiction writers might be helping the lawyers to grasp all the possible implications of the laws they want to concoct.

Other Treaties

The U.S. has ratified several other treaties that have some affect on what we can and cannot do in space.

Partial Test Ban Treaty, 1963. This treaty prohibits testing nuclear weapons in Earth's atmosphere, under water or in space.

Nuclear Nonproliferation Treaty, 1970. Signed by more than sixty-two nations, this treaty requires the nations that already have nuclear weapons (United States, Russia, Britain, France, China, India) refrain from assisting other nations in acquiring nuclear arms, while the nonnuclear nations agree not to develop or acquire nuclear weapons. Nations that have *not* signed this treaty include Israel, France, Argentina, Brazil, India, Pakistan, China, Cuba, South Africa, South Korea, Saudi Arabia, Iran, Iraq, and several other Middle Eastern states.

However, there is no treaty prohibition against sharing (or selling) information on how to build rocket boosters. Or selling the boosters themselves. Rocket technology is spreading all across the world; within a few years, any nation that wants to will be able to build or buy boosters capable of launching payloads into orbit—or delivering warheads over intercontinental distances.

SALT I Accord, 1972. Like earlier arms-control agreements, SALT I requires that the signatories (the U.S. and U.S.S.R.) refrain from interfering with "national technical means of verification" of the treaty's provisions. In other words, neither side will try to prevent the other side from using observation satellites to check on the number and type of ballistic missiles being fielded.

ABM Treaty, 1972. Prohibits development, testing, or deployment of an antiballistic-missile defense system in space (or on the ground, or at sea). However, as we shall see in the next chapter, there is some argument as to whether the treaty would actually prohibit a "Star Wars" type of defense system in orbit.

Registration Convention, 1975. Information about the designation and function of all launches of vehicles into space must be registered with the U.N. Secretary General.

ENMOD Convention, 1977. The signatories agree not to deliberately alter the Earth's environment or natural processes for purposes that are aimed at harming another nation.

SALT II, 1979. The U.S. and U.S.S.R. agreed not to develop, test or deploy weapons of mass destruction in space, including fractional orbit bombardment systems (FOBS). Although the U.S. never ratified the treaty, and the U.S.S.R. has ceased to exist, both the United States and Russia have agreed to honor its provisions.

Many other treaties and agreements impinge on our activities in space. For example, in the ITU Convention of 1984, the signatory nations (including the U.S.) agreed to avoid harmful interference of other nations' satellite signals.

Undoubtedly, as human activities expand across the frontier of space, more legal problems will arise and more international agreements will be suggested for solving them. The basic questions of ownership and use of extraterrestrial resources will have to be updated from the concepts expressed in the 1967 Outer Space Treaty, sooner or later.

CHAPTER 14

Military Uses of Space

May the shoreless cosmic ocean be pure and free of weapons of any kind.

Leonid Brezhnev

When Brezhnev made that statement in 1981, he was General Secretary of the Communist Party and President of the Soviet Union. The U.S.S.R. had already tested and made operational a weapons system designed to destroy satellites in orbit, a so-called ASAT (antisatellite) weapon.

They had also developed a fractional orbit bombardment system (FOBS), a ballistic missile that went into orbit temporarily (a fractional orbit), then de-orbited to deposit its nuclear-bomb warhead on its target. FOBS had two advantages: (1) it gave the defense only a few seconds of warning time, since the defenders could not know that it was not really a peaceful satellite; and (2) it got around the limitations of the 1967 Outer Space Treaty (just barely) which banned placing nuclear weapons in orbit.

Ballistic Missiles and the Cold War

Space became an arena for military use in 1944, when Nazi Germany fired the first V-2 rockets at London and Antwerp. The V-2, a ballistic missile designed and built by Werner Von Braun's team at Peenemunde, on Germany's Baltic coast, spent most of its five-minute flight time above the sensible atmosphere—in space.

During the long decades of the Cold War, the U.S. and U.S.S.R. both built arsenals of thousands of intercontinental ballistic missiles—ICBMs—rocket vehicles powerful and accurate enough to drop multiple hydrogen bomb warheads on targets more than five thousand miles from their launch points. To these, both sides added submarine-launched ballistic missiles. Not as powerful or accurate as the ICBMs, the SLBMs still could rain cataclysmic destruction on their targets.

These ballistic missiles spent most of their flight times in space, well above the atmosphere. And it wasn't long before military men on both sides of the Iron Curtain began using those rocket boosters to place other kinds of hardware in orbit.

Military Satellites

We saw in chapter 3 that satellites are used to relay communications, observe weather, provide navigational data, and to survey the ground and the oceans for purposes ranging from seeking natural resources to making oceanographic studies. Satellites also perform a wide variety of scientific observations.

Military forces also need to communicate over global distances, predict the weather, get navigational fixes, and observe actual and potential battlefields, whether on land or at sea. Ballistic missiles need precise geographic coordinates to find their targets; the military pioneered the use of satellites for geodesy and mapmaking. As we saw in chapter 5, global positioning satellites were crucial to the American-led military success over Iraq in the 1990-1991 Gulf War.

Surveillance satellites are also on the lookout for missile launches. During the Cold War, when both East and West feared a massive attack by thousands of ICBMs and SLBMs, "early warning" satellites offered the chance of getting perhaps as much as thirty minutes' warning time of an attack's launch. The hope was that the warning would give enough time to launch a counterstrike, and that fear of a massive counterstrike would deter the attacker from launching his missiles in the first place.

This was the policy of Mutual Assured Destruction (MAD), which was aimed at deterring nuclear attack by threatening nuclear counterattack. The idea behind FOBS was to cut down the warning time and thus prevent a counterstrike.

Thus the military began using satellites for all these purposes, and still do. Increasingly, a general's (or admiral's) intelligence information comes from satellite imagery, relayed perhaps from halfway across the world by military commsats.

ASAT Weapons

Satellites are extremely valuable military assets and may well be targets in any war involving nations with space capabilities. A war between space-capable nations might begin with the aggressor attacking the other nation's surveillance and communications satellites, thereby effectively blinding the enemy and destroying his long-range communications.

The Soviet Union developed an antisatellite (ASAT) weapon in the 1970s. It was basically a rocket booster that delivered a high-explosive bomb into an orbit close to the targeted satellite. The system destroyed target satellites during several Soviet orbital tests. The U.S. was developing an ASAT missile to be carried aloft under the wing of an F-15 jet fighter and then fired into orbit. That development was stopped by an act of Congress, which feared extending the arms race into orbital space.

The Soviets also used powerful ground-based lasers to damage surveillance satellites overflying their territory or degrade their optical systems.

Arms Control Efforts

As we saw in the previous chapter, the Nuclear Nonproliferation Treaty was aimed at preventing the spread of nuclear weaponry. However, nations that want nuclear weapons will work to acquire them. Israel, for example, is widely acknowledged to have a clandestine nuclear arsenal. Iraq was working on nuclear weaponry before, during and—some say—after the Gulf War of 1990-1991.

The arms control agreements reached between the U.S. and former U.S.S.R. depended on "national technical means of verification." In plain words, American and Soviet surveillance satellites looked down on each other's territory and kept watch over the numbers of missile silos, submarines, research facilities, airfields, and other parts of the military establishments.

The earliest surveillance satellites used film cameras and ejected the film cartridges from orbit. They re-entered the atmosphere in their own little capsules, popped parachutes once they had reached the proper altitude, and were snagged in midair by specially equipped cargo planes. Modern satellites send their imagery back to Earth electronically.

Other satellites, such as the Vela series, were put into orbit to watch out for clandestine nuclear tests not only on Earth, but in space, as well. No space tests were ever detected, but the satellite sensors did discover high-energy natural phenomena that have helped astronomers understand more about the universe.

The Strategic Defense Initiative

Although the nuclear arms race between East and West (basically, between the U.S.S.R. and U.S.) continued through the 1960s, 1970s and 1980s, both sides tried to work out some ways of controlling the growth of their own nuclear arsenals and preventing the spread of nuclear know-how to other nations.

The arms control agreements worked out under the Strategic Arms Limitation Talks (SALT I and II) were based on the concept of Mutual Assured Destruction—MAD. Under the MAD policy the U.S. maintained such a huge nuclear arsenal that, even if the Soviet Union launched a full nuclear strike that would wipe out North America, we would still have enough weaponry (and enough warning time) to launch a counterstrike that would wipe out the U.S.S.R.

The Soviets seemed to be following the same policy. The hope was that each side would be deterred from launching a strike, for fear of the other side's counterstrike. One unintended result of MAD, however, was to constantly escalate the nuclear arms race. How many weapons do you need to *assure* the total destruction of the other side? Both the U.S. and U.S.S.R. kept building more nuclear weapons and more missiles to launch them.

The assumptions of MAD became a fundamental part of American thinking about arms control: The idea of defending ourselves against a Soviet strike was therefore seen as "unbalancing." If we could defend ourselves, then we could attack the U.S.S.R. without worrying about their counterstrike. Thus, if we started to build defenses, the Soviets would most likely attack us at once, thinking they had nothing to lose.

That was the basis for the 1972 ABM Treaty; both sides promised *not* to defend anything more than one chosen site in their territories. The Soviets built a "primitive" missile defense system around Moscow. The U.S. decided that 1970s-era missile-defense technology could not stop a full-scale attack and built no defenses at all. On both sides, the cities and population of each country were offered as nuclear hostages to the other.

These assumptions and the entire MAD policy were challenged by President Ronald Reagan in 1983 when he announced the

Strategic Defense Initiative: mounting weapons on satellites that could destroy ballistic missiles while in flight, long before they reached their targets. The aim of SDI was to defend against an attack by destroying the attacking missiles, rather than hoping to deter a nuclear attack by promising to rain an equal holocaust on the U.S.S.R. To allay Soviet fears, Reagan offered to share the defense system with the U.S.S.R.

There were two competing approaches within the SDI concept: using lasers or other types of "beam weapons" to destroy the ballistic missiles, or using small hypervelocity missiles to destroy the ICBMs by impact, called the "kinetic kill" approach. See my nonfiction book *Star Peace: Assured Survival* for all the technical and political details.

Many politicians, diplomats and scientists saw SDI as anathema, a crazy space-nut scheme that would unbalance MAD and lead to a nuclear holocaust. They dubbed it "Star Wars." However, experiments and tests moved ahead, and the kinetic kill system called Brilliant Pebbles (smarter and smaller than "smart rocks") seemed to be making progress.

Critics said that if we deployed SDI-type satellites it would be a violation of the ABM Treaty. SDI supporters retorted that the treaty does not cover the kinds of technology that SDI would use, and even if it does, we could withdraw from the treaty.

As things turned out, the Soviet Union collapsed from within and a space-based SDI system was not needed. Not yet.

Ground-Based Missile Defenses

In 1991, during the Gulf War, Iraq fired Scud missiles at Israel and Saudi Arabia. Little better than updated V-2s, the Scuds did more damage than the entire Iraqi army and air force. A jury-rigged defense system based on the Patriot missile[1] was brought into action, with results that are still being debated as this is written. Whether they actually shot down the Scuds or not, the Patriots were fed targeting information from data that originated in surveillance satellite sensors.

Now the U.S. is pushing the development of groundbased defenses against ballistic missiles and cruise missiles, while the U.S. Air Force is pursuing development of an airborne laser system, a jumbo jet transport plane carrying a multimegawatt laser that can destroy missiles over ranges of hundreds of miles.

The fighter plane of the future may look more like the Goodyear blimp than a sleek jet-jockey's dream!

Peacekeepers in Orbit

As more and more nations acquire ballistic missiles and nuclear, chemical or biological warheads for them, the need for missile defenses grows more urgent.

Defensive satellites, armed with sensors that can detect missile firings and weapons that can destroy the missiles in flight, may become vitally necessary to world peace. Remember, satellites orbit over the entire world. They could be used to protect every nation on Earth against missile strikes, no matter where the missiles are launched. The question is, who would control such satellites in a way that guarantees that they will be used to defend any nation being attacked?

The political problems are usually more difficult to solve than the technical ones. Slowly, painfully, the world is inching toward a true, permanent international peacekeeping force, armed and ready to prevent aggression anywhere in the world. Or perhaps, anywhere in the Solar System. I dealt with one possible scenario for the birth of an IPF in my novel *Peacekeepers*.

The Limitations of Treaties

History has shown that nations will live up to the treaties they sign only as long as they perceive the treaties to be working in their best interests. In 1839 the nations of Europe solemnly pledged to respect the neutrality of Belgium. In 1914, however, when Germany wanted to invade France via Belgium, that treaty pledge was characterized as "a scrap of paper" by German chancelor Theobald von Bethmann-Hollweg.

Unless and until a real world government comes into power (itself a theme worthy of countless science fiction tellings), national governments will agree to treaties when it suits them and resort to force when it doesn't.

This has serious implications for the peaceful development of space.

One of the arguments against development of SDI-type space defenses is that weapons in orbit could easily be used against fragile, unprotected satellites—and space stations.

Clementine and DC-X

However, not all military operations are warlike. Military research in the SDI program has led to improvements in massively paralleled computer systems, adaptable optics, and many other technological breakthroughs.

The first spacecraft to study the Moon since the Apollo days was SDI's Clementine "smallsat," launched on January 25, 1994. SDI was seeking to develop new, lightweight sensors and satellites that would be small and cheap enough to launch in large numbers. Clementine was a "proof of concept" mission, showing that the "small is beautiful" approach could work, that a new generation of miniaturized sensors could perform admirably well, and—as a bonus—give us a new look at the Moon.

The entire Clementine spacecraft weighed only 3720 pounds, including the satellite's actual "dry weight" of 500 pounds, plus the hardware mating it to its Titan IIG booster and the kick motor to boost it from LEO to a lunar trajectory. That is ten times less than the weight of previous satellites with the same capability.

And Clementine proved that a highly successful scientific space mission could be done in less than three years from the starting gun, for a cost of *less than* its planned $80 million budget, which is some ten times lower than earlier planetary probes had cost.

After weeks of mapping the Moon with an array of sensors, Clementine was intended to go off and study an asteroid, but a software error sent it instead into a solar orbit. Dreadful sorry, Clementine!

Clementine 2 is being built by the Air Force Space Command and will inspect three asteroids that cross Earth's orbit in 1998.

As we saw in chapter 8, the Delta Clipper SSTO program began with SDI's need to develop a cheaper, faster way to put large tonnages of payload into orbit.

This concept of doing things "cheaper, faster, better" is now the byword at NASA—and in the fast-growing private sector of space development. The old days of massive, Apollo-type projects that take decades to complete and cost billions of dollars may be a thing of the past. The military led the way into space in the first place and now has been a leader toward operating in space "cheaper, faster, better."

ASATS and Economics

It is not only the military who should be worried about being "blinded" by attacks on communications and observation satellites.

As more and more of the world's economic welfare comes to depend on commsats, geographic information systems and other types of space facilities, these satellites and space stations will become increasingly lucrative targets for military or terrorist attack.

Imagine what would happen to the world's interlinked stock markets *today* if key commsats were knocked out by terrorists. Or if observation satellites were destroyed by one or more nations opposed to being "spied" upon from space.

Imagine a future in which a good share of the world's electrical power is provided by Solar Power Satellites. Wouldn't the SPSs be juicy targets for an aggressor who wants to cripple a nation at one blow?

Or how about holding a whole space station full of scientists and astronauts hostage in order to negotiate a political point or two?

It's been said that where your purse is, there your heart will be also. The economic value of our growing investment in space will one day make it prudent to be prepared to defend those facilities. Just as navies came into existence millennia ago to defend the ability to travel and trade across seas and oceans, so will—sadly, perhaps—military forces eventually be needed in space to protect the right to travel and trade.

May the shoreless cosmic ocean be pure and free of weapons of any kind, as Brezhnev said. Yes. But keep your powder dry.

◆ ◆ ◆

[1] The Patriot was originally designed as part of an antimissile system, then downgraded to be used against jet airplanes when the U.S. scrapped its antimissile work in the 1970s. It had to be quickly upgraded again to be able to work against the Scuds.

The true era of space flight is just beginning. What has happened so far is merely the hesitant infant steps into this vast new domain. Soon we will stride across the void with all the confidence of strong, knowing adults. We will expand the space frontier—a frontier that begins a scant hundred miles over your head.

In his book *A Moment on the Earth*, Gregg Easterbrook said, "Once thinking beings spread to many other worlds, no people-caused malfeasance in any one place—no war, dictatorship, resource collapse, pestilence, or pollution—would be able to wipe out . . . life. No natural badness in any one place—no ice age, volcanic eruptions, comet strikes, or other catastrophes—would be able to wipe out life. The risk of the extinction of life may for all intents and purposes end."

That is the true promise of space flight.

These are exciting times, and as a writer you should consider yourself lucky that so much is happening that can be used as grist for your story mill.

Science fiction has always been interlinked with scientific research in a positive feedback loop. Scientists discover new knowledge, and science fiction writers produce stories that speculate about how this new knowledge will affect us. Scientists and students read these works of science fiction, and the stories stimulate their imaginations, move them toward more research, more new knowledge.

How many careers in science and technology began with reading science fiction stories? Each of the astronauts who walked on the Moon read science fiction in his formative years.

How many careers in writing have been triggered by the fascinating new knowledge that science gives us? Many science fiction writers began as teenagers who were thrilled by the exploration of space.

Planetary probes, space stations, industries growing in orbit, discoveries of planets around distant stars—a cornucopia of story material is being poured out for us. And the stories we write will help to inspire still more exploration and utilization of the space frontier.

It's a great time to be writing.

It is also a great time to be reading. The information flow available to you in books, magazines, research journals, the internet, and even television is enormous and constantly growing. Our knowledge of the universe and our abilities to live and work in space are changing very rapidly. Even as we wrote this book, scientists found possible life forms from Mars, the *Galileo* probe entered Jupiter's atmosphere, extrasolar planets were discovered, and the first low-orbit commsats were lofted.

It is important to you, as a writer, to stay abreast of this rapidly changing situation. Read as widely as you can. Don't confine your reading to science fiction; don't limit yourself to the works cited in the bibliography and reference sections of this book. Stay current or you will quickly fall out of date. Read about the scientific research itself. Follow the thrilling new discoveries made as we explore the Solar System and the stars. There is excitement and adventure in the continuing exploration of the universe—and wonderful material for great science fiction stories.

Keep reading.

Keep learning.

And above all, *keep writing.*

BIBLIOGRAPHY

Listed below are books and journal articles that can help to supply more details about space travel. Please remember that the fields of astronomy and astronautics are expanding and changing constantly: New ideas, information and data are being generated all the time. Stay abreast of these new developments by reading some or all of the journals given at the end of this section.

Abell, George O., David Morrison and Sidney C. Wolff. *Exploration of the Universe* (Sixth Edition). Philadelphia: Saunders College Publishing, 1991.

America at the Threshold, Report of the Synthesis Group on the Space Exploration Initiative. Superintendent of Documents, U.S. Government Printing Office, 1991.

Barrow, John D. *The Origin of the Universe*. New York: Basic Books, 1994.

Bova, Ben, and Byron Preiss, eds. *First Contact: The Search for Extraterrestrial Intelligence*. New York: NAL Books, 1990.

—. *Welcome to Moonbase*. New York: Ballantine Books, 1987.

—. *The High Road*. New York: Houghton Mifflin, 1981; Pocket Books, 1983.

—. *Star Peace: Assured Survival*. New York: Tor Books, 1984.

Burrows, William E. *Exploring Space*. New York: Random House, 1990.

Clarke, Arthur C. *Interplanetary Flight*. New York: Berkley, 1985 (originally published by Harper & Row, 1950).

—. *The Exploration of Space*. New York: Pocket Books, 1979 (originally published by Harper & Row, 1951).

Davies, Paul. *The Last Three Minutes: Conjectures About the Ultimate Fate of the Universe*. New York: Basic Books, 1994.

—. *Are We Alone?* New York: Basic Books, 1995.

Easterbrook, Gregg. *A Moment on the Earth*. New York: Viking, 1995.

Forward, Robert. *Future Magic*. New York: Avon, 1988.

Halpern, Paul. *Cosmic Wormholes: The Search for Interstellar Shortcuts*. New York: Dutton, 1992.

Hartmann, William K. *Moons and Planets* (Third Edition). Belmont, CA: Wadsworth Publishing Co., 1993.

Henbest, Nigel. *The Planets*. New York: Viking, 1992.

Krauss, Lawrence M. *The Physics of Star Trek*. New York: Basic Books, 1995.

Lazio, T. Joseph W., and James M. Cordes. "Pulsars, Planets, and Genetics," *Mercury*, March-April 1995.

Linde, Andrei. "The Self-Reproducing Inflationary Universe," *Scientific American*, November 1994.

Mallove, Eugene F., and Gregory L. Matloff. *The Starflight Handbook: A Pioneer's Guide to Interstellar Travel.* New York: John Wiley & Sons, 1989.

Margulis, Lynn, and Dorion Sagan. *What Is Life?* New York: Simon & Schuster, 1995.

McDonough, Thomas R. *The Search for Extraterrestrial Intelligence.* New York: Wiley, 1987.

Neal, Valerie, Cathleen S. Lewis, and Frank H. Winter. *Spaceflight: A Smithsonian Guide.* New York: Macmillan USA, 1995.

O'Neill, Gerard K. *The High Frontier.* New York: Anchor Books, 1982.

Ordway III, Frederick I., and Randy Lieberman, eds. *Blueprint for Space.* Washington, DC: Smithsonian Institution Press, 1992.

Pogue, William R. *How Do You Go to the Bathroom in Space?* New York: Tor Books, 1991.

Ruzic, Neil P. *Where the Wind Sleeps.* New York: Doubleday, 1970.

Rycroft, Michael, ed. *The Cambridge Encyclopedia of Space.* New York: Cambridge University Press, 1990.

Schmidt, Stanley, and Robert Zubrin. *Islands in the Sky: Bold New Ideas for Colonizing Space.* New York: John Wiley & Sons, 1996.

Shklovskii, I.S., and Carl Sagan. *Intelligent Life in the Universe.* Boca Raton, FL: Holden-Day, 1966; New York: Dell/Delta, 1968.

Stine, G. Harry. *The Third Industrial Revolution.* New York: Ace Books, 1979.

Trimble, Virginia, and George Musser. "Clusters, Lensing, and the Future of the Universe," *Mercury*, May-June 1995.

Watters, Thomas R. *Planets: A Smithsonian Guide.* New York: Macmillan, 1995.

Up-to-date information about astronomy and astronautics can be found in the following journals:

Ad Astra, published bimonthly by the National Space Society, 922 Pennsylvania Ave. SE, Washington, DC 20003-2140.

Mercury, published bimonthly by the Astronomical Society of the Pacific, 390 Ashton Ave., San Francisco, CA 94112-1787.

The Planetary Report, published bimonthly by the Planetary Society, 65 N. Catalina Ave., Pasadena, CA 91106-2301.

Science News, published weekly by Science Service Inc., 1719 N Street NW, Washington, DC 20036.

Sky & Telescope, published monthly by Sky Publishing Corp., P.O. Box 9111, Belmont, MA 02178-9111.

REFERENCES

Listed below are the stories referred to in the text. In sadly all too many cases, it is quite difficult to find them in bookstores or even libraries.

The original publication is given. As you will see, most of them originally appeared in science fiction magazines. Many of these stories have been reprinted in collections and anthologies. However, few of these books remain in print and what is on the bookstore shelf now will almost certainly be pushed off for something else in a few months. If there is a specialty bookstore in your area that deals in science fiction, look there. Libraries are also an excellent place to find the "classic" anthologies.

The cutting edge of the field is in the magazines. You should buy them (subscriptions are better because newsstand distribution is spotty) and read them to see where science fiction is going.

The major science fiction magazines being published today include:

Analog Science Fiction and Fact, Penny Press, 1270 Avenue of the Americas, New York, NY 10020.

Isaac Asimov's Science Fiction, Penny Press, 1270 Avenue of the Americas, New York, NY 10020.

The Magazine of Fantasy & Science Fiction, Mercury Press, 143 Cream Hill Rd., West Cornwall, CT 06796.

Science Fiction Age, Sovereign Media Co., Inc., 457 Carlisle Drive, Hernden, VA 22070.

We have tended to reference the more well-known writers because you will have a better chance of finding their works than those of less well-known ones. The choices are illustrative and not necessarily based entirely upon literary quality, although most of these stories stand up quite well decades after they were written.

Anderson, Poul. "Call Me Joe," *Astounding Science Fiction*, April 1957.

—. "Supernova," *Analog Science Fiction and Fact*, January 1967 (retitled "The Day of Burning" in subsequent collections and anthologies).

Asimov, Isaac. "The Martian Way," *Galaxy*, November 1952.

—. "My Son, the Physicist," *Scientific American*, February 1962. This was part of an advertisement by Hoffman Electronics Corp.

—. "Planet of the Double Sun," *The Magazine of Fantasy & Science Fiction*, June 1959; also in *Fact and Fancy*. New York: Doubleday, 1962.

—. "Runaround," *Astounding Science Fiction*, March 1942.

Bova, Ben. "Answer, Please Answer," *Amazing Stories*, October 1962; also in *First Contact: The Search for Extraterrestrial Intelligence*. Edited by Ben Bova and Byron Preiss. New York: New American Library, 1990.

—. *As On a Darkling Plain*. New York: Dell, 1972; New York: Tor Books, 1985.

—. *Colony*. New York: Pocket Books, 1978; New York: Tor Books, 1988.

—. *Empire Builders*. New York: Tor Books, 1993.

—. *The Exiles Trilogy*. New York: Berkley, 1980; Riverdale, NY: Baen Books, 1994.

—. "Fifteen Miles," *The Magazine of Fantasy & Science Fiction*, May 1967; also in *The Craft of Writing Science Fiction That Sells*. Cincinnati: Writer's Digest Books, 1994.

—. "Inspiration," *The Magazine of Fantasy & Science Fiction*, April 1994.

—. "Life As We Know It," *The Magazine of Fantasy & Science Fiction*, September 1995.

—. "The Man Who Hated Gravity," *Analog Science Fiction and Fact*, July 1989; also in *Challenges* (story collection). New York: Tor Books, 1989.

—. *Mars*. New York: Bantam Books, 1992.

—. *Orion Among the Stars*. New York: Tor Books, 1995.

—. *Peacekeepers*. New York: Tor Books, 1988.

—. *Privateers*. New York: Tor Books, 1985.

—. "Sam's War," *Analog Science Fiction and Fact*, July 1994.

—. *Test of Fire*. New York: Tor Books, 1982.

—. "Vacuum Cleaner," *The Magazine of Fantasy & Science Fiction*, June 1991; also in *Sam Gunn, Unlimited*. By Ben Bova, New York: Bantam Books, 1993.

—. *Voyagers*. New York: Bantam Books, 1981; New York: Tor Books, 1990.

—. *Voyagers II: The Alien Within*. New York: Tor Books, 1986.

—. *Voyagers III: Star Brothers*. New York: Tor Books, 1990.

—. *The Winds of Altair*. New York: E.P. Dutton, 1973; New York: Tor Books, 1983.

—. "Zero Gee," *Again, Dangerous Visions*. Edited by Harlan Ellison, New York: Doubleday, 1972; also in *Prometheans* (story collection). By Ben Bova, New York: Tor Books, 1986.

Bova, Ben, and A.J. Austin. *To Fear the Light*. New York: Tor Books, 1994.

Bova, Ben, and A.J. Austin. *To Save the Sun*. New York: Tor Books, 1992.

Bova, Ben, and Bill Pogue. *The Trikon Deception*. New York: Tor Books, 1992.

Bradbury, Ray. "Kaleidoscope," *Thrilling Wonder Stories*, October 1949; also in *The Illustrated Man*. New York: Doubleday, 1951; New York: Bantam, 1983; Cutchogue, NY: Buccaneer Books, 1991.

—. *The Martian Chronicles*. New York: Doubleday, 1946; New York: Bantam, 1984; Cutchogue, NY: Buccaneer Books, 1991.

Burroughs, Edgar Rice. *A Princess of Mars*. (originally published as *Under the Moons of Mars* by Normal Bean, in *All-Story*, February 1912) McClurg, 1917; New York: Ballantine, 1985.

—. *The Warlord of Mars*. McClurg, 1919; New York: Ballantine, 1985; Cutchogue, NY: Buccaneer Books, 1976.

Campbell, John W., Jr. "Who Goes There?" (originally as by Don A. Stuart), *Astounding Science Fiction*, August 1938.

Clarke, Arthur C. *2001: A Space Odyssey*. New York: NAL-Dutton, 1968; New York: NAL-Dutton, 1993.

—. *2010: Odyssey Two*. New York: Ballantine Books, 1984.

—. *Earthlight*. Denver: Muller 1955; New York: Ballantine, 1955.

—. *Fountains of Paradise*. UK: Gollancz, 1979; Orlando: Harcourt Brace Jovanovich, 1979; New York: Bantam, 1991.

—. "The Hammer of God," *Time*, Fall 1992.

—. "A Meeting With Medusa," *Playboy* 1971.

—. "The Star," *Infinity*, November 1955.

Clement, Hal. "Dust Rag," *Astounding Science Fiction*, September 1956.

—. "Proof," *Astounding Science Fiction*, June 1942.

Cook, Rick, and Peter L. Manly. "Symphony for Skyfall," *Analog Science Fiction and Fact*, July 1994.

de Bergerac, Cyrano. *The Other World*. 1657.

Forward, Robert. *Dragon's Egg*. New York: Ballantine, 1983.

Heinlein, Robert A. The chart of future history appeared in the May 1941 issue of *Astounding Science Fiction*.

—. "The Green Hills of Earth," *Saturday Evening Post*, February 8, 1947.

—. *The Man Who Sold the Moon*. San Rafael, CA: Shasta, 1950; also in *The Past Through Tomorrow: "Future History" Stories*. New York: G.P. Putnam's Sons, 1967; New York: Ace Books, 1988.

—. *Time for the Stars*. New York: Scribner's, 1956.

—. "Universe," *Astounding Science Fiction*, May 1941.

Herbert, Frank. *Dune*. Serialized in *Analog Science Fiction and Fact*, starting December 1963; Radnor, PA: Chilton, 1965; New York: Ace Books, 1990.

Hubbard, L. Ron. "Return to Tomorrow." *Astounding Science Fiction*, February and March 1950 (originally titled *To the Stars*).

Ing, Dean. "Down and Out on Ellfive Prime," *Omni*, March 1979.

Kingsbury, Donald M. "To Bring in the Steel," *Analog Science Fiction and Fact*, July 1978.

Knight, Damon. "To Serve Man," *Galaxy*, November 1959.

Kornbluth, C.M. (as Cecil Corwin). "The Rocket of 1955," *Stirring Science Fiction*, April 1941.

LeGuin, Ursula. "The Word for the World Is Forest," *Again, Dangerous Visions*. Edited by Harlan Ellison, New York: Doubleday, 1972.

Leinster, Murray. "First Contact," *Astounding Science Fiction*, May 1945.

Martin, George R.R. "With Morning Comes Mistfall," *Analog Science Fiction and Fact*, May 1973.

Niven, Larry. "Becalmed in Hell," *The Magazine of Fantasy & Science Fiction*, July 1965.

—. "The Green Marauder," *Destinies*, February 1980.

—. *Ringworld*. New York: Ballantine, 1970, 1985.

Niven, Larry, and Jerry Pournelle. *Lucifer's Hammer*. Chicago: Playboy Press, 1977; New York: Fawcett, 1985.

Nourse, Alan E. "Brightside Crossing," *Galaxy*, January 1956.

Pohl, Frederik. *Gateway*. New York: Ballantine, 1977, 1987.

—. *Man Plus*. New York: Random House, 1976; Riverdale, NY: Baen Books, 1994.

Pournelle, Jerry. "High Justice," *Analog Science Fiction and Fact*, March 1974.

Robinson, Kim Stanley. *Blue Mars*. New York: Bantam Books, 1996.

—. *Green Mars*. New York: Bantam Books, 1994.

—. *Red Mars*. New York: Bantam Books, 1993.

Schmidt, Stanley. *The Sins of the Fathers*. New York: Berkley Medallion, 1976.

Simak, Clifford. "Construction Shack," *Worlds of If*, February 1973.

Smith, Cordwainer. "Think Blue, Count Two," *Galaxy*, February 1963.

Smith, George O. *Venus Equilateral*. Philadelphia: Prime Press, 1947 (an 11th story, "Interlude," was published in *Astounding, John W. Campbell Memorial Anthology*. Edited by Harry Harrison, New York: Random House, 1973).

Stine, G. Harry (as Lee Correy). *Shuttle Down*. Serialized in *Analog Science Fiction and Fact*, starting December 1980.

Wells, H.G. *The Time Machine*. New York: Holt, 1895; Portsmouth, NH: Heinemann, 1895; available in *The Complete Science Fiction Treasury of H.G. Wells*, Avenel Books, 1978; New York: Tor Books, 1992.

—. *The War of the Worlds*. New York: Harper, 1898; available in *The Complete Science Fiction Treasury of H.G. Wells*, Avenel Books, 1978; New York: Tor Books, 1993.

Williamson, Jack (as Will Stewart). "Collision Orbit," *Astounding Science Fiction*, July 1942.

—. "Minus Sign," *Astounding Science Fiction*, November 1942.

—. "Opposites—React!" *Astounding Science Fiction*, January and February 1943.

—. "Seetee Shock," *Astounding Science Fiction*, February, March and April 1949.

GLOSSARY

ablation: The loss of material by erosion; in particular, ablative heat shields "boil away" during reentry, carrying the friction-generated reentry heat away from the spacecraft.

absolute magnitude: The brightness that a star would show from Earth if it were at 10 *parsecs'* distance. Contrasted to *apparent magnitude.*

absolute zero: The coldest temperature possible, at which all molecular motion stops; -273.15°C on the Celsius scale; -459.67°F on the Fahrenheit scale.

accretion: The process of gradually accumulating matter; for example, planets are formed by capturing smaller chunks of matter from the interplanetary medium.

anhydrous: Without water; rocks that contain no dissolved water or water molecules chemically linked to other molecules in the rock are anhydrous.

antimatter: The mirror image of normal matter. Where a normal electron carries a negative electrical charge, an anti-electron has a positive charge, and is thus called a *positron*. Antiprotons have negative charge. For every normal particle discovered, an antiparticle mirrors it. When antimatter meets normal matter they annihilate each other in an explosion that turns 100 percent of their mass into energy.

aphelion: The point on a planet's or spacecraft's orbit where it is farthest from the Sun. (See also *perihelion.*)

apogee: The point on a satellite's orbit where it is farthest from Earth. (See also *perigee.*)

apparent magnitude: The brightness of a star as seen from Earth; this brightness depends on the star's intrinsic *luminosity* and its distance from Earth. (See also *absolute magnitude.*)

asteroid: A minor planet; also called (more correctly) a *planetoid.*

Asteroid Belt: The region between the orbits of Mars and Jupiter where most of the Solar System's asteroids orbit.

astroblemes: Literally, "star scars"; craters on Earth's surface caused by meteoroid strikes, usually very weathered.

astronautical unit (AU): The average distance between the Earth and the

Sun, rounded off to 93 million miles. The AU is a convenient yardstick for discussing distances within the Solar System.

Big Bang: Cosmological theory that pictures the universe beginning in a single explosive event.

black hole: Matter collapsed to such density that not even light can escape its titanic gravitational pull.

brown dwarfs: Astronomical objects of a size between a planet and a star; brown dwarfs are not massive enough to trigger nuclear fusion reactions in their cores, but they radiate in the infrared due to the heat generated by their continued slow gravitational contraction.

carbonaceous chondrite: A type of *meteorite* or *asteroid* that contains carbon compounds and is composed of chondrules, small spheres about the size of a pea.

centrifugal force: An apparent (but not real) force that acts radially outward from a spinning or orbiting body.

chemical rockets: Rocket engines that produce thrust from the chemical reaction of propellants, such as burning hydrogen and oxygen.

cislunar space: The space between Earth and the Moon's orbit.

conjunction: The position of a planet when it is exactly on the opposite side of the Sun from Earth's position (*superior conjunction*), or when it is between the Earth and the Sun (*inferior conjunction*).

cosmic background radiation: Microwave radiation that pervades the universe, considered to be the remnants of the original *Big Bang.*

cosmic rays: Actually not rays, but the enormously energetic nuclei of atoms apparently generated in vast stellar explosions.

cryogenic: Very cold; cryogenics deals largely with liquified gases, such as liquid oxygen, nitrogen, hydrogen, etc.

cryonics: The technique of preserving human bodies by immersing them in *cryogenic* fluid.

Delta v (δv): Change in the *velocity* of a spacecraft.

Doppler-Fizeau Effect: The shift in the wavelength of a light source as it approaches or retreats from the observer. (See also *redshift.*)

Doppler shifts: The shift in the pitch of a sound as its source either approaches or retreats from the observer.

Dyson sphere: Freeman Dyson proposed that a technologically advanced society could construct a spherical shell around its sun, to capture all of its radiant energy.

ecological niche: The set of environmental conditions that allows a species of organism to live and reproduce, including the species' particular habitat, range, food sources, etc.

electromagnetic radiation: A broad band of energy that includes radio waves, microwaves, infrared, visible light, ultraviolet, X-rays and gamma rays.

elongation: The separation of a planet's observed position from the position in the sky of the Sun.

escape velocity: The velocity needed to get away from a body; Earth's escape velocity is 7 miles per second. (Contrast to *orbital velocity.*)

event horizon: The perimeter around a collapsing body (such as a star) beyond which escape velocity is greater than the speed of light. Inside the event horizon is a black hole.

failed star: A very massive body that did not attain enough mass to trigger nuclear fusion reactions in its core. (See also *brown dwarfs.*)

fuel cells: Electrochemical devices that generate electricity from the chemical reactions of their fuels. Fuel cells that run on hydrogen and oxygen produce water as a byproduct.

fusion rockets: Rockets that employ *nuclear fusion* reactions to generate thrust.

g: Symbol used to denote the force of gravity, usually Earth's surface gravity, which equals 32 feet per second squared. High rocket accelerations are often discussed in terms of *g*s, and low-gravity environments are given as fraction of a *g:* The Moon's surface gravity is one-sixth *g*, for example. (See also *zero g.*)

Gaia: The concept that a planet's biosphere (all its living organisms) actively regulates the planetary environment to keep conditions optimal for life.

galaxy: A system of billions of stars that include spirals (such as our own Milky Way galaxy), ellipticals (spherical or semispherical in shape) and irregulars.

gas giants: Large planets made up primarily of gaseous materials. In our Solar System, Jupiter, Saturn, Uranus and Neptune are gas giants.

gas-core reactor: A *nuclear fission* reactor in which the fissionable material (usually uranium or plutonium) is in the form of a gas, rather than a solid.

generations ships: Interstellar arks travelling at speeds much less than light, therefore spending thousands of years in transit; many generations of crew and/or passengers will be born and die aboard the ship before it reaches its destination.

geographic information systems (GIS): Satellites and associated ground equipment used for mapping, searching for natural resources, detecting lightning strikes, weather observation, news gathering and other surveillance and observation tasks.

geomagnetosphere: The Earth's magnetic field.

geosynchronous earth orbit (GEO): The 24-hour orbital region 22,300 miles above the equator. Satellites in GEO remain stationary over a spot on the equator.

Global Positioning System (GPS): A network of satellites that provides precise location information to receivers on land, sea or in the air.

heat engine: Any engine that converts heat energy into mechanical work.

Hohmann minimum energy orbits: Interplanetary trajectories that require the least energy, and therefore the least propellant.

horizontal takeoff and landing (HOTOL): Spacecraft that take off and land horizontally, like an airplane.

Hubble constant: The estimated value for the speed with which the universe is expanding. The inverse of the Hubble constant provides an estimate for the age of the universe.

hydroponics: The technique of growing plants without soil, using nutrient baths instead.

hypergolic: Chemicals that ignite spontaneously on contact.

inclination: The angle between the plane in which a planet orbits and the plane of the ecliptic. (See also *plane of the ecliptic*.)

interstellar ramjets: Nuclear fusion engines that scoop their fuel from the hydrogen in interstellar space.

ion thruster: A low-thrust rocket system in which an electrically-conductive *working fluid* is accelerated by electrical energy; one of several types of electrical rockets.

ionizing radiation: Radiation such as X-rays and gamma rays that can ionize atoms within the body (i.e., strip electrons from the atoms) causing harmful physiological effects.

isotope: A variation of an element that has the same number of protons and electrons, and is therefore chemically identical, but a different number of neutrons, and therefore has a different atomic weight.

Kuiper Belt: A region at the outer edge of our Solar System populated by icy bodies; the source of most *short-period comets*; the innermost part of the *Oort Cloud.*

L-4 and L-5: Lagrange points along the orbit of the smaller of the two bodies in a system such as Earth-Moon or Jupiter-Sun, and equidistant from both bodies.

Lagrange points: Points between any two astronomical bodies where the gravitational forces from those two bodies (such as the Earth and the Moon) tend to balance one another; also called *libration points.*

LGM: "Little Green Men," a euphemism for intelligent extraterrestrial creatures.

libration points: See *Lagrange points.*

lightsails: Large, ultrathin surfaces that use the pressure of light to propel spacecraft; also called *solar sails.*

lightspeed: The speed of light in vacuum, approximately 186,000 miles per second.

lightyear: The distance that light travels in one year, nearly six trillion miles. Used as a yardstick for interstellar distances. (See also *parsec.*)

low earth orbit (LEO): Orbits from approximately 60 to 300 miles' altitude.

luminosity: In astronomy, a star's intrinsic luminosity is the measure of how much light it is radiating.

magnetic bottle: The technique of containing electrically conducting gases in magnetic fields, rather than solid walls.

magnetic storm: Disruptions in the *geomagnetosphere* caused by a solar flare.

magnetohydrodynamic (MHD) generators: Devices that convert the heat energy of a high-speed, high-temperature *plasma* to electrical energy.

magsails: Electrically-conductive sails that use the energy of interplanetary or interstellar magnetic fields to propel a spacecraft.

main sequence star: A star that remains stable for billions of years.

Manned Maneuvering Unit (MMU): A one-man propulsion system that allows astronauts to maneuver themselves in space without needing to be tethered to their spacecraft.

maria: Large flat plains on the Moon, thought to be seas before telescopic observations. (Plural of *mare.*)

mascon: Concentrations of mass beneath several lunar maria.

mass: The amount of material an object possesses. On Earth mass and weight are interchangeable terms. Not so in space or on other planets.

mass driver: A form of electrical catapult, proposed for launching shipments of ore and other cargo from the Moon.

mass driver reaction engine (MDRE): A mass driver used as a rocket engine, firing solid pellets to propel the spacecraft.

mass ratio: The ratio of a spacecraft's *payload* (crew, passengers, cargo) to its total liftoff weight.

medium earth orbit (MEO): Orbits between *LEO* and *GEO*; therefore between 300 and 22,300 miles' altitude.

meteor: The flash of light in the sky made when a *meteoroid* enters the atmosphere and burns.

meteorite: The remains of a *meteoroid* that has reached the ground.

meteoroid: A small object in space, from the size of a dust grain to a few yards across.

microgravity: Very low gravity, such as experienced in orbital flight. (See also *zero g.*)

mission specialist: An astronaut who is not a spacecraft pilot, but a member of the crew who deals with the performance of the mission. (See also *payload specialist.*)

neutrino: A subatomic particle of no electrical charge and vanishingly small (if any) mass.

neutron stars: Stars that have collapsed to diameters of only a few miles; at this point the protons and electrons of their atoms have been crushed into neutrons. Such material is called neutronium. (See also *pulsars.*)

nova: A type of exploding star that suddenly increases in brightness.

nuclear fission: The splitting of the nuclei of very massive elements such as uranium and plutonium, thereby releasing energy.

nuclear fusion: Merging nuclei of elements to produce energy. Solar energy is produced by hydrogen fusion in the Sun's core.

Nuclear-MHD torch: A proposed space propulsion system that employs a *gas-core nuclear reactor* combined with an *MHD power generator.*

Occam's Razor: The principle that selects the simpler of two possible explanations for a phenomenon.

occultation: The passage of a large astronomical object in front of a smaller one, such as the Moon passing in front of a star. ("Large" and "small," in this sense, refer to the apparent sizes of the objects in Earth's sky, not necessarily their true sizes.)

Oort Cloud: A spherical cloud of icy cometary bodies orbiting between 20,000 and 100,000 *AUs* from the Sun. The inner region is called the *Kuiper Belt.*

opposition: The position of a planet when it is exactly opposite the position of the Sun in the sky.

orbital eccentricity: An orbit's difference from a perfect circle.

orbital maneuvering system (OMS): Two liquid rocket engines on the space shuttle orbiter, of 6000 pounds' thrust each, that help the orbiter to maneuver in space and slow it down for de-orbit and return to Earth.

orbital velocity: The velocity an object must have to attain a stable orbit around a planet or star. Minimal orbital speed for satellites of Earth is five miles per second.

oxidizer: A chemical that supports combustion of fuel.

parsec: 3.26 *lightyears.*

payload: The crew, cargo and passengers carried by a vehicle.

payload specialist: A non-pilot astronaut whose duties are concerned with the spacecraft's payload. (See also *mission specialist.*)

perigee: The point on a satellite's orbit that is closest to Earth. (See also *apogee.*)

perihelion: The point on a planet's or spacecraft's orbit that is closest to the Sun. (See also *aphelion.*)

plane of the ecliptic: The plane in which the Earth orbits around the Sun.

planetesimals: Bodies that existed early in the Solar System's history, sized from ten to hundreds of miles across, that eventually were *accreted* by the planets and moons.

planetoid: A minor planet, more often called an *asteroid.*

plasma: A gas that is ionized and can therefore react to electromagnetic forces.

plasma thruster: A type of electrical rocket that employs electromagnetic fields to accelerate a plasma *working fluid.*

plate tectonics: The geologically-slow movement of continent-sized slabs of crustal rock across the hotter, denser rocks of the deeper mantle.

positron: The *antimatter* version of the electron; positrons have positive electrical charges, whereas electrons are negatively charged.

precession: The motion of a planet's axis of rotation, similar to the "wobble" of a spinning top.

propellants: The chemicals or other types of *working fluids* accelerated in a rocket system to produce thrust.

protoplanet: A planet that is still in the process of *accreting* additional material and has therefore not reached its eventual size and mass.

protostar: Dark clumps of interstellar gas and dust, sometimes a lightyear in diameter, that are condensing and will eventually become true stars, shining by the energy of *nuclear fusion* in their cores.

pulsars: *Neutron stars* that emit pulses of radio energy, visible light, and higher-frequency electromagnetic energy.

quasars: Enigmatic objects that display large *redshifts* and emit copious radio, visible, and other wavelengths of electromagnetic energy.

radio-isotope thermal generators: Devices that generate electricity from the heat caused by the natural decay of radioactive elements.

reaction control system (RCS): Small rocket engines on the space shuttle orbiter for making attitude changes in space.

rectennas: Coined from "receiving antennas"; antennas that receive microwave energy beamed from *solar power satellites.*

red giant: Stars that have evolved beyond their *main sequence* phase and expanded to hundreds of times their original sizes.

redshift: A Doppler-Fizeau shift in the wavelengths of light from distant galaxies deduced to mean that the universe is expanding.

regolith: The topmost layer of dirt on the Moon (or any airless body) that has been pulverized by meteoric infall. It is incorrect to call regolith "soil," since soil connotes living creatures such as worms, insects, etc.

relativistic velocity: Speeds so close to the speed of light that *time dilation* effects come into play.

resistojet: A simple form of electrical rocket, where an electrical heating element heats a *working fluid* to produce thrust.

retrograde: Backward motion, compared to the other bodies of the solar system; counterclockwise when viewed from the north.

seed ship: An interstellar spacecraft that carries frozen embryos, or fertilized ova, or even preserved sperm and separate ova, to be brought to term upon arrival at the destination star and thereby provide human colonists.

short-period comets: Comets that regularly return to the inner Solar System in periods less than 200 years. Halley's Comet is the most famous example.

single stage to orbit (SSTO): A rocket booster that can fly from Earth's surface to orbit in one jump, without needing second or third stage rockets.

singularity: A hypothetical object that has collapsed to a point of zero volume and infinite density, thereby creating a *black hole.*

skyhook: A tower extended from *GEO* to the surface, used to support electrical elevators to carry people and cargo into space without the need for rockets.

solar power satellites (SPS): Satellites that convert solar energy to electricity and then beam the energy in the form of microwaves (or laser beams) to *rectennas.*

solar sail: See *lightsails.*

solarvoltaic: The process of converting sunlight directly to electricity; solar cells are more accurately called *solarvoltaic* cells.

solid-core reactor: A *nuclear fission* reactor that is fueled by solid uranium or plutonium.

space adaptation syndrome (SAS): "Space sickness," the nauseous, dizzy feeling that afflicts the body when it first experiences *microgravity.*

space habitat: A facility in space where people can live permanently.

space station: A facility in orbit where people can live and work for months at a time.

spacetime: The three dimensions of space (length, breadth, height) plus time; modern physics considers spacetime as a single entity, or continuum.

specific impulse: The length of time that a pound of propellants will produce a pound of thrust, measured in seconds; a measure of a rocket system's efficiency.

spectral classes: The various colors of the stars, which are determined by their surface temperatures.

superluminal velocity: A velocity higher than the speed of light.

supernova: A star-wrecking explosion, so bright that supernovas can be seen in galaxies far beyond the Milky Way.

tachyons: Hypothetical particles that always move faster than light.

tardyons: Ordinary particles that cannot move faster than light.

terraforming: Planetary engineering that transforms an alien planet into a terrestrial environment.

thrust: The force that accelerates a rocket, spacecraft, etc.

time dilation: When flying at *relativistic velocity,* the rate that time flows becomes slower, compared to the rate of time flow on Earth.

transfer orbits: Trajectories that go from one orbit to another, or from Earth orbit to *escape velocity.*

Transfer Orbital Stage (TOS): A rocket system designed to move a spacecraft from one orbit to another, or to *escape velocity.*

transit: The passage of a small astronomical object in front of a larger one, such as when the planet Venus *transits* across the face of the Sun.

Trojan asteroids: Groups of *asteroids* located at the *L-4* and *L-5* positions along Jupiter's orbit.

twin paradox: If one twin flies into space at *relativistic velocity* it will age more slowly than the twin who remains at home, because of the *time dilation* effect.

Van Allen belts: Zones of charged particles trapped in a planet's magnetosphere.

velocity: The speed and direction of an object.

Vernier RCS engines: The smallest of the space shuttle orbiter's maneuvering engines, with 25 pounds of thrust.

walled plains: Very large lunar craters that lack the central peak seen in true craters.

white dwarf: An aged star that has collapsed to about the size of Earth.

working fluid: A liquid or gas that receives energy (as from a nuclear reactor or electrical generator) and is thereby accelerated, creating *thrust*.

wormhole: A hypothetical warp in spacetime that connects two parts of the universe; often used in science fiction to produce *superluminal* trip times.

zero g: Zero gravity; this term is often used mistakenly in a *microgravity* environment such as experienced in orbital flight.

INDEX

More Great Books
to Help You Get Published!

Science Fiction and Fantasy Writer's Sourcebook—Discover how to write and sell your science fiction and fantasy! Novel excerpts, short stories and advice from pros show you how to write a winner! Then over 300 market listings bring you publishers hungry for your work! Plus, you'll get details on SF conventions, on-line services, organizations, and workshops. #10491/$19.99/480 pages

World-Building—Filled with facts to help you write believable fiction that transports readers from this world to another . . . of your making. You'll learn how to mix elements and build planets with chemically credible and geologically accurate characteristics. #10470/$16.99/208 pages

Aliens & Alien Societies—Gain a better understanding of extraterrestrial life and develop viable creatures with well-founded cultures using these thoroughly fascinating facts. #10469/$17.99/240 pages

The Writer's Ultimate Research Guide—Save research time and frustration with the help of this guide. Three hundred fifty-two information-packed pages will point you straight to the knowledge you need to create better, more accurate fiction and nonfiction. Hundreds of listings of books and databases reveal how current the information is, what the content and organization is like and much more! #10447/$19.99/336 pages

The Fiction Dictionary—The essential guide to the inside language of fiction. You'll discover genres you've never explored, writing devices you'll want to attempt, fresh characters to populate your stories. *The Fiction Dictionary* dusts off the traditional concept of "dictionary" by giving full, vivid descriptions, and by using lively examples from classic and contemporary fiction . . . turning an authoritative reference into a can't-put-it-down browser. #48008/$18.99/336 pages

The Writer's Guide to Creating a Science Fiction Universe—An easy-to-read guide for writers to put the science back in science-fiction. You'll find contemporary science tailored to the needs of writers plus the "wrong science" you must avoid to be credible in this demanding market. #10349/$18.95/336 pages

How To Write Science Fiction and Fantasy by Orson Scott Card—You'll discover how to break into this ever-expanding market as you share in vital marketing strategies that made this author a bestseller! #10181/$14.99/176 pages

The Craft of Writing Science Fiction That Sells by Ben Bova—You'll discover how to fascinate audiences (and attract editors) with imaginative, well-told science fiction. Bova shows you how to market your ideas, submit your manuscripts and more! #10395/$16.99/224 pages

Description—Discover how to use detailed description to awaken the reader's senses; advance the story using only relevant description; create original word depictions of people, animals, places, weather and much more! #10451/$15.99/176 pages

How to Write Like an Expert About Anything—Find out how to use new technology and traditional research methods to get the information you need, envision new markets and write proposals that sell, find and interview experts on any topic and much more! #10449/$17.99/224 pages

Voice & Style—Discover how to create character and story voices! You'll learn to write with a spellbinding narrative voice, create original character voices, write dialogue that conveys personality, control tone of voice to create mood and make the story's voices harmonize into a solid style. #10452/$15.99/176 pages

How to Write Tales of Horror, Fantasy & Science Fiction—Explore the worlds of the weird, the fantastic and the unknown to create extraordinary speculative fiction! Masters of the craft give you their writing secrets in 27 succinct chapters. #10245/$14.99/242 pages/paperback

The Complete Guide to Writing Fiction—This concise guide will help you develop the skills you need to write and sell long and short fiction. You'll get a complete rundown on outlining, narrative writing details, description, pacing and action. *#10158/$19.99/312 pages*

Setting—Expert instruction on using sensual detail, vivid language and keen observation will help you create settings that provide the perfect backdrop to every story. *#10397/$14.99/176 pages*

Conflict, Action & Suspense—Discover how to grab your reader with an action-packed beginning, build the suspense throughout your story and bring it all to a fever pitch through powerful, gripping conflict. *#10396/$15.99/176 pages*

Creating Characters: How to Build Story People—Grab the empathy of your reader with characters so real they'll jump off the page. You'll discover how to make characters come alive with vibrant emotion, quirky personality traits, inspiring heroism, tragic weaknesses and other uniquely human qualities. *#10417/$14.99/192 pages/paperback*

Writing Mysteries—Sue Grafton weaves the experience of today's top mystery authors into a mystery writing "how-to." You'll learn how to create great mystery, including making stories more taut, more immediate and more fraught with tension. *#10286/$18.99/208 pages*

1997 Novel & Short Story Writer's Market—Get the information you need to get your short stories and novels published. You'll discover listings on fiction publishers, plus original articles on fiction writing techniques; detailed subject categories to help you target appropriate publishers; and interviews with writers, publishers and editors! *#10493/$22.99/672 pages*

Writing the Modern Mystery—If you're guilty of plot, character and construction murder, let this guide show you how to write tightly crafted, salable mysteries that will appeal to today's editors and readers. *#10290/$14.99/224 pages/paperback*

Fiction Writer's Workshop—In this interactive workshop, you'll explore each aspect of the art of fiction including point of view, description, revision, voice and more. At the end of each chapter you'll find more than a dozen writing exercises to help you put what you've learned into action. *#48003/$17.99/256 pages*

38 Most Common Fiction Writing Mistakes—Take steps to diagnose and correct the 38 most common fiction writing land mines that can turn dynamite story ideas into slush pile rejects. *#10284/$12.99/118 pages*

Writing the Blockbuster Novel—Let a top-flight agent show you how to weave the essential elements of a blockbuster into your own novels with memorable characters, exotic settings, clashing conflicts and more! *#10393/$18.99/224 pages*

The Writer's Complete Crime Reference Book—Now completely revised and updated! Incredible encyclopedia of hard-to-find facts about the ways of criminals and cops, prosecutors and defenders, victims and juries—everything the crime and mystery writer needs is at your fingertips. *#10371/$19.99/304 pages*

Write Tight—Discover how to say exactly what you want with grace and power, using the right word and the right number of words. Specific instructions and helpful exercises will help you make your writing compact, concise and precise. *#10360/$16.99/192 pages*

Handbook of Short Story Writing, Volume II—Orson Scott Card, Dwight V. Swain, Kit Reed and other noted authors bring you sound advice and timeless techniques for every aspect of the writing process. *#10239/$13.99/252 pages/paperback*

Freeing Your Creativity—Discover how to escape the traps that stifle your creativity. You'll tackle techniques for banishing fears and nourishing ideas so you can get your juices flowing again. *#10430/$14.99/176 pages/paperback*

The Writer's Digest Guide to Good Writing—In one book, you'll find the best in writing instruction gleaned from the past 75 years of *Writer's Digest* magazine! Phenomenally successful authors like Vonnegut, Steinbeck, Oates, Michener and over a dozen others share their secrets on writing techniques, idea generation, inspiration and getting published. *#10391/$18.99/352 pages*

A Beginner's Guide to Getting Published—This comprehensive collection of articles will calm your worries, energize your work and help you get published! You'll find in-depth, expertly written articles on idea generation, breaking into the business, moving up the ladder and much more! *#10418/$16.99/208 pages*

How to Write a Book Proposal—Don't sabotage your great ideas with a so-so proposal. This guide includes a complete sample proposal, a nine-point Idea Test to check the salability of your book ideas, plus hot tips to make your proposal a success! *#10173/$12.99/136 pages/paperback*

The Writer's Digest Guide to Manuscript Formats—No matter how good your ideas, an unprofessional format will land your manuscript on the slush pile! You need this easy-to-follow guide on manuscript preparation and presentation—for everything from books and articles to poems and plays. *#10025/$19.99/200 pages*

The Writer's Digest Character Naming Sourcebook—Forget the guesswork! 20,000 first and last names (and their meanings!) from around the world will help you pick the perfect name to reflect your character's role, place in history and ethnicity. *#10390/$18.99/352 pages*

Get That Novel Started! (And Keep It Going 'Til You Finish)—If you're ready for a no-excuses approach to starting and completing your novel, then you're ready for this get-it-going game plan. You'll discover wisdom, experience and advice that helps you latch on to an idea and see it through, while avoiding common writing pitfalls. *#10332/$17.99/176 pages*

Mystery Writer's Sourcebook—This updated market guide and resource book takes the mystery out of mystery writing! You'll get in-depth market reports on 120 mystery publishers, 125 agent listings for mystery writers and techniques from top writers and editors. Two novel excerpts and an award-winning short story are also included for your inspection with comments on why they sold! *#10455/$19.99/475 pages*

Make Your Words Work—Loaded with samples and laced with exercises this guide will help you clean up your prose, refine your style, strengthen your descriptive powers, bring music to your words and much more! *#10399/$14.99/304 pages/paperback*

30 Steps to Becoming a Writer—This informational, inspirational guide helps you get started as a writer, develop your skills and style and get your work ready for submission. *#10367/$16.99/176 pages*